Annie Lennox

Retrospective

New York · Paris · London · Milan

Contents

16 Introduction

p.20 **1976–79**

p.42 **1980–84**

p.90 **1985–86**

p.132 **1987–89**

p.148 **1990–94**

p.178 **1995–98**

p.204 **1999–**

246 Index

The cart horse standing in front of my great grandfather's dairy
farm – Cowsrieve, Peterhead Aberdeenshire Scotland.

My great grandmother Paton.

My great grandfather Paton.

A family gathering with my mother as a young girl.
My great grandparents, my great aunt, my great uncle,
my grandparents, my uncle Alistair, and my second cousin.

My great aunts Bessie and Elsie standing with my Grandmother
Dora, who was the youngest daughter.

Overleaf: My maternal Grandmother with her primary school class — third little girl from the right in the third row back.

My father and mother.

A wedding group, with my Grandma and Granda Lennox seated on the left hand side. My uncle Alistair standing. My mother and father. My aunt Jean (Lennox) and my Grandma and Granda Ferguson seated..

My parents on the day they got engaged.

My mother holding her newborn baby outside my Grandparents' (Lennox) council house in Manor Avenue, Aberdeen.

Baby Ann in my pram with Mickey Mouse.

Three years old.

Dressed for a wedding outside Hutcheon Street tenement.

Playing with the chickens at my grandparents' cottage – The Grantlands, Aberlour Speyside.

Enjoying an ice-cream cone, holding hands with Granda Ferguson in the park.

With Grandma and Granda Ferguson outside The Grantlands.

Outside the kitchen window at Hutcheon Street.
Socks and shoes SO pristine white and clean.
My mother looking striking in a dark green 1950s summer dress from a visit to Petticoat Lane, London.

At four and a half – wearing an oversized uniform with navy-blue velour hat for my first day at Aberdeen High School for Girls.

Singing in Miss Aughinachie's junior school choir at the Music Centre in Aberdeen, next to my little friend Isla Munroe.

Shyly standing in the school playground.

Four years old, standing in front of the front door of the Hutcheon Street tenement block.

utside my grandmother and grandfather's
Esquibuie, Aberlour.

fish on the loch side in the Highlands

standing on the riverbank in beautiful Deeside,

Introduction: Annie Lennox

I'VE ALWAYS WANTED TO RELEASE A BOOK, but it was never quite the right time, place or situation to go ahead with the notion. I love books. I love picking them up and turning through the pages - usually starting at the back and working through till the beginning.

I do lots of things in a 'back-to-front' kind of way. I've always been like that. Maybe it has something to do with being left-handed… or because I'm apprently neurodivergent (a fact I recently discovered after being tested for ADHD and coming out with flying colors!). It explains why I've always had a tendency to daydream, and why I often have difficulty concentrating on subjects I have no capacity for, like maths, sports and science. My boredom threshold is pretty low; but then I rarely get bored because there's always something that interests me.

In my seventh decade I think it's time to unleash this book into the world.

There have been countless images flying in the ether somewhere - in magazines, newspapers, through live performances, television and video clips. Several years ago an angel called Rosie Crombie came along, to collate as many of those images as possible to be chronicled and uploaded to the 'cloud.' A couple of years ago, I finally went ahead and started exploring them. They illustrate parts of the spaces of days and weeks and months and years of my life, from the very beginning going forwards till this very day.

Beginning with my great-grandparents (on my mother's side), without whom there would have been no A.L. I'm grateful and appreciative for each and every one of them. Only three generations before, when most women had to cook and clean and do all the domestic chores by hand, come rain, hail, or shine. They ALL had to work extremely hard in this way and I wish to honor them, as I'm probably the first in my female lineage to have ended up under the bright lights of the stage.

*

1976–79

The very first Tourists album…

It took a TREMENDOUS amount of 'blood sweat and tears' to actually arrive at this place.

Having an actual 'record' felt like a huge accomplishment at the time. There were SO MANY ways for it to fail and fall apart at EVERY juncture. I look back at it now with a sense of incredulity.

We were totally focused on the mission of creating a band, while having to learn and make things up as we went along this aspirational adventure… on a shoestring.

Much credit goes to Dave, who was something of a 'mastermind' and driving force, along with Peet's copious songwriting output.

There were so many people in Crouch End who loved us and came along to every gig we played in London throughout those years.

Early Tourists days. Dave and I in a London back garden wearing matching 'mullets.' I thought I might as well turn into a statue on impulse. Why not?

Most of my clothes came from second-hand charity shops, where you could find treasures hanging on the racks just waiting to be discovered for next to nothing. And I love nothing better than wandering into random places, looking to find things to wear.

I met Dave through Paul Jacobs, who ran a record stall in Camden Lock market, before it became the great heaving throng it's turned into now. I used to find thrift-store clothes in Aberdeen and bring them down to London in a suitcase to sell on a little stall run by my friend. I got to know Paul and mentioned to him that I wrote songs and had actually been offered a publishing contract, but I didn't have a clue what to do about it. Paul said, "You should meet my friend Dave. He'll know."

You never know what might come from introductions.

Dave had been writing songs with his friend Peet Coombes, so he took me along to meet him, and before really discussing anything properly I became a kind of 'plus one.' So I put the publishing contract I'd been offered in a drawer and that was the beginning of what became The Catch.

Peet was a gifted and prolific writer. A kind of North-Eastern ragamuffin-poet- musician-bard. He had two little boys – Robin and Joey – with his sweet girlfriend, Sue. They all lived in a basement squat in Finsbury Park, back in the day when 'squatting' was a means of shelter if you had no money and couldn't afford to rent a place.

Not long after we all met and I'd learned quite a few of Peet's songs, Dave put a call in to someone he knew, Rob Gold, who was interested in hearing what we were doing. So the three of us headed down to St Martin's Lane in central London to meet him in his office, where he'd just started working for a new independent record label – Logo Records.

I'd never set foot in a building like that before. I'd never been inside an 'office,' and felt completely out of my depth. It felt like entering another world. He asked if we could play him some songs. I don't even think we'd made any demos at that point. But Dave and Peet had brought their acoustic guitars and I was more than happy to sing, so we just played a few songs for him in the room, right there on the spot.

We were only a song or two in when the door cracked open and two heads peered in. The owners of the new record company had heard music coming through the walls and wanted to see what was going on…

(The next part sounds surreal.)

They asked us who we were, if we had any more songs, and were we looking for a record deal?

Our first record signing in an Oxford Street record store.
An early dip into the world of 'fame.'
Slightly intimidating, admittedly.
Me and Peet signing girls' arms.
I'm wearing a silver boiler suit with a leopard-skin printed belt.
I thought it was pretty 'snazzy' at the time.

Our second Tourists record, *Reality Effect*.

The photograph was taken by Gered Mankowitz in his beautiful studio – a converted old chapel in Kentish Town.

Gered had painstakingly created a pristine white set with matching furniture, a white table and chairs for us to sit on, all dressed in white. The idea was to gradually introduce a selection of different colors, with each of us having been given giant bottles of liquid paint. We sat down in place, ready to start shooting. Paint bottles in hand and at the ready.

Peet had been drinking earlier that day and, without paying any attention to what we were actually supposed to do, started squeezing his bottle exuberantly, everywhere around the set, before Gered had given us the 'get-go.'

As you can see, there's a predominance of blue…

It wrecked Gered's concept, but looking at Peet's hands I think it made a suitably anarchic statement.

We played every club and venue on the circuit... The Hope and Anchor, The Nashville Rooms, Dingwalls, The Electric Ballroom, The famous Marquee Club... Hauling gear. Driving in vans up and down every treacherous motorway in every kind of weather condition. Life on the road, where you truly earned your stripes.

New York…
Just like I pictured it!
Our very first encounter with America in the mid-seventies.
We look more seasoned here… and we were.
It was thrilling and overwhelming.
We were like cats let out of a bag.
Slightly disoriented, but ready to conquer.
Savvy but incongruous in this mighty Big Apple,
with its crazy-paced throngs of people –
Constant traffic roar.
Cockroaches in bathrooms and on window ledges.
Muggers in Central Park – too dangerous a place to enter.
Ordering heaps of pancakes with maple syrup in delis.
Drinking copious cups of bitter coffee.
Plates piled with far more food than you could handle.
It was a wild playground ride.

Our first taste of Baskin Robbins ice cream!
So many flavors.
This was AMERICA for real!

My very first time in Disney Land!
I go for the 'safer' rides.
Swirling blue teacups and 'It's a Small World After All.'
Corporate Mickey Mouse.
Annie in Wonderland.
The U S of A... Makes your head spin!

Recorded over a couple of weeks in George Martin's studio on the Island of Montserrat – *Luminous Basement* was to be the last Tourists album.

Differences in temperaments were becoming more evident, and at times it felt burdensome and contentious.

This is something many 'bands' go through.
The expectation that four or five individuals can survive the experience of being 'stuck together' through endless demands and dramas is something of a misconception. Small differences, resentments and irritations eventually turn into a pressure cooker of tension and general disagreeability. We were bound to go our separate ways after this album.

Eventually the Tourists broke up…

It was inevitable.

We were heading for a club tour of Australia when our flight was forced to land in Thailand. There'd been a strike at Sydney airport and our connecting flight had been cancelled.

After disembarking, we were taken through customs and passport control then driven by taxi to a Bangkok hotel. The airline had arranged accommodation for all the delayed passengers until the situation was resolved.

Over the years, Peet had steadily become more and more reliant on 'mood enhancers' and, as he couldn't risk taking anything illegal, decided to sequester himself in his room with a strange-looking bottle of ginseng root brandy as a kind of substitute for class-A drugs, which are strictly forbidden in Thailand – there are still severe penalties for anyone caught breaking the rules, with absolutely no exceptions.

And so Peet remained out of sight. No one caught the faintest glimpse of him. After a while it started to feel really odd. Dave and I both had a weird feeling about this and kept calling him until eventually he picked up the phone and agreed to meet us in the hotel bar. We waited for a while until he finally showed up, to announce that he'd decided to leave the band and was going fly back to London right away. It was something of a bombshell… But Peet had made up his mind, and that was that.

The following morning, word came through that the airport dispute had been settled and we could catch the next available flight to Australia. So… FOUR Tourists boarded the flight, minus the main man.

Somehow we managed to figure out how to cover for Peet. I'd have to take his place and sing without him. It was quite a giant-sized leap, as we'd been singing together for a few years and our set list consisted mainly of Peet's songs. There really was no alternative – so I did what I had to do and sang the songs without him.

Without Peet, however, it felt pretty weird. Like a table with a missing leg. It just didn't add up anymore. Somehow, we managed to valiantly scrabble through the Tourists tour, minus the lead Tourist. Most of the audiences hadn't even heard of us, so I doubt it really made any difference anyway. After a few gigs it started to feel intolerable. Australia was the last place on earth I wanted to be. I was miserable, but we had to muster through somehow. Then something quite magical happened…

Dave randomly found a solid gold bracelet lying on the pavement outside a café. He took it to the manager to ask if anyone had come looking for it. No one had. So he gave them his contact number and said they should call him if anyone came to claim it. A couple of days passed and no one called. So Dave took the bracelet to a local pawn shop and, with the money made by the exchange, he managed to buy a small handheld film camera. Dave is a brilliantly gifted fast adapter, so he quickly learned how to use the camera. Although it wasn't obvious at that point how it would be put to use, that camera marked the beginning of an entirely new concept… We would form a duo between the two of us. We'd have to invent a name.

And that was the birth of Eurythmics.

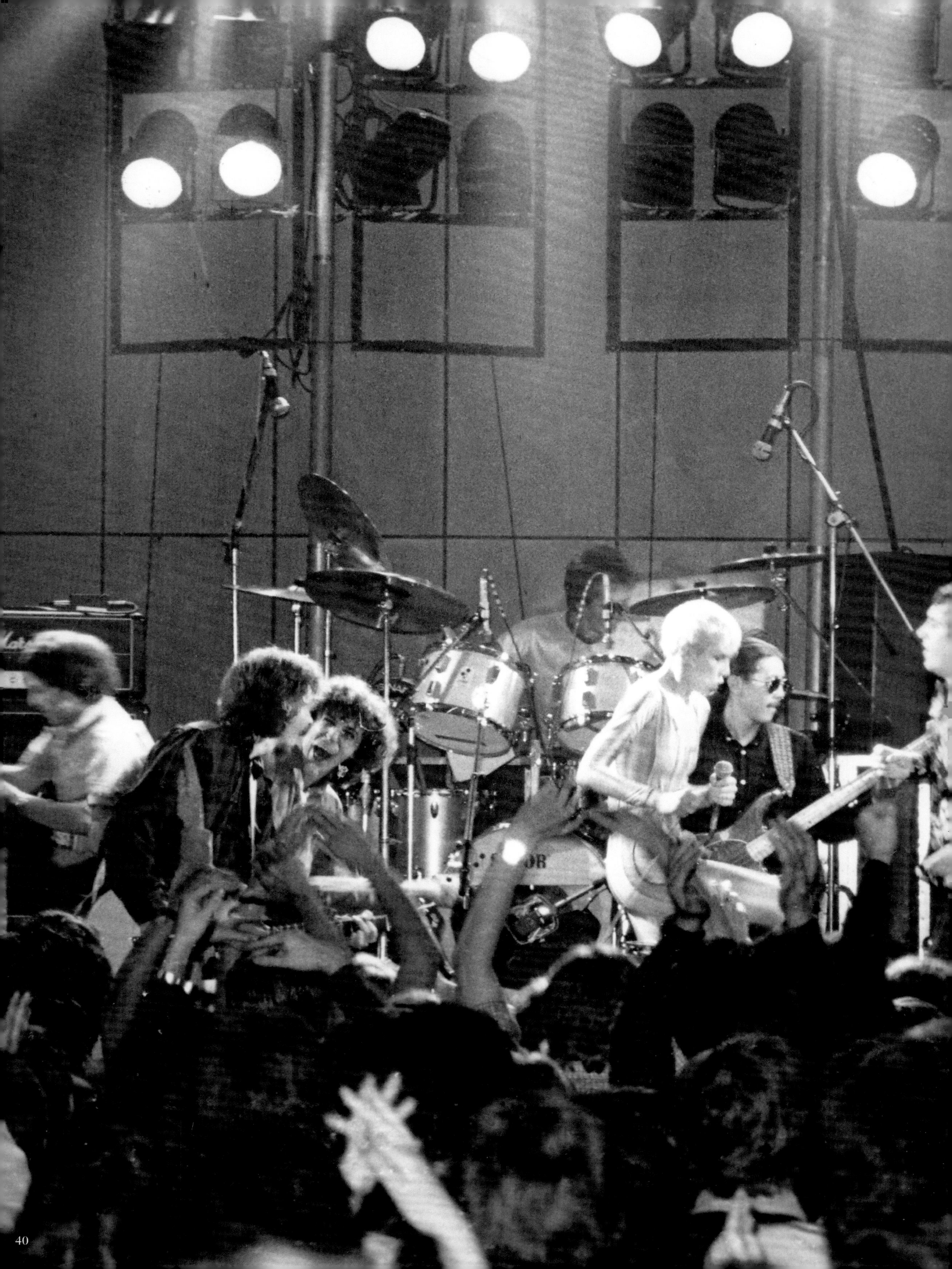

41

1980–84

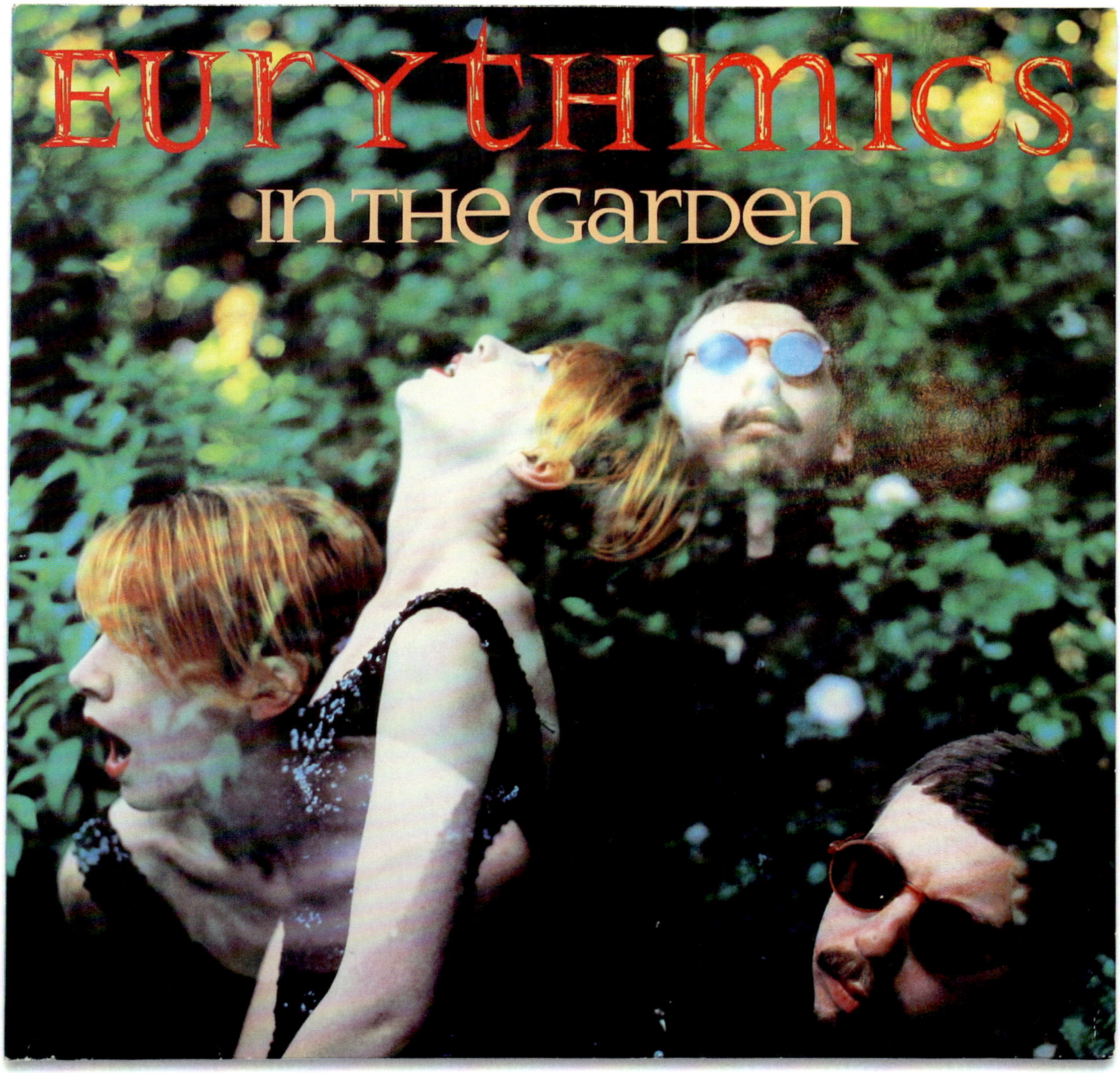
EURYTHMICS
IN THE GARDEN

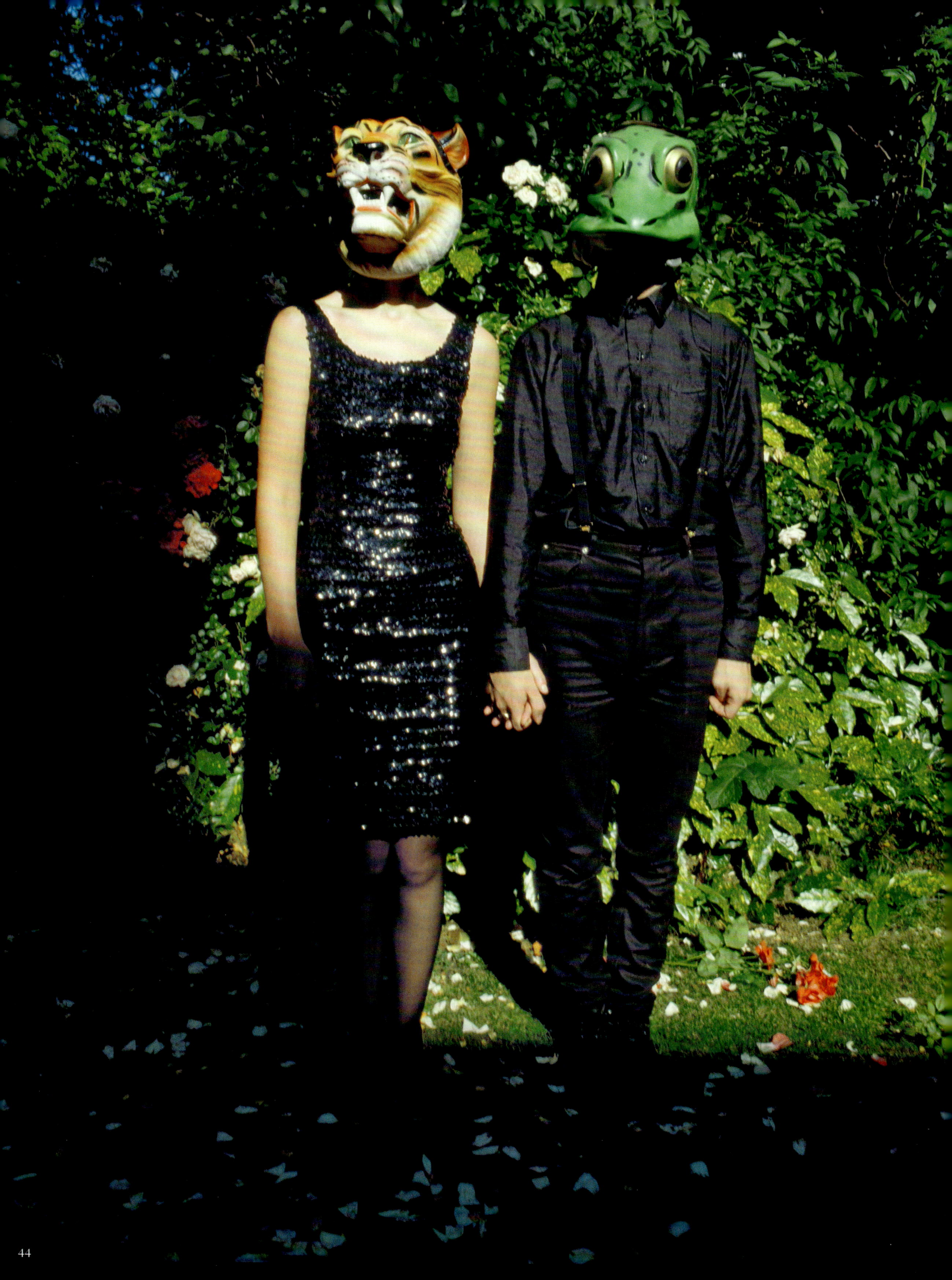

Dave and I had been together
As a couple
For about four years.
Not long after the Tourists disbanded
We broke up too.
It was very sad
But at that time
There were so many changes
Taking place
It was all part of the general upheaval

One thing we never questioned
Was staying together
For the music
Needless to say
It wasn't easy.

We were saddled
With the Tourists' debt
From the advance we'd received
From the record company
But somehow
We managed to cover our costs
And reinvented ourselves
As Eurythmics

We went to Germany
To record our first album
In the Garden
Produced by Conny Plank
Who, as well as being a friend,
Became something
Of a mentor
To Dave and I

46

It was a very experimental album
We pushed boundaries
And tried recording ideas
That were very out-of-the-box.

RCA records
Weren't thrilled by it.
We heard later
That they were about to drop us
When a new A and R man
Stepped in
And told them
We were the only band
On the roster
That he actually wanted
To work with.

Thank you Jack Steven.

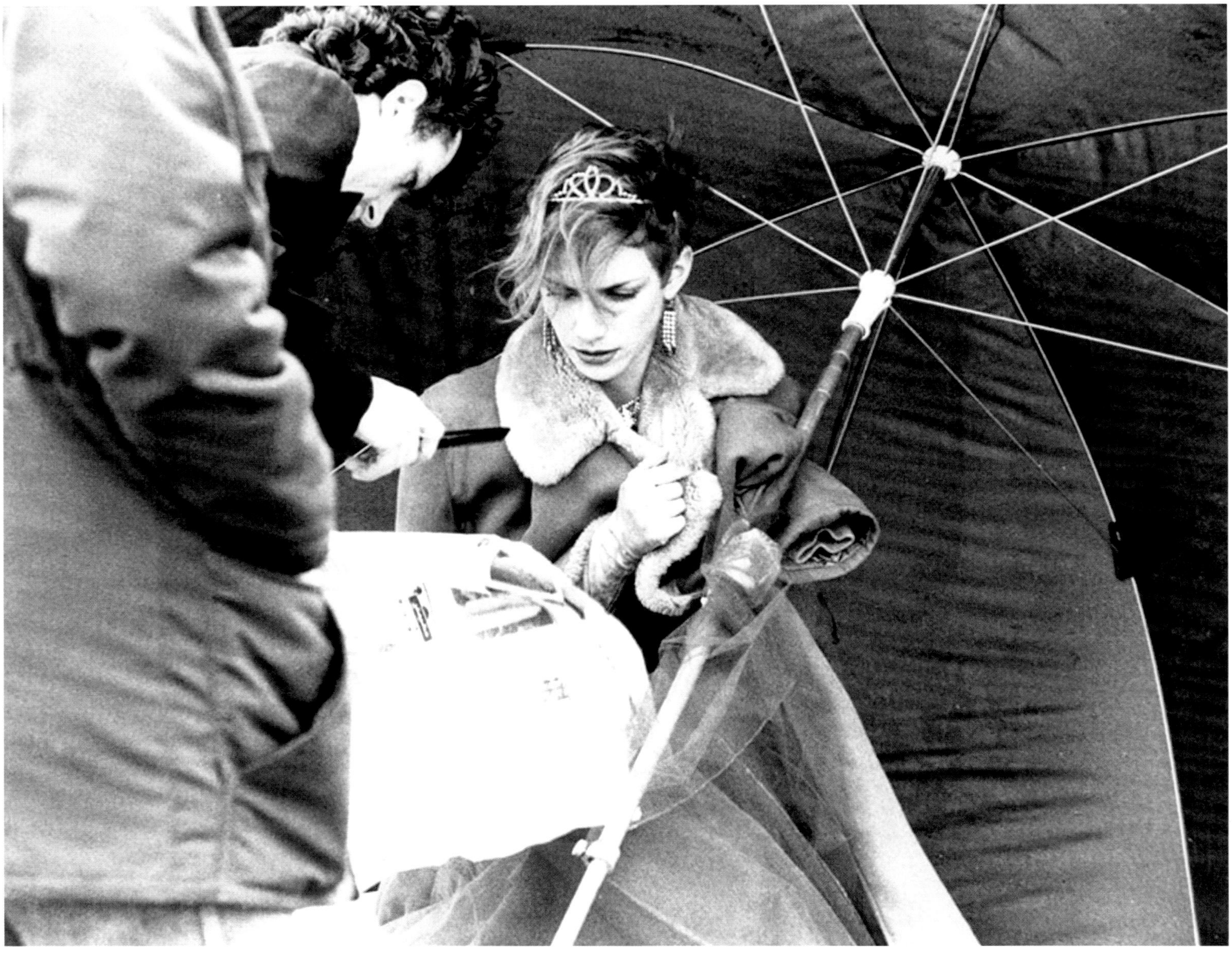

I'm never gonna cry again
I'm never gonna die again
I shed some tears for you
I shed more tears for you than the ocean
The ocean

I didn't wanna let you know
I didn't wanna take your time
I didn't wanna bring you down
I didn't want to hang around you
Around you

So we're livin' in desperate times
Oh such an unfortunate time
I can't relate to you
I just can't find a place to be near you
To be near you

We performed so many concerts.
It's all something of a blur to me now.
This was clearly taken around the time we were recording 'Sweet Dreams.'
I can tell because my hair is distinctly shorn. Cropped and bright orange, despite the picture being in black and white.
After years of varying hair styles, I finally came upon the *one* that I've pretty much kept ever since.
At first, I would bleach my hair as white as it would go.
Then I'd make up a thick paste with hot water mixed with henna powder, which I'd layer all over my head.
It was a messy process, with the unwieldy globs of henna paste dropping everywhere.
But the striking effect made it all worth the effort.
Cutting your hair short often feels like a sort of relief.
There's no styling involved for weeks.
No taming, persuading or blow drying.
It's the easiest way to wear your hair and you spend almost no time on it.
Practically, it wins every time – hands down!
Later on, I discovered a magic potion called Crazy Colour.
It replaced the henna and was a *much* easier process all round.

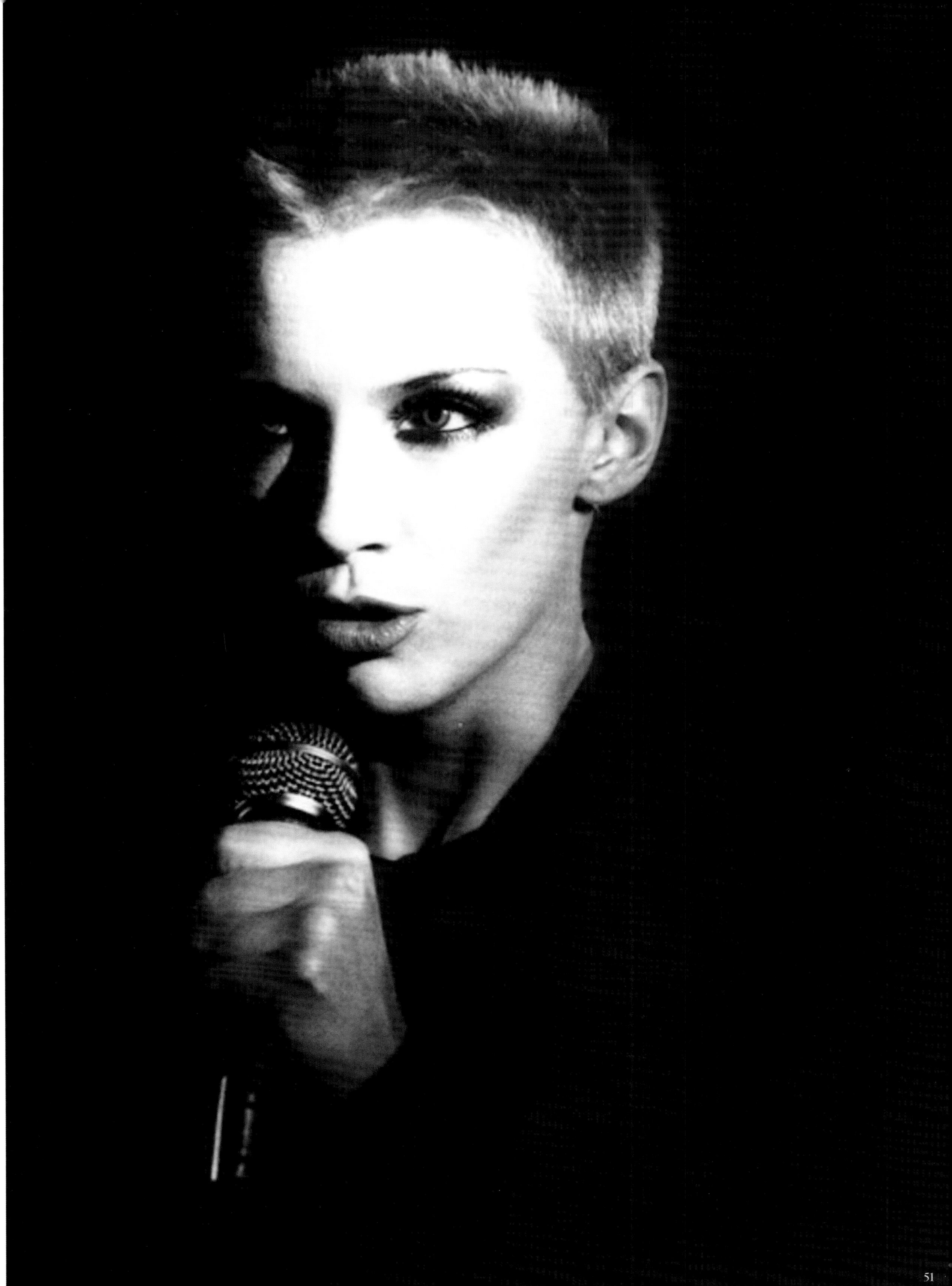

Holding a chocolate-box heart
The contents unseen
Like the one behind the mask
L'amour
What does it mean?
Your chocolate-box heart
With the contents
Unseen…

EURYTHMICS

SWEET DREAMS —are made of this·»

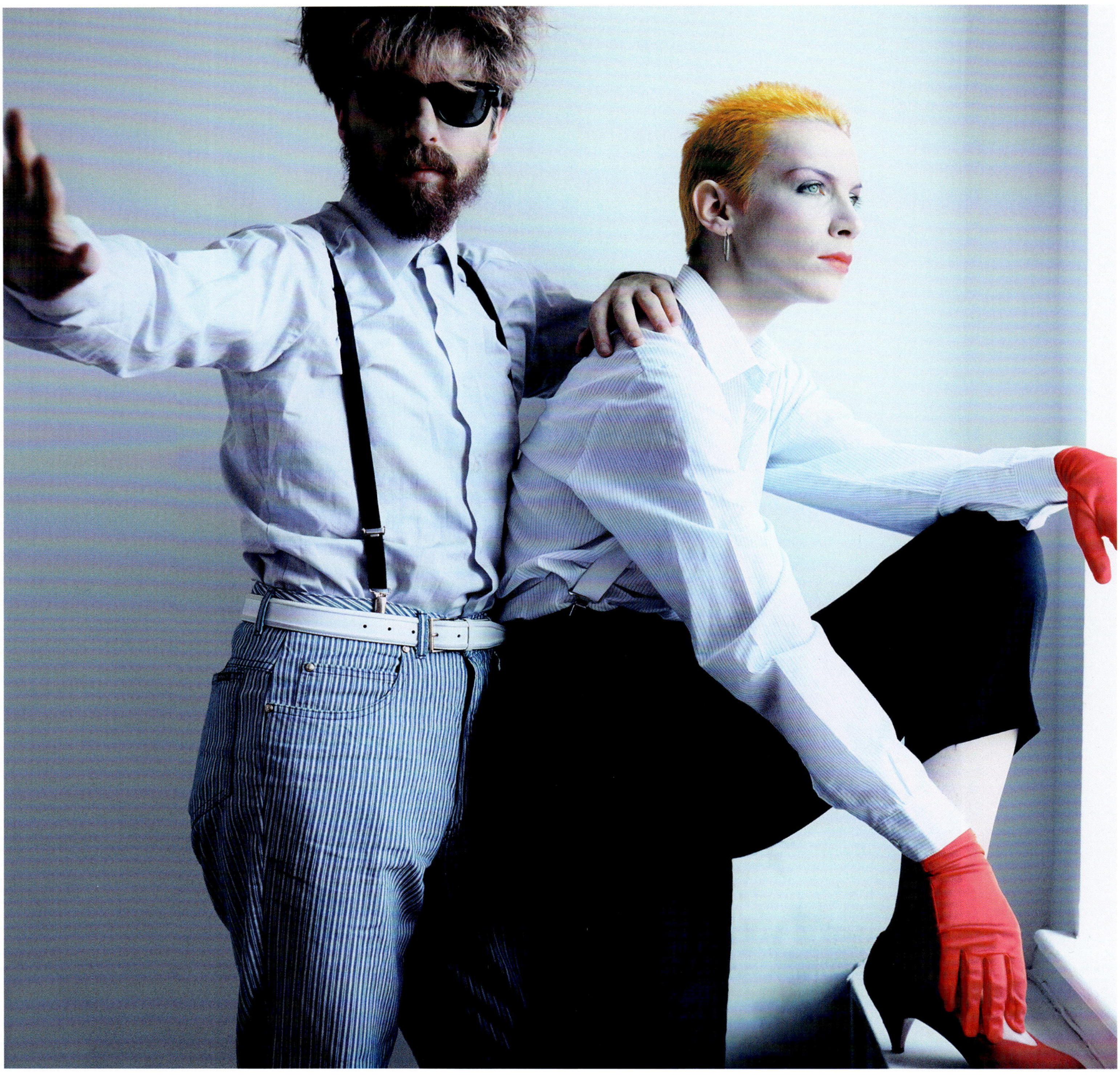

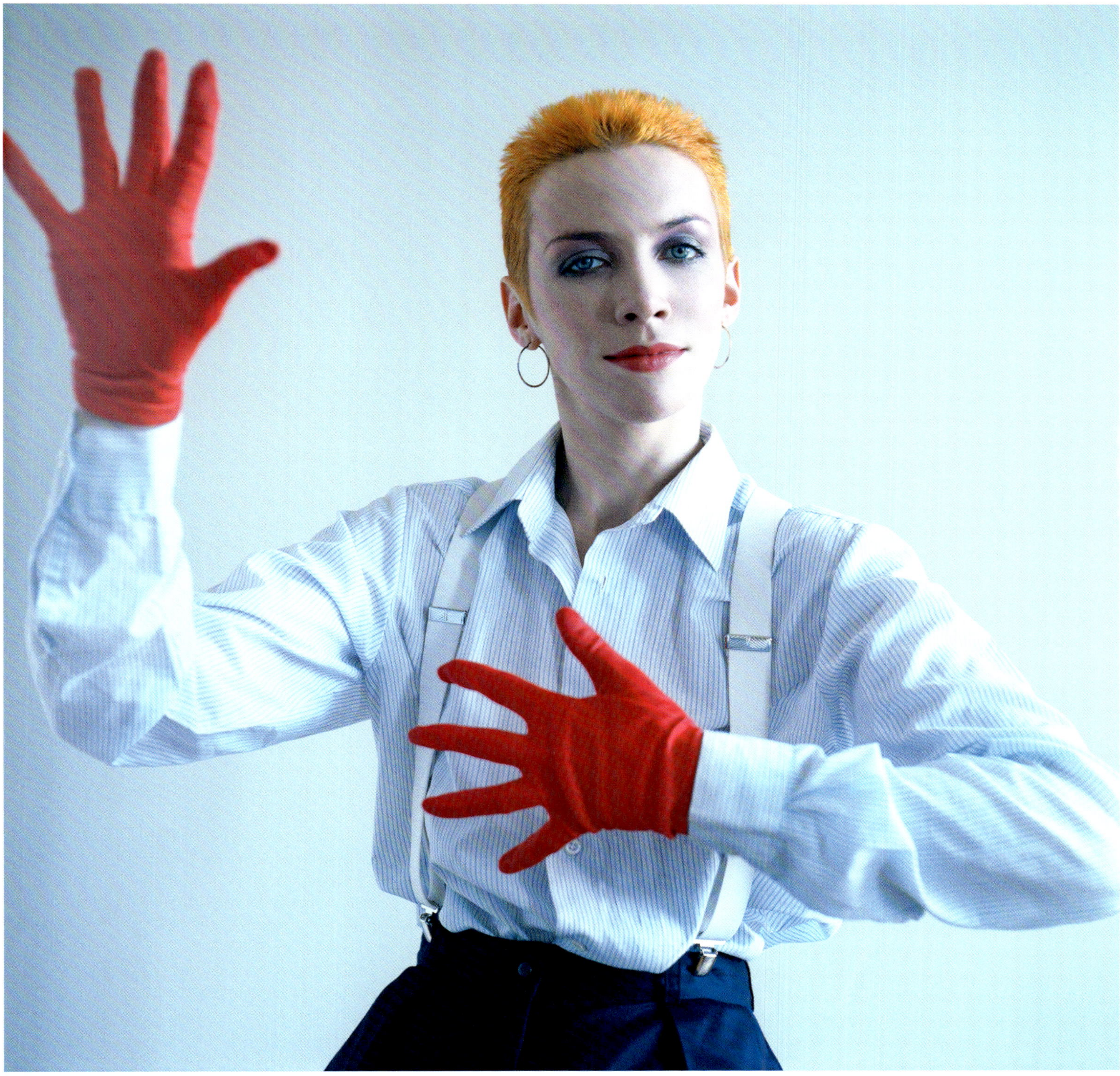

56

Sweet dreams are made of this
Who am I to disagree
I travel the world and the seven seas
Everybody's lookin' for something

Some of them want to use you
Some of them want to get used by you
Some of them want to abuse you
Some of them want to be abused

Even as I look at these photographs now, I see a particular kind of courage and confidence it takes to look directly into a camera lens like this. The gaze seems impermeable and almost defiant. I think it was borne out of all the experiences that had gone before that very moment in time, just before the shutter clicked.

We bought two matching suits from a cheap gentlemen's outfitters. With white shirts and formal ties, we took our places in front of Lewis Ziolek's camera, standing on a background of white paper.

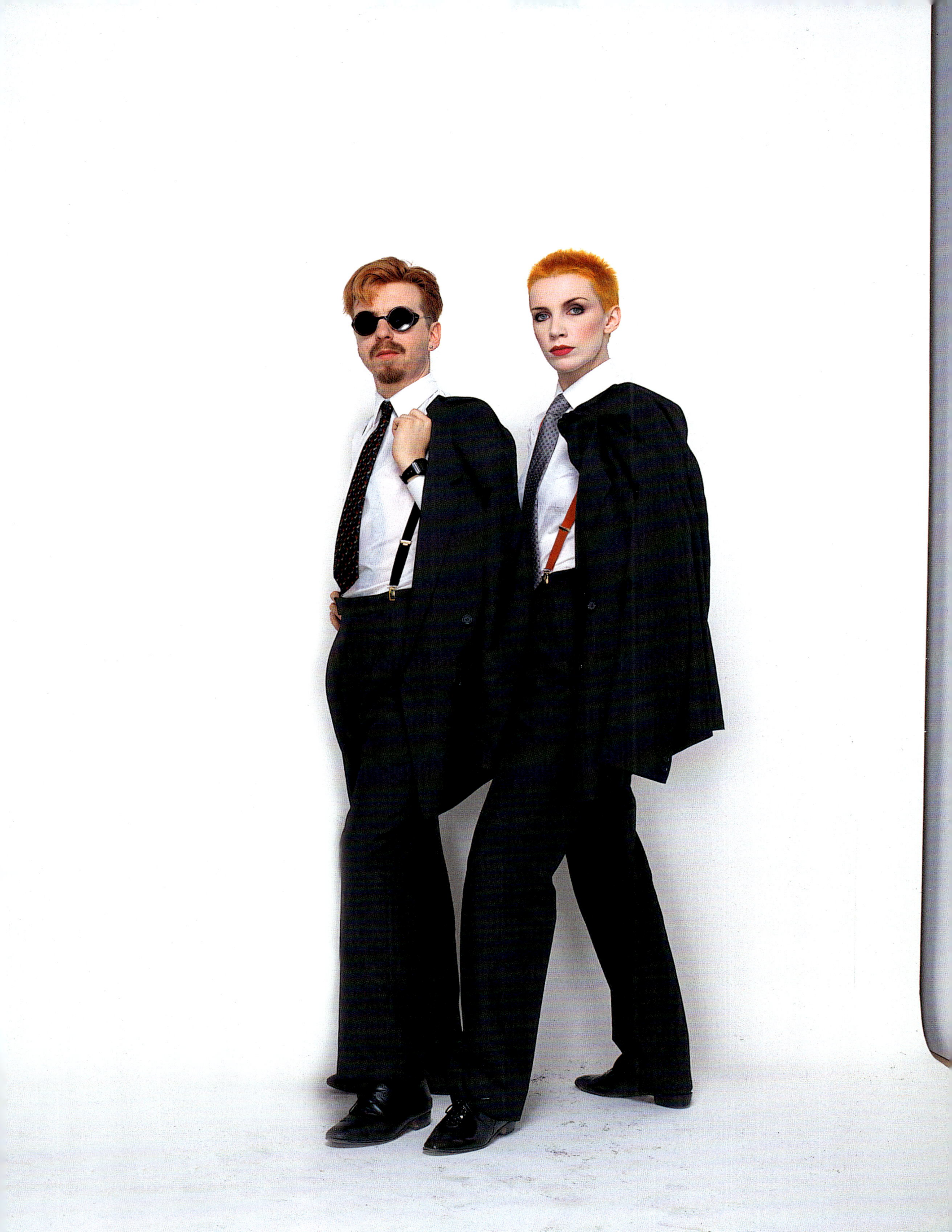

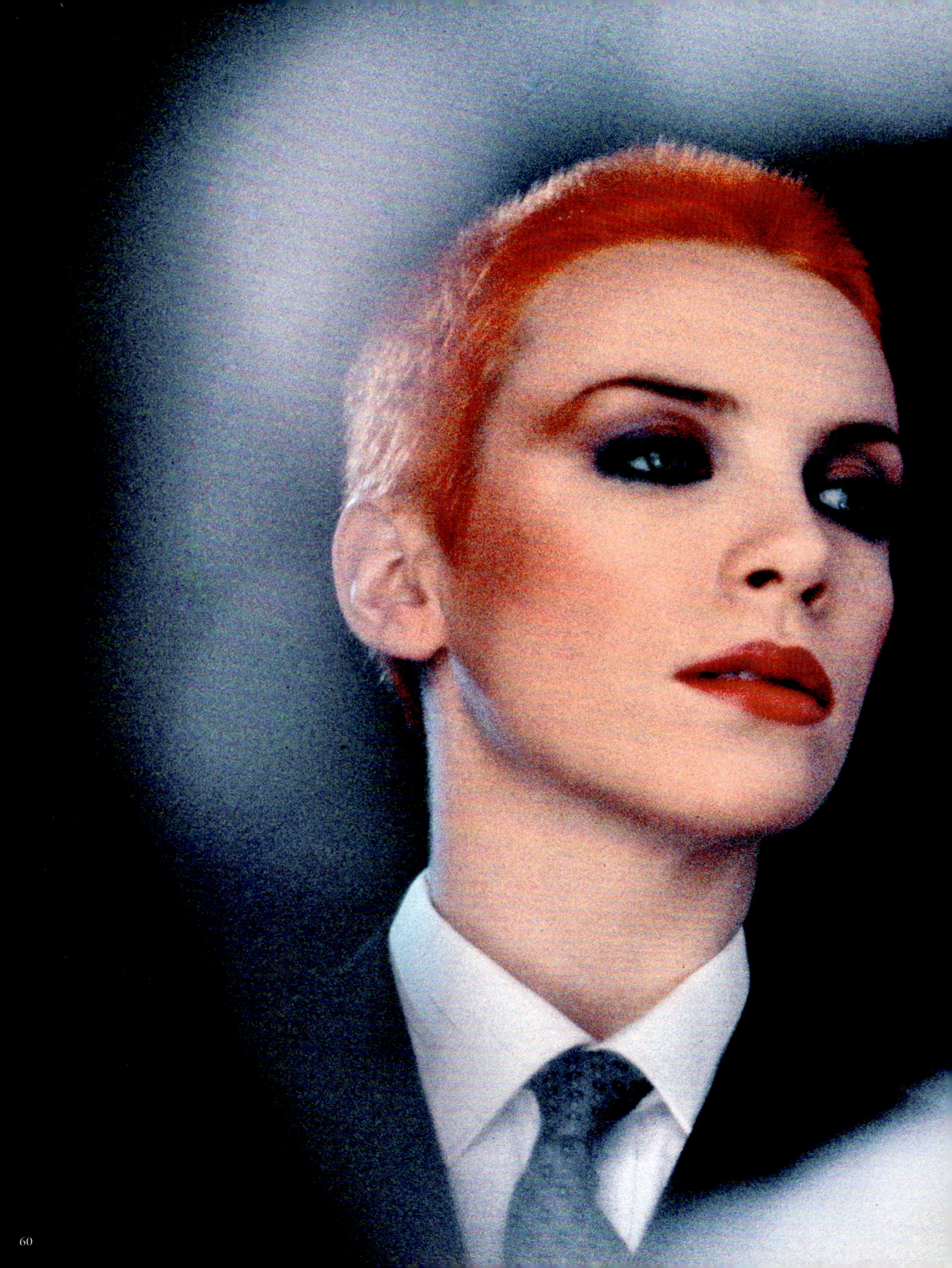

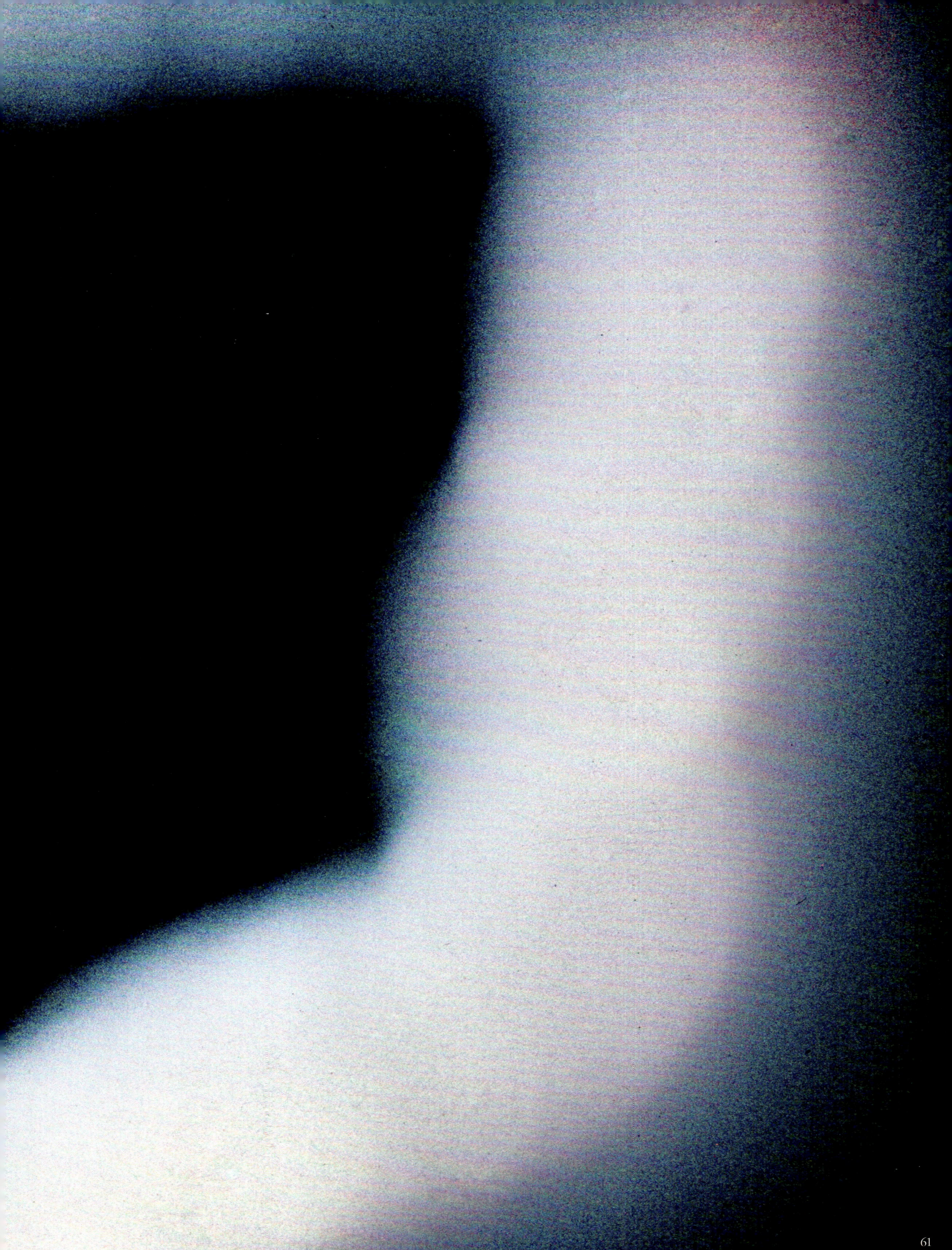

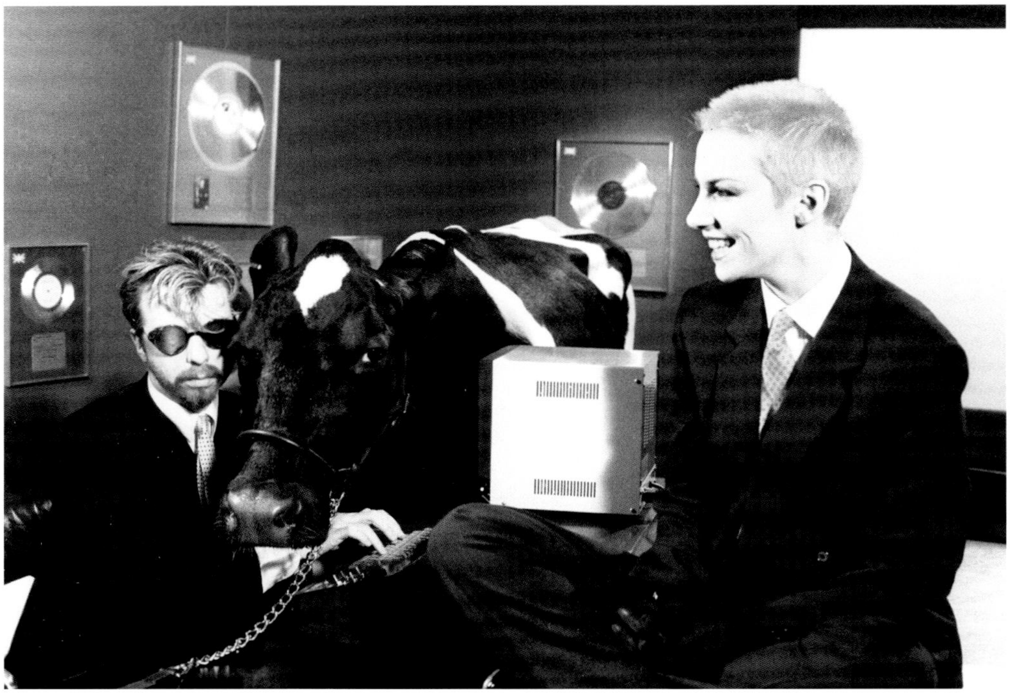

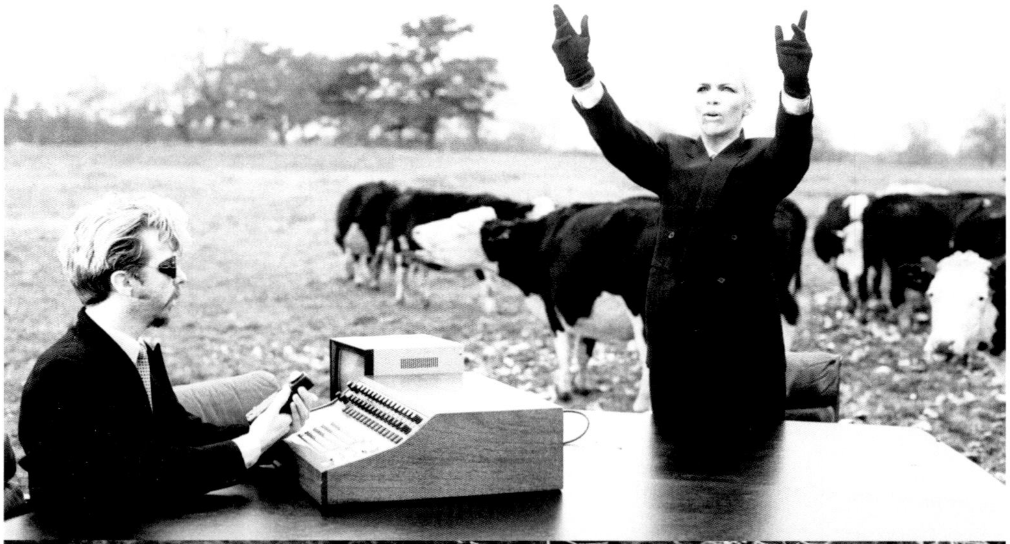

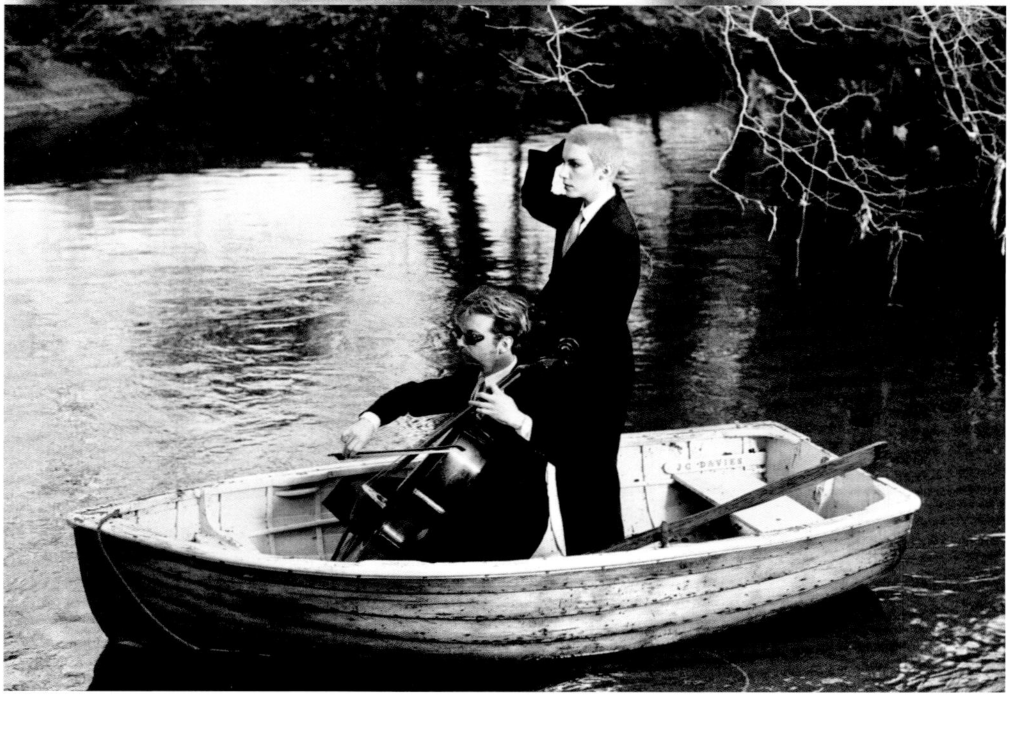

These photographs were taken on set, during the filming of Eurythmics' 'Sweet Dreams' video. We started in a tiny basement room in London's Soho. The Friesian cow was taken down very carefully in a goods lift, while everyone looked on with bated breath.

Dave's concept of having a cow in a boardroom became manifest right there and then. The room went so silent you could have heard a mouse squeak.

(I don't know what was in that cup, but it made my hair grow right away!)

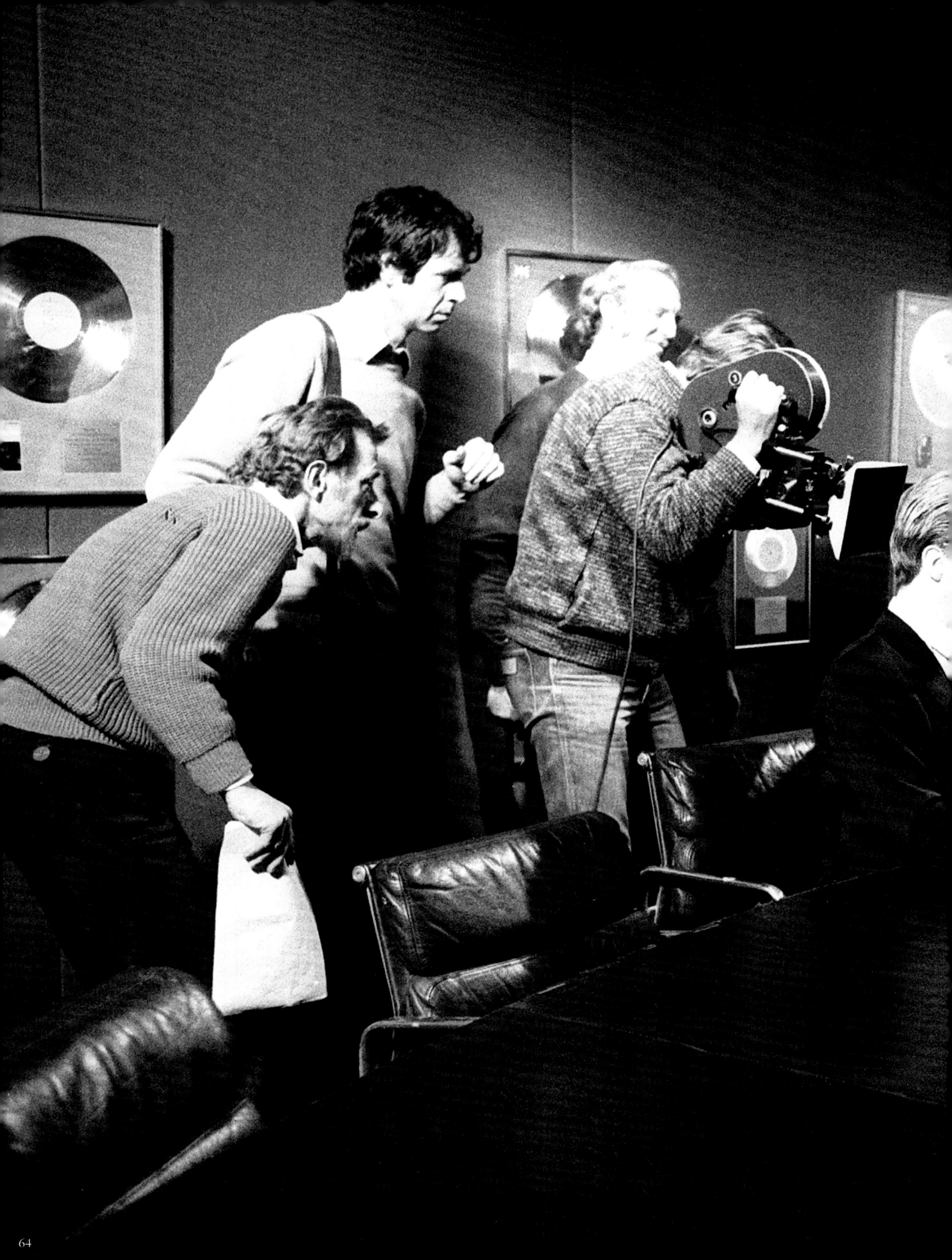

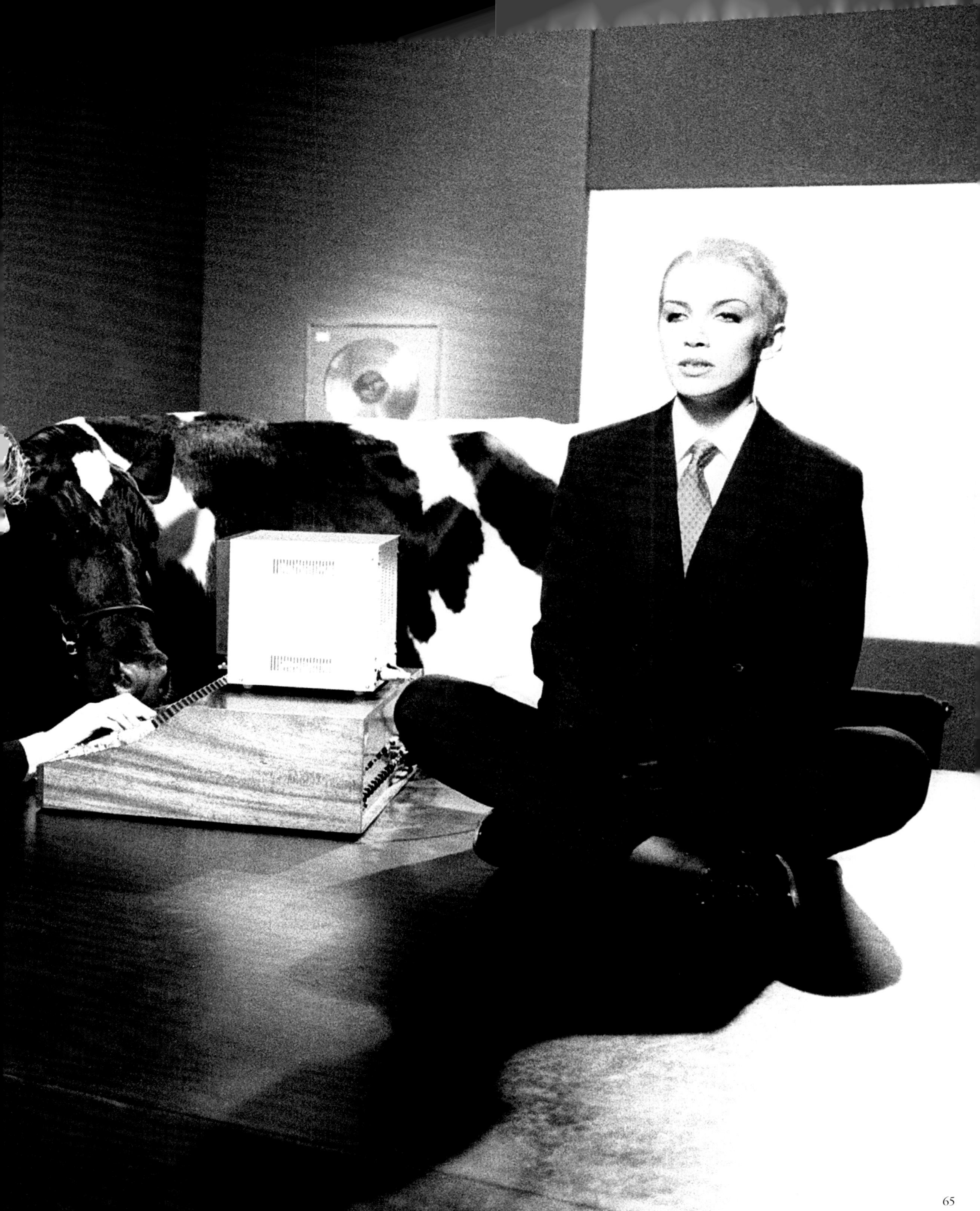

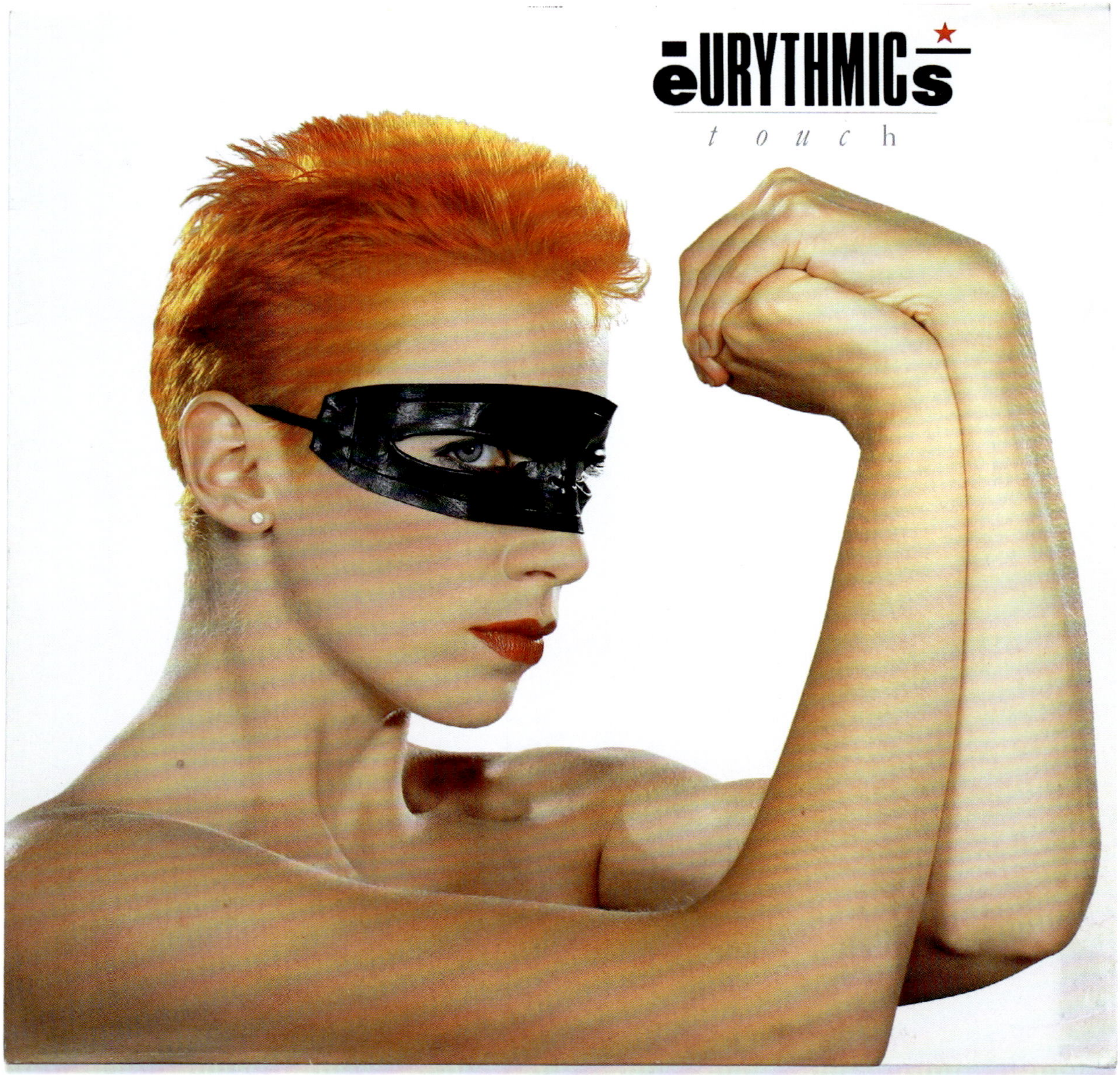
EURYTHMICS
touch

Three Polaroids from a session with Peter Ashworth, a photograph from which became the front cover for the Eurythmics album *Touch*. Progressing from the velvet beaded mask of 'Sweet Dreams' to a harder-edged black leather.

67

Apart from the occasional magazine article, I've actually rarely ever worked with a stylist. I brought my own clothes to wear in most of the photographs in this book. Sometimes I'd go to a costume-hire store or warehouse to trawl through the racks, looking for elements to bring to photo sessions. I found this fantastic pink ballroom dance gown, a gold lamé suit, and red-and-gold platform boots in a shop in King's Cross in London, as well as this somewhat disquieting plastic see-through mask of a 1940s gentleman's face.

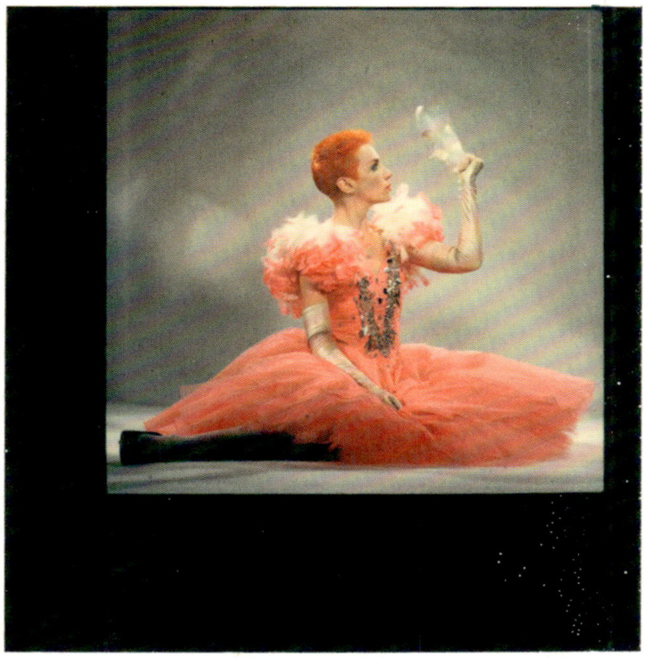

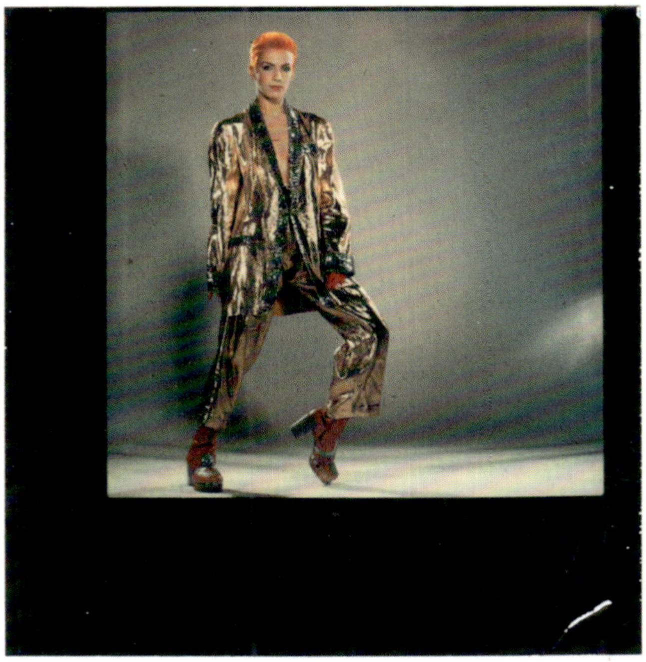

70

71

Going a little experimental, with shimmering makeup and matching metallic earrings. A cross between a 1930s ingenue and a 1980s punkish rocker.

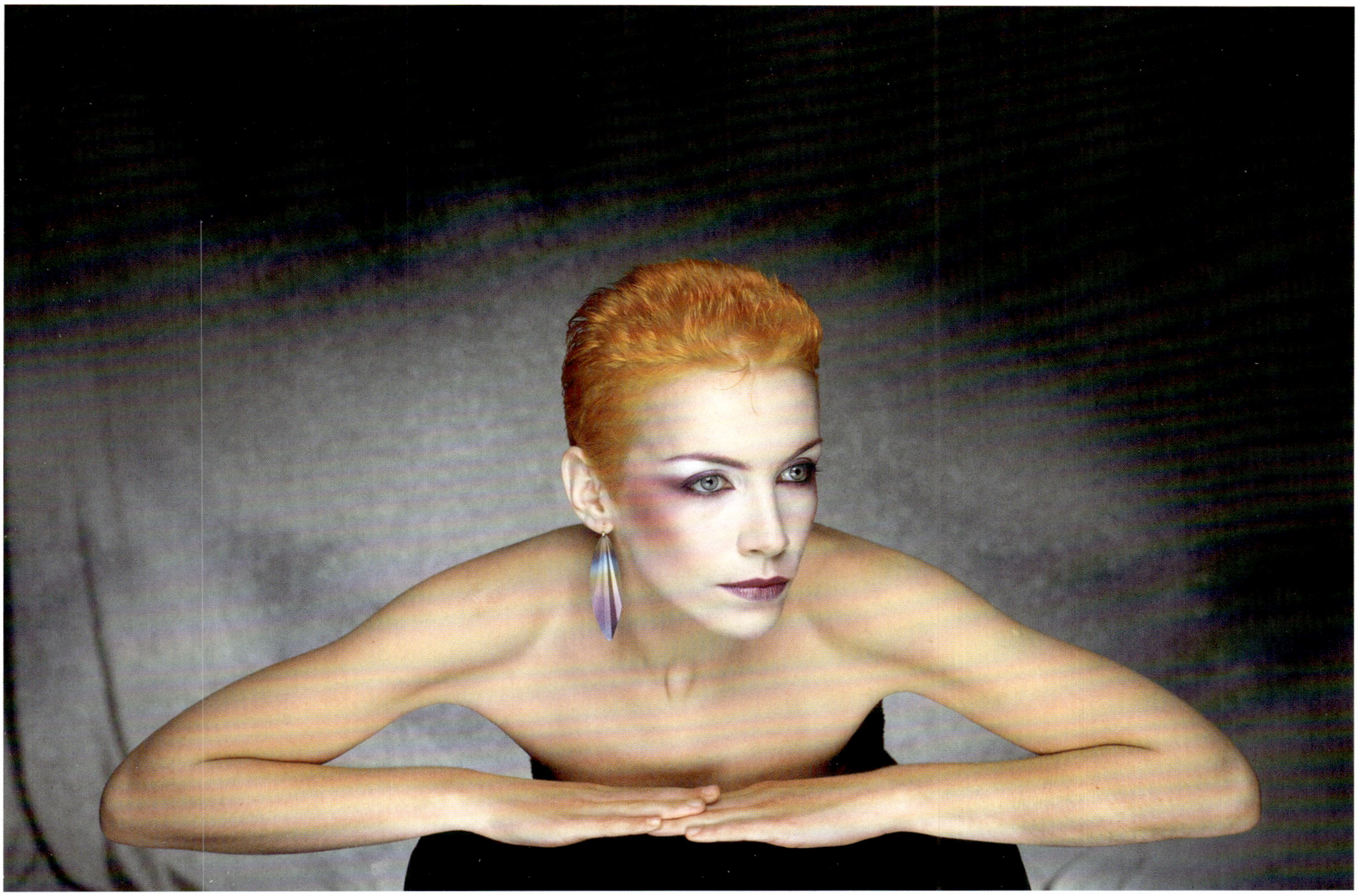

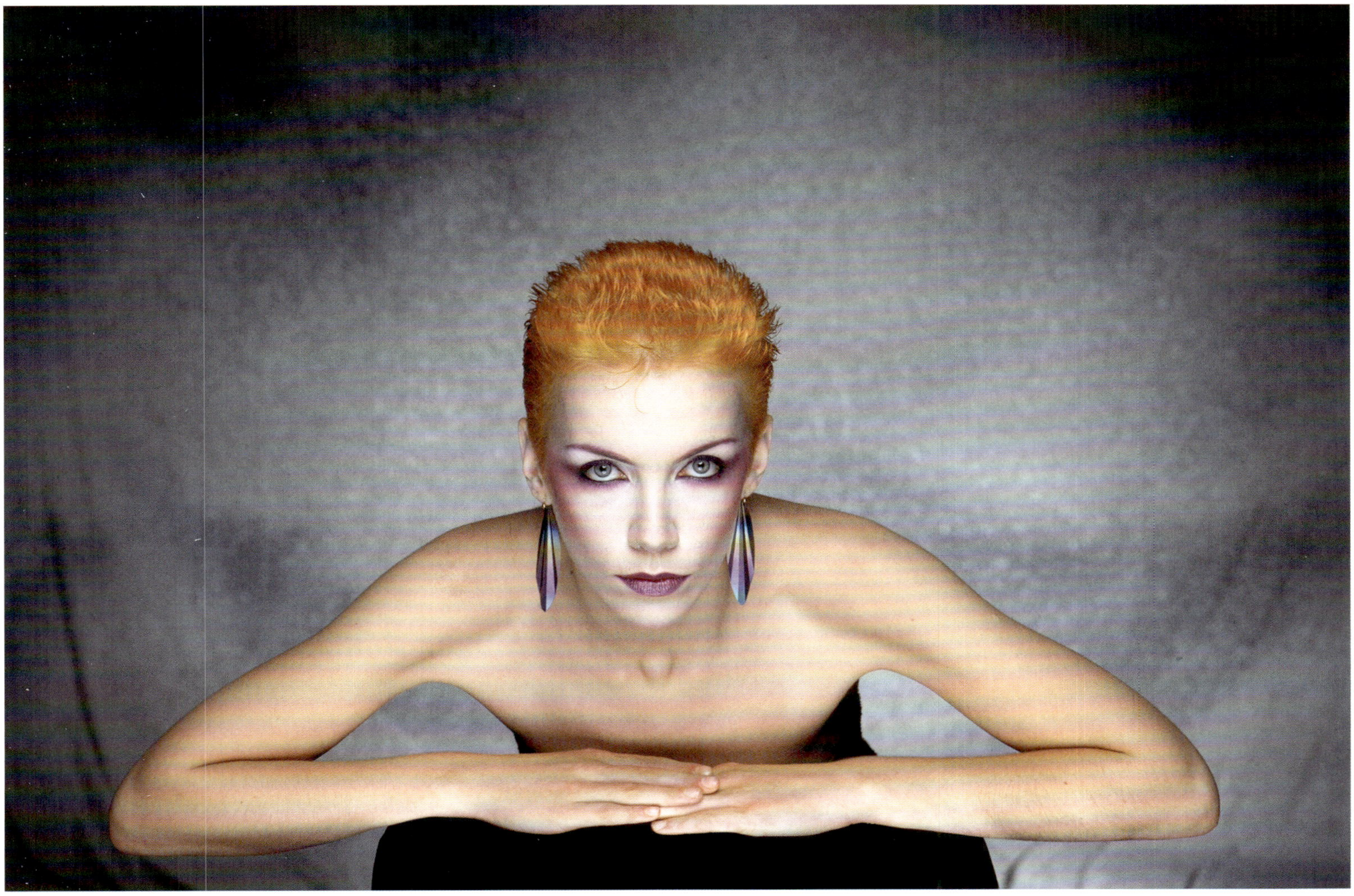

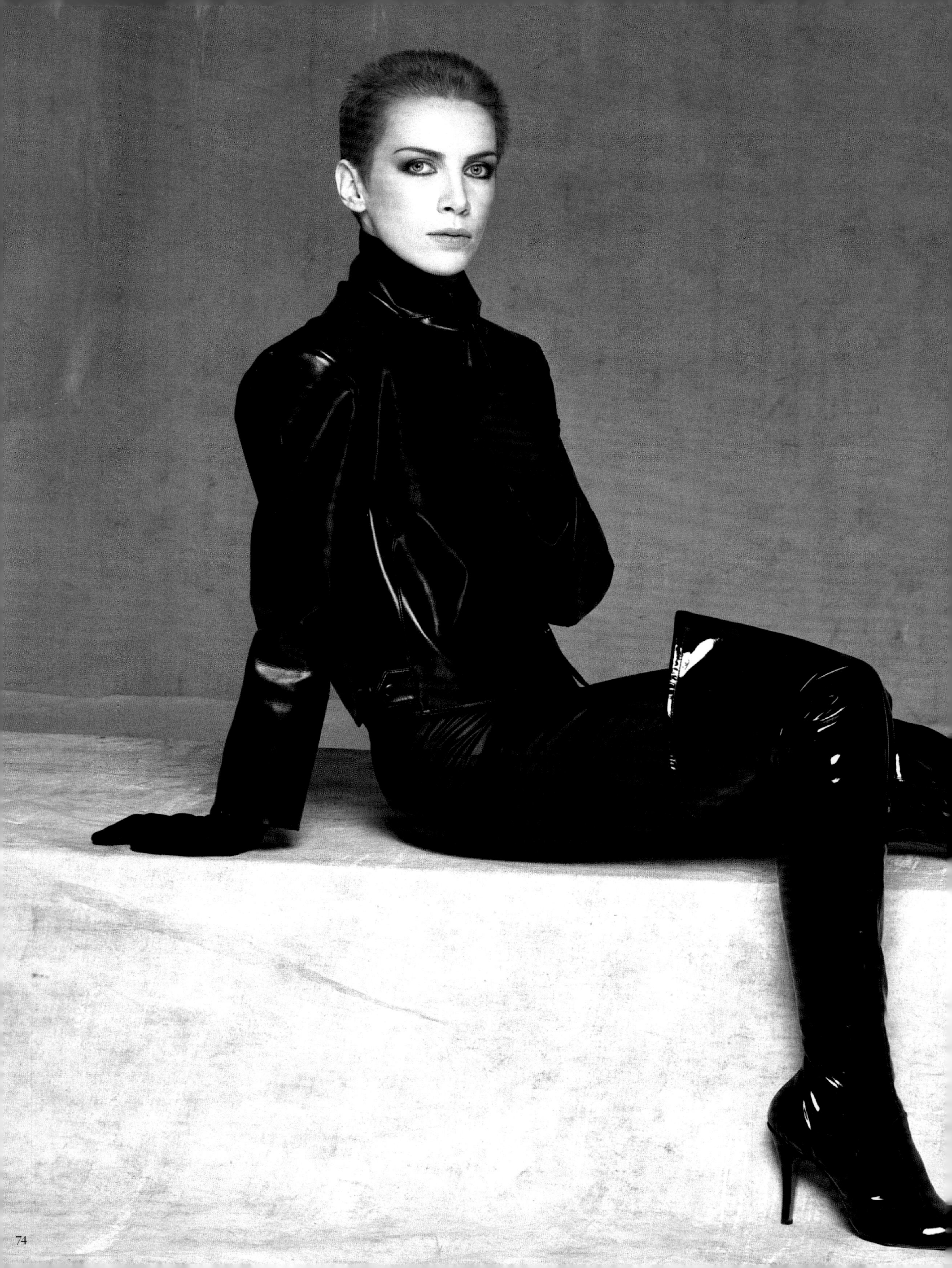

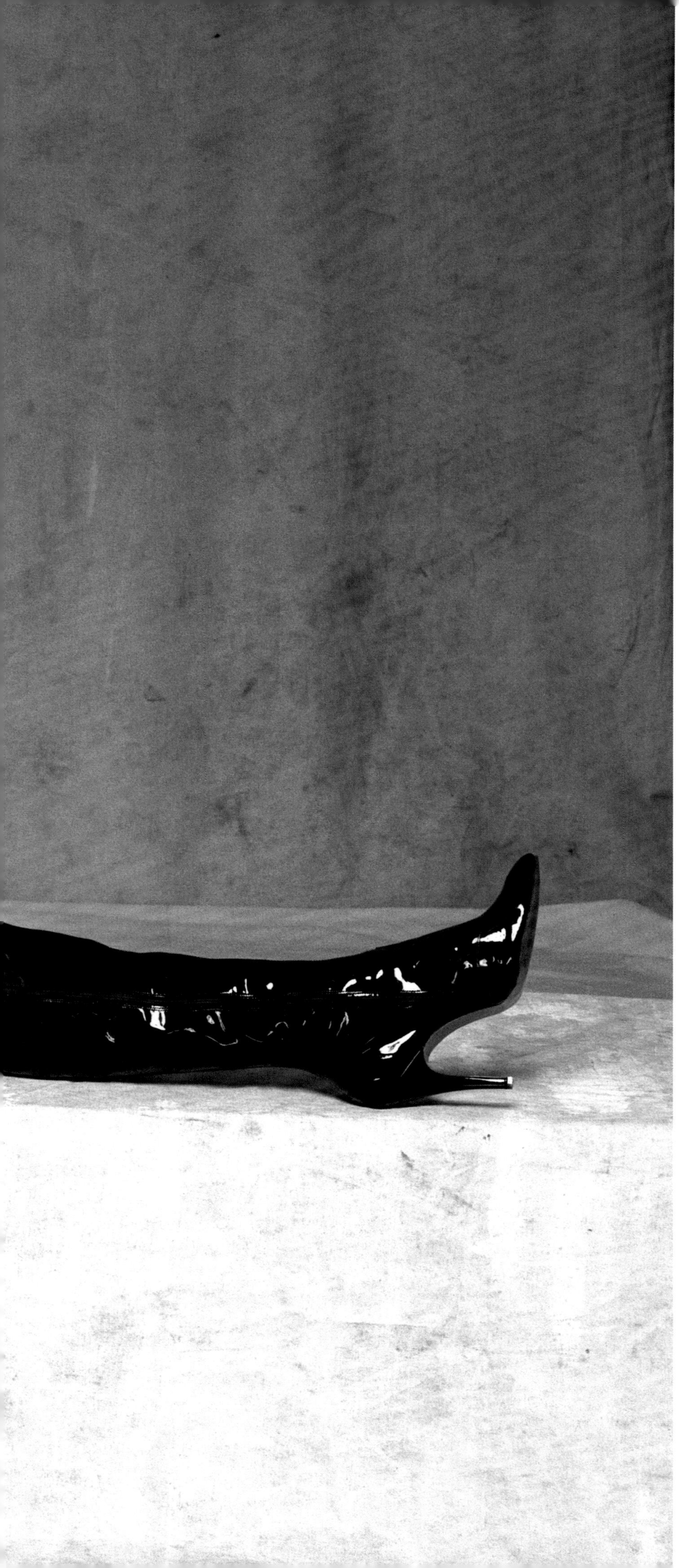

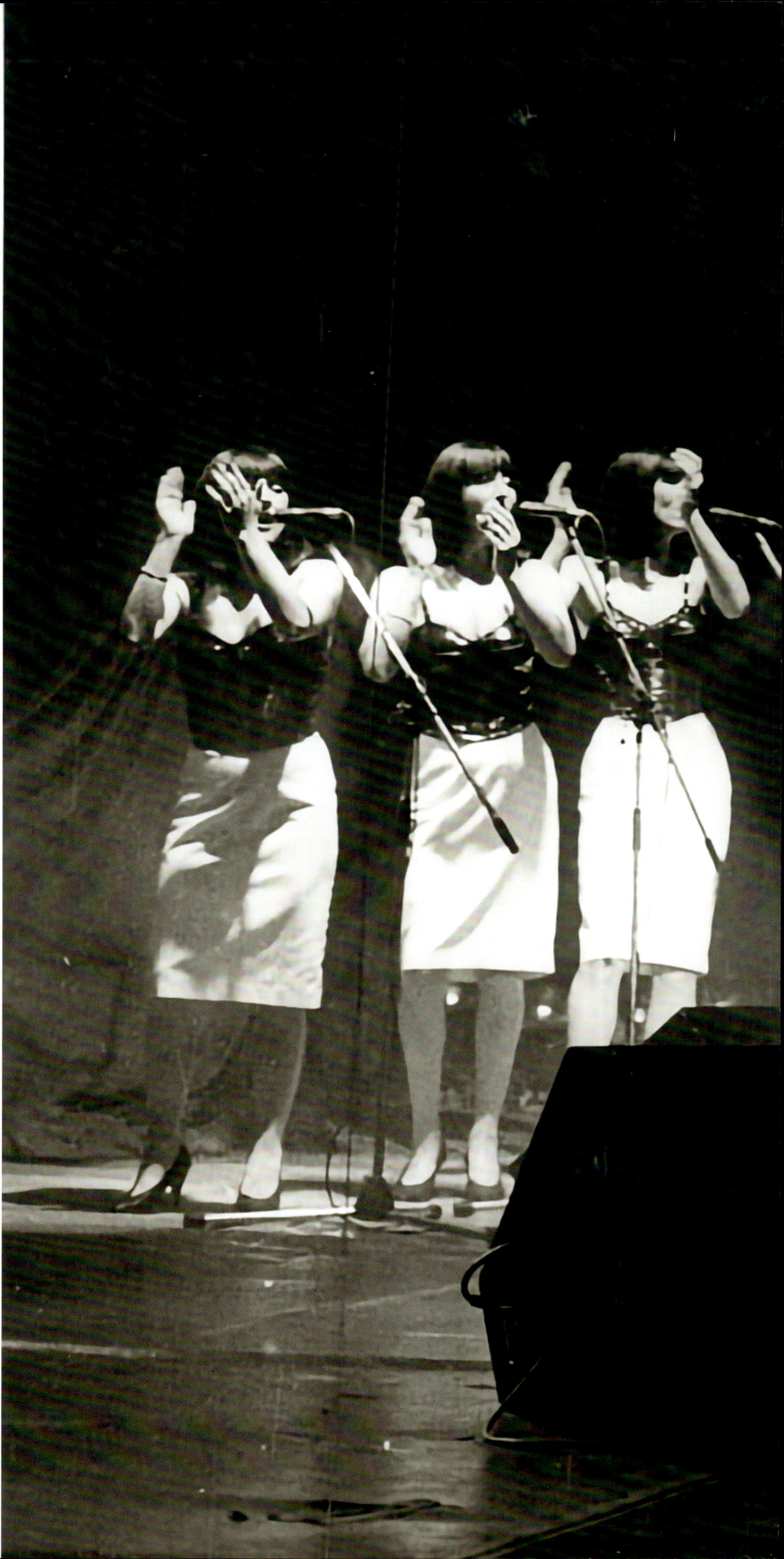

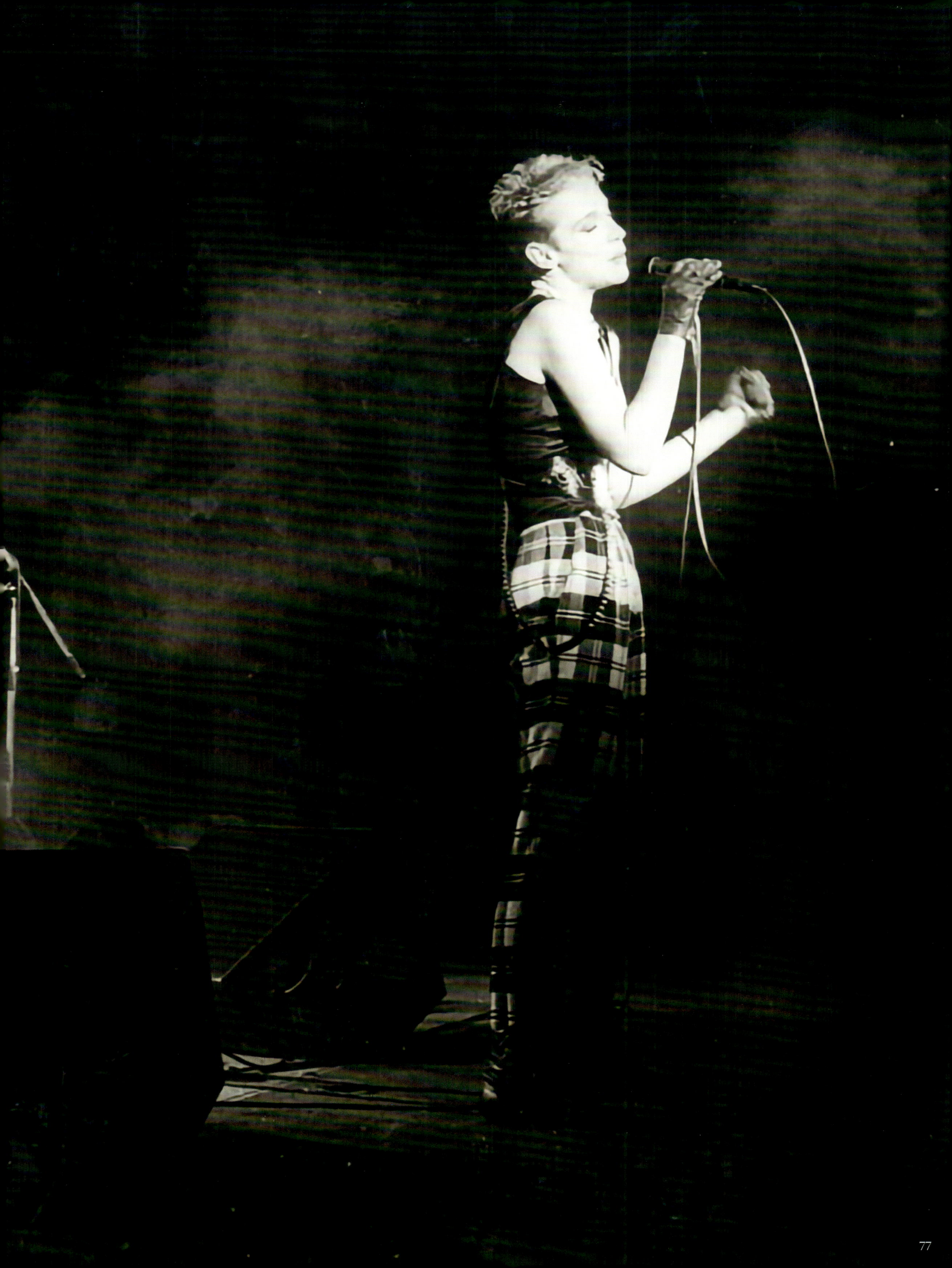

In many ways, I realize now that all the experiences I'd gone through with the Tourists had been a very intense learning curve. That even if it had felt like an overwhelm of setbacks, the struggle had also given Dave and me an intense drive to create music and imagery that would resonate powerfully in the zeitgeist. We upped our game, almost without realizing it. Anything that didn't fit with our vision was swiftly discarded.

We were on a serious mission to carve out and create the very best songs and concepts we possibly could.

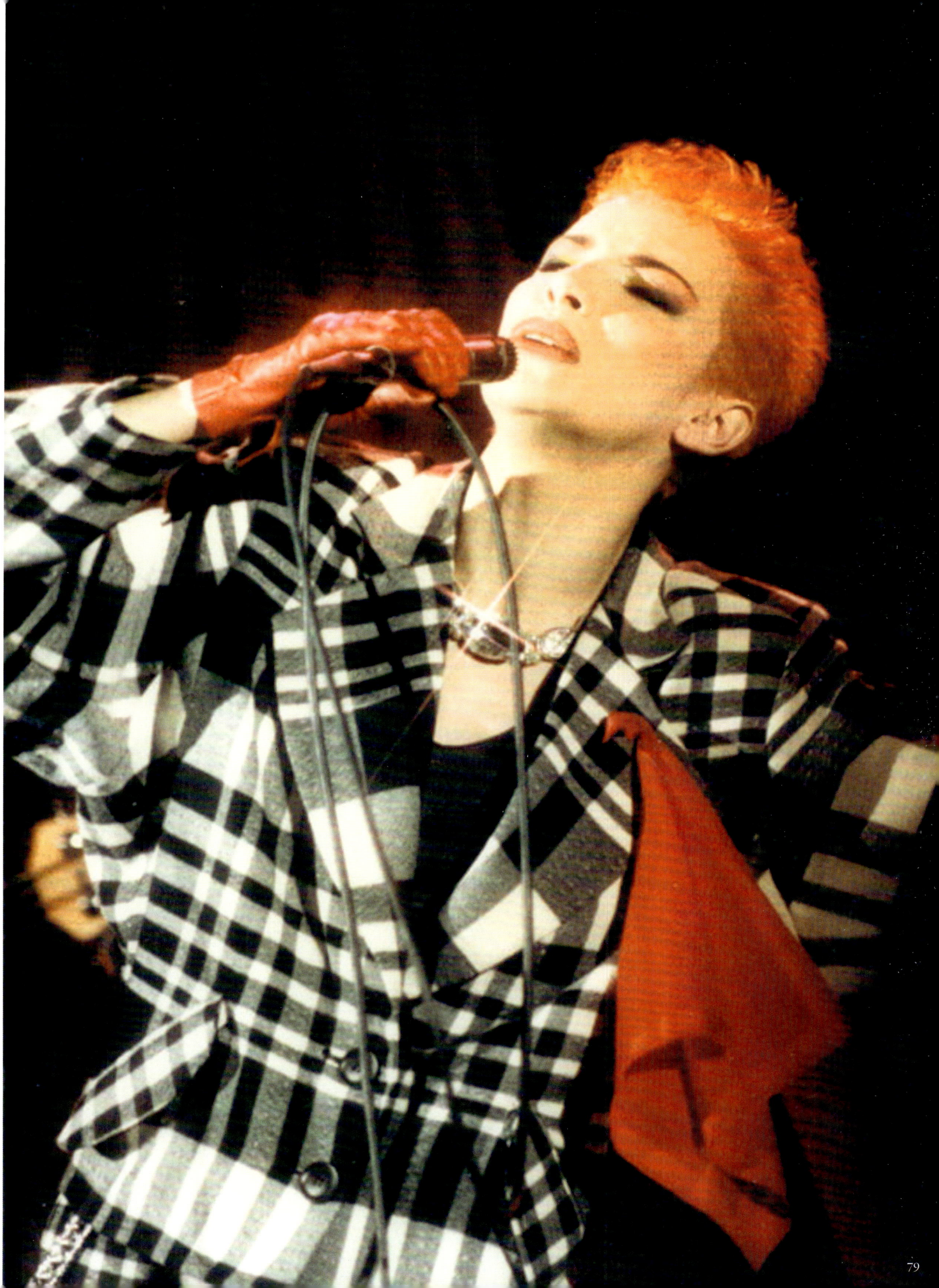

These shots were taken during the video shoot for 'Here Comes the Rain Again,' which was filmed on the Island of Orkney, off the North coast of Scotland.
Orkney is a wild and rugged place.
Staggeringly beautiful – dark, ancient, and melancholic.
It was teeth-chatteringly cold, in that way where it's almost impossible to access any effective source of heat, while your very bones have turned to ice. The shoot was a long and tough one, starting just before sunrise and going on for the rest of the day, until the final roll of film had been taken.
That was the moment when Dave and I jumped for joy!

81

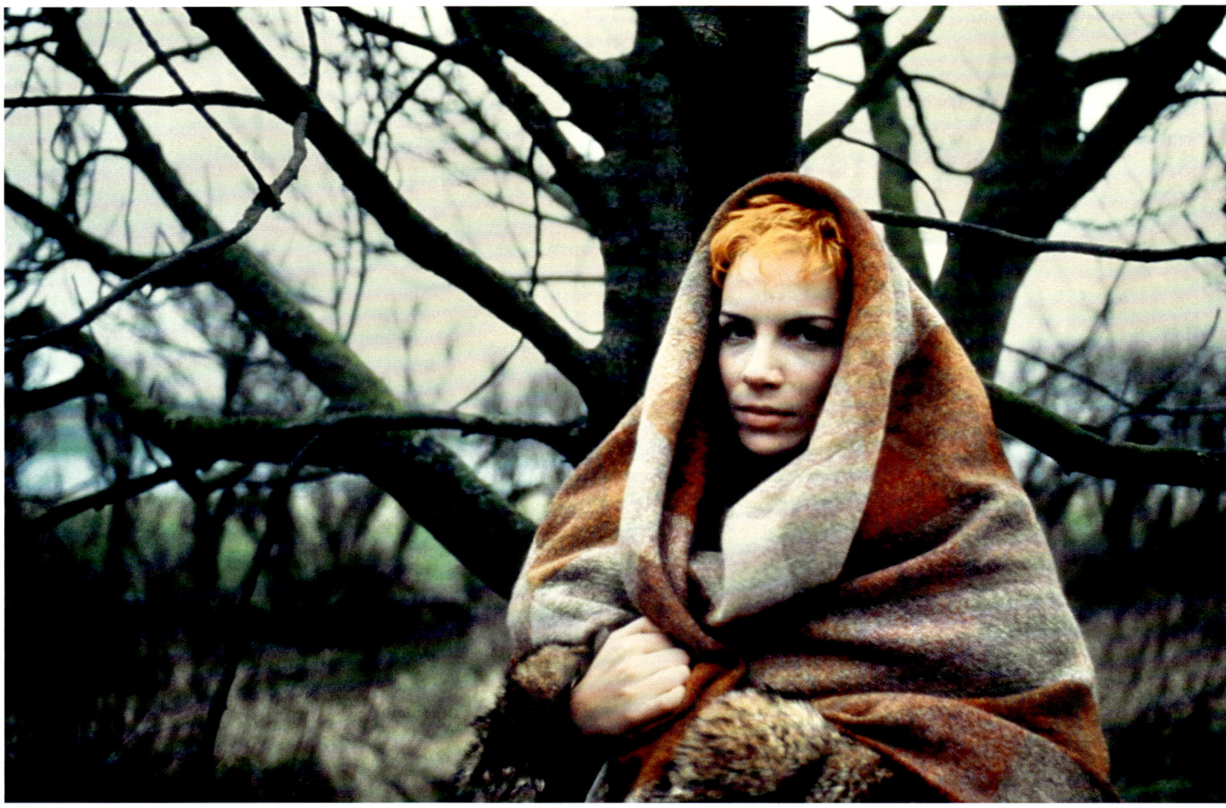

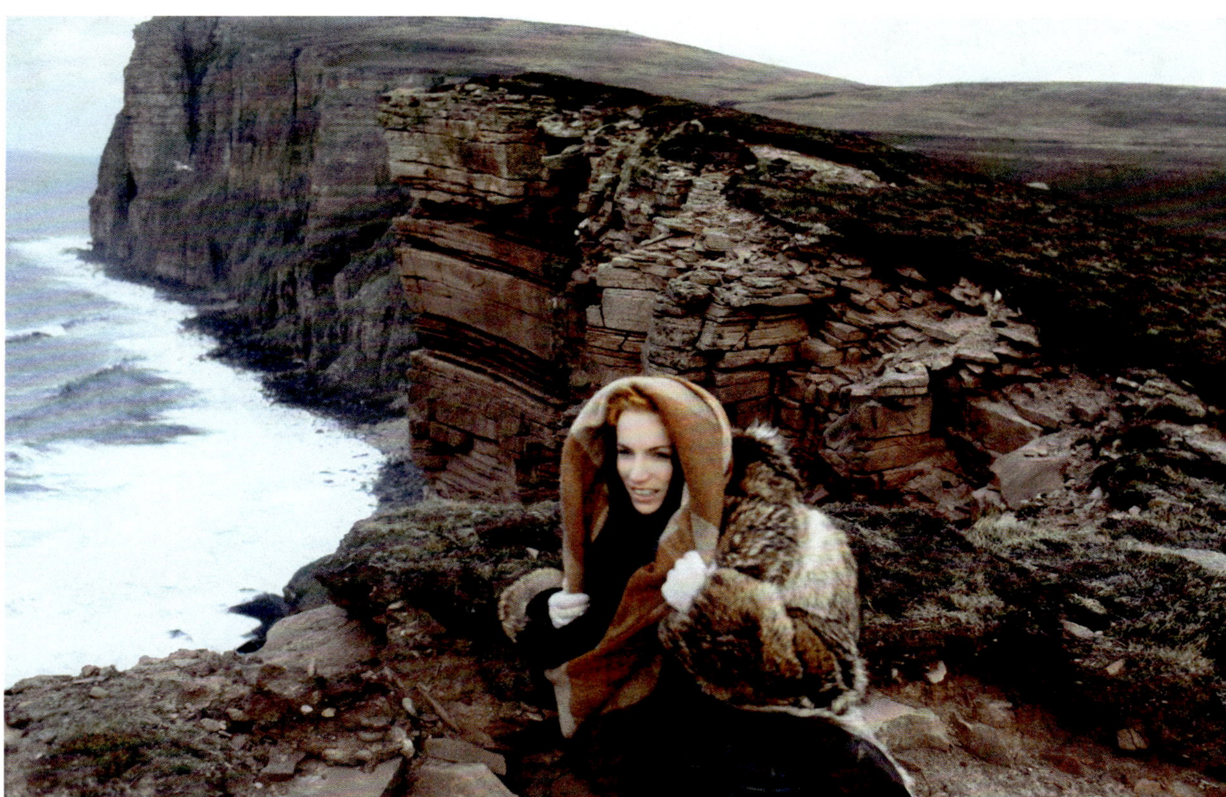

Here comes the
rain again
Raining in my head
like a tragedy
Tearing me apart like
a new emotion

I want to breathe in the
open wind
I want to kiss like
lovers do
Want to dive into
your ocean
Is it raining with you?

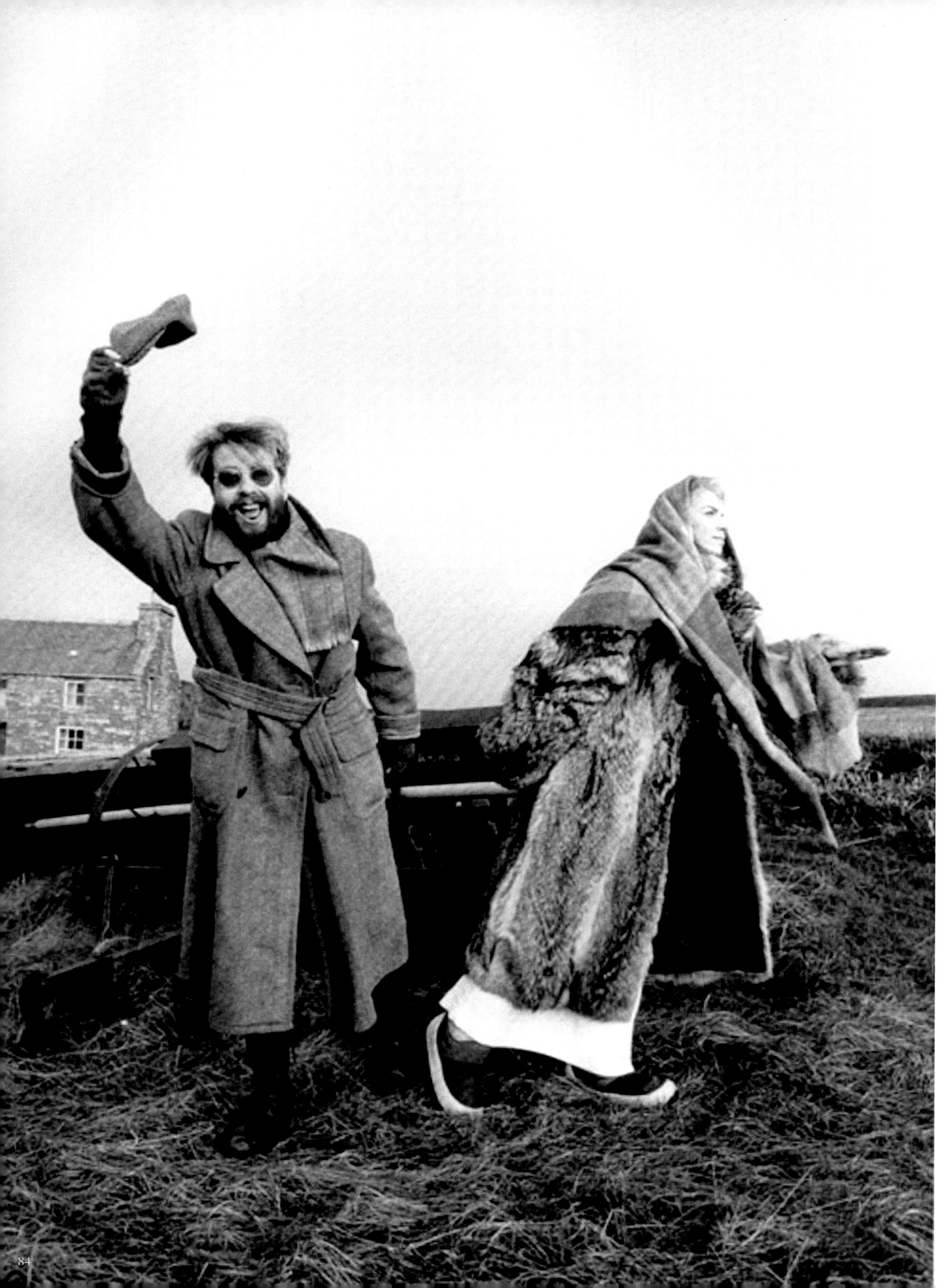

85

1984
WRIT LARGE
THE FACE
BEST, WORST, UPS, DOWNS; ALL THE ANGLES ON '84
ANNIE LENNOX FACE INTERVIEW
SPITTING IMAGES
PAUL YOUNG
DAN AYKROYD
HEALTH CLUB DISCOS
JAMES TRUMAN NY '84

There was a controversy around Eurythmics recording the music for *1984*. When Virgin Films asked us to do it, they omitted to tell us that the director of the film, Michael Radford, had already had an orchestral score composed and recorded that they didn't actually like. They were asking us to replace it, without telling us the 'truth' about the situation. 'Rescuing their investment,' as they saw it. If we'd had any idea there'd have been an issue, we'd never have agreed to come on board.

We were both in complete shock when, out of the blue, the director publicly denounced Eurythmics and our music, to a room filled with assembled press. We'd been unwittingly scapegoated by the director and Virgin films, by being drawn into an issue that had absolutely nothing to do with us. It was hurtful and baffling, especially because we loved the album we'd recorded and every song on it.

Years later… I went to a very festive Christmas party when a total stranger approached me, introducing himself as Michael Radford. I was taken completely off-guard, as I'd mostly forgotten about the whole debacle. Somewhat bashfully he said he wanted to apologize for the entire thing and any subsequent unpleasantness caused. I was touched by this gesture and immediately accepted his apology. All was well that ended well.

Life can be strange like that… We go through challenges we didn't ask for, but then events can gradually come around to instantly release all the resentment or bitterness that might have been easily let go, with an explanation and apology.

Filming the video for *Sexcrime* (1984) in Battersea Power Station in London while it was still in a state of impressive dereliction.

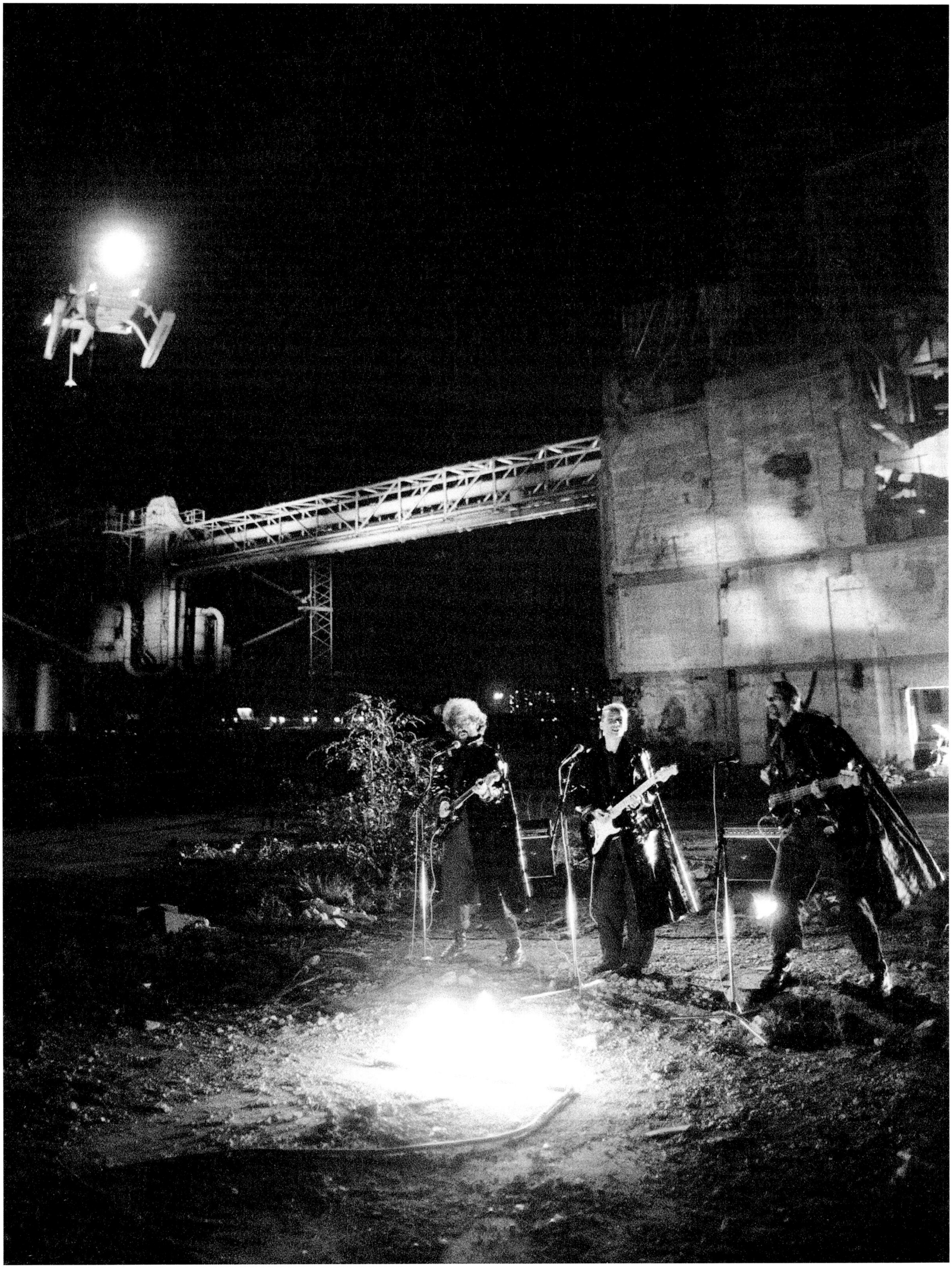

1985-86

Polaroids were absolutely novel. Everyone loved them – long before the digital revolution changed the way everything could be done. There's a special magic about watching film come to life before your eyes. We've become so acclimatized to instant gratification now that we want the next new event before the NOW has barely been digested.

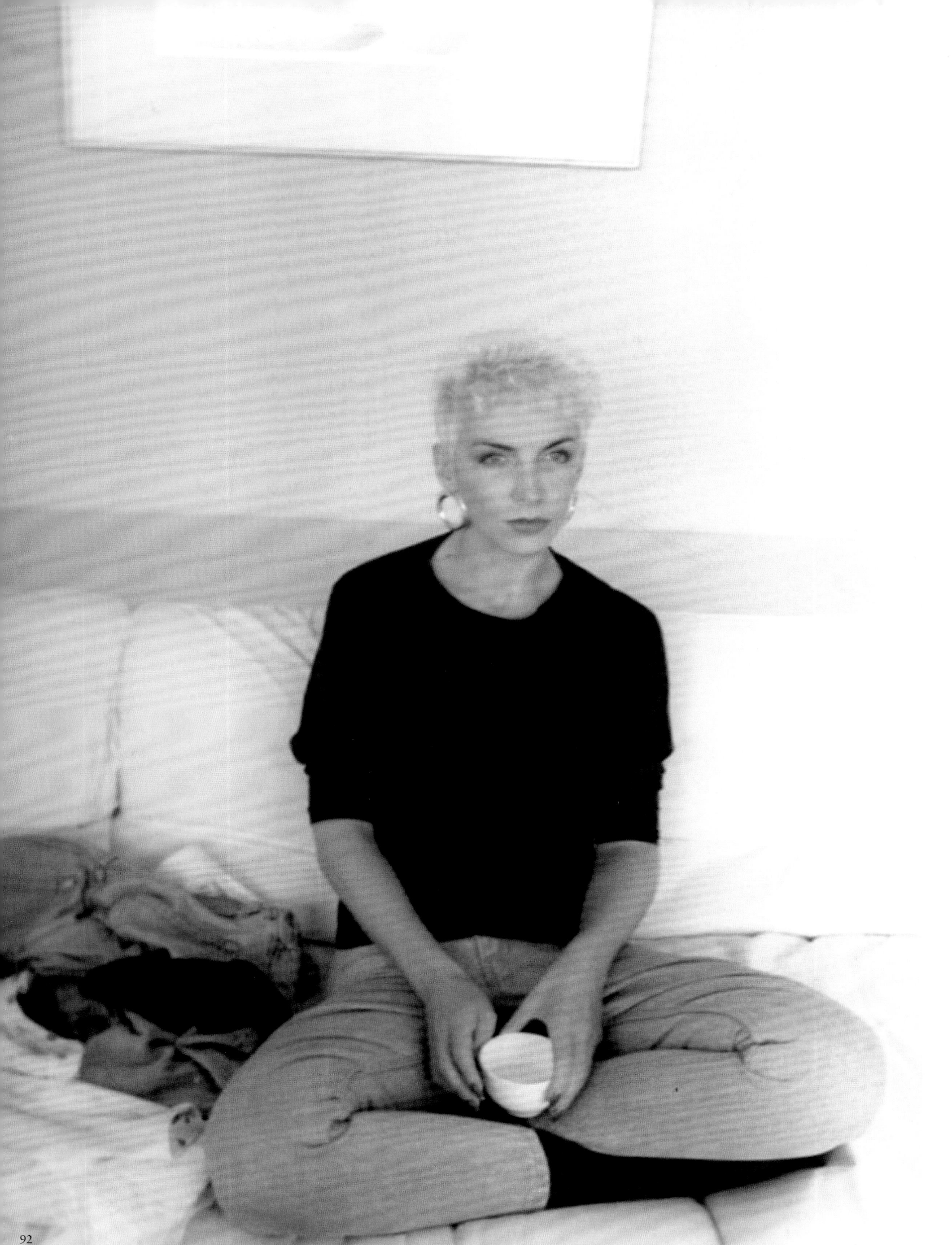

Caught daydreaming in a Tokyo hotel room, 1987.

87 G   87 G

SEE AND SPEAK NO EVIL – SPEAK AND SEE NO EVIL

The spoken word is powerful. Our minds shape-shift and chatter away, while our tongues serve whatever thoughts, ideas, words, and phrases that come to us.
We're unskillful, clumsy and inarticulate.
Stumbling, mumbling, stammering and grumbling.
We are poor communicators.
We don't listen. We can't wait for the other person to stop talking so we can steam in with our own pearls of wisdom, funny jokes or anecdotes.
We charm, seduce and flatter. We drop hints, manipulate and control. We put down, offend and insult. We are shy. We say little and it comes out the wrong way.
We are tactless, we blunder, we hurt others. We scream, we rage, we roar.
We are rude, proud and incorrect. We talk endlessly. We drone on. We complain.
We snap, we bark, we are sarcastic. We demand, we order, we are snobbish in tone.
We are gentle. We are quiet. We are soft and kind.
We whisper, we soothe, we sing lullabies.

96

Director Hugh Hudson discussing a scene with Al Pacino during the filming of *Revolution* in 1985.

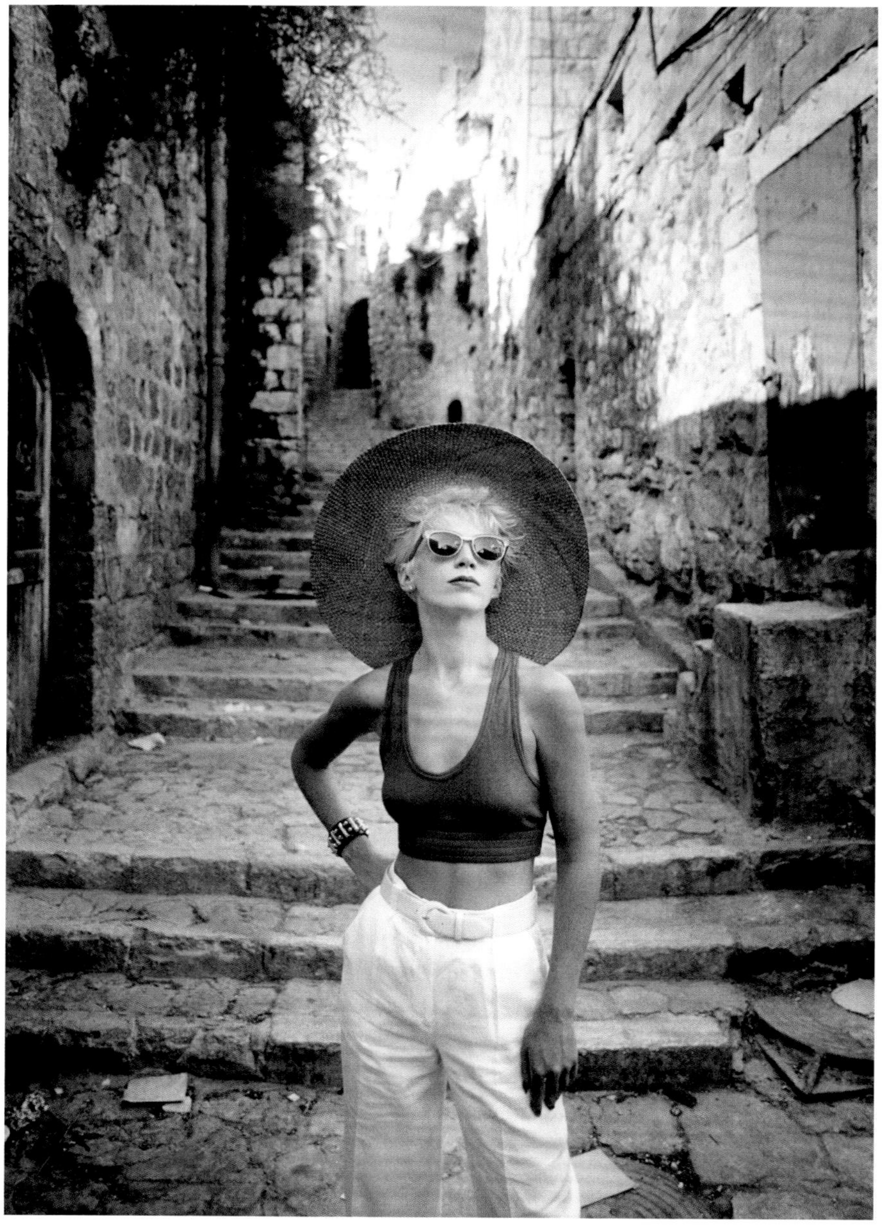

My mama told me good
My mama told me strong
She said "be true to yourself
And you can't go wrong"

But there's just one thing
That you must understand
You can fool with your brother
But don't mess with
The missionary man

EURYTHMICS

Eurythmics released our fifth album, *Revenge*, in 1986. The artist Eric Scott painted from photographs in exquisite fine detail.

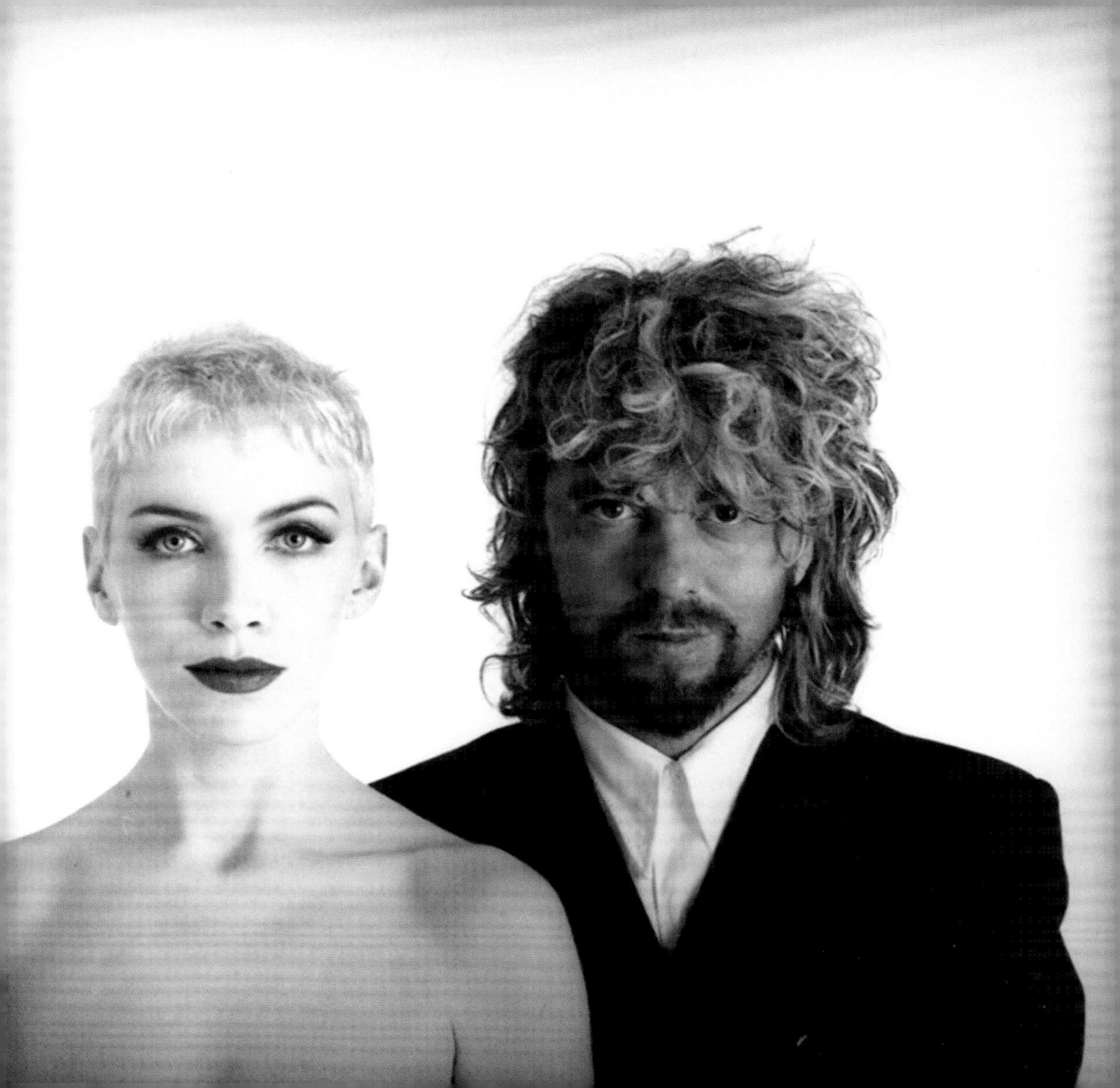

102

103

We decided to become full-blown 'rockers' for *Revenge*...
These photographs were taken on set from the 'Missionary
Man' video, directed by our pal Willy Smax.

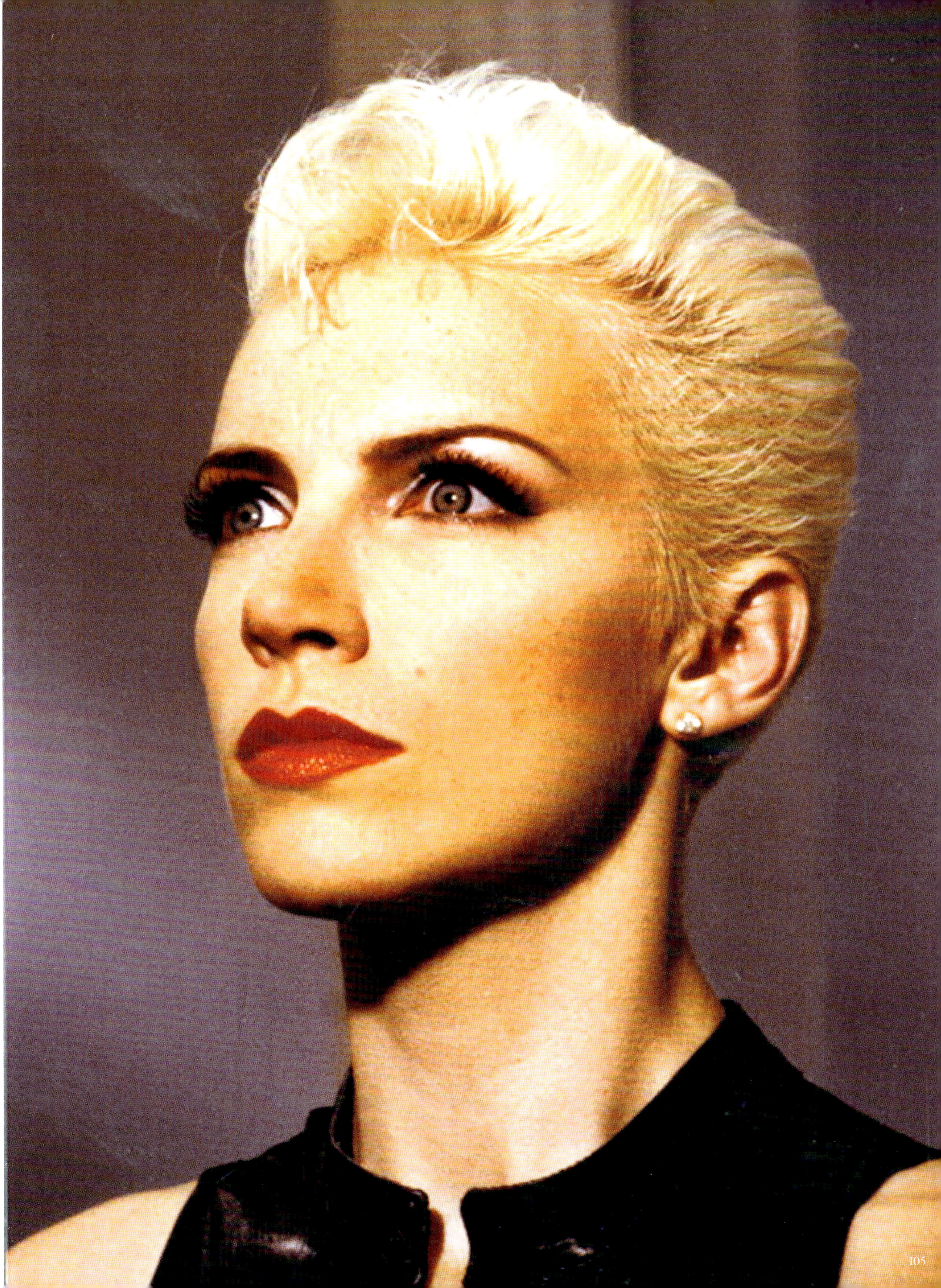

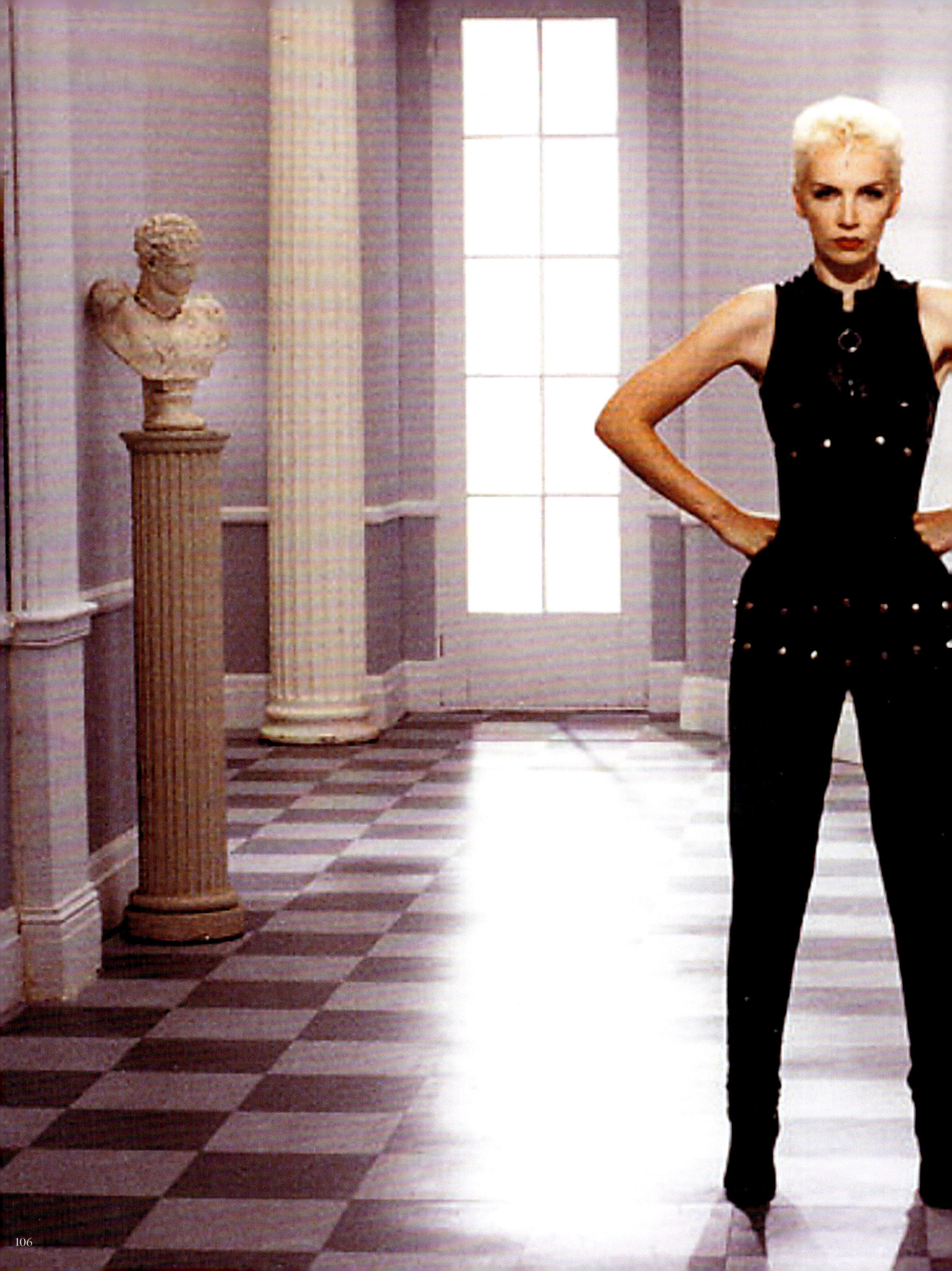

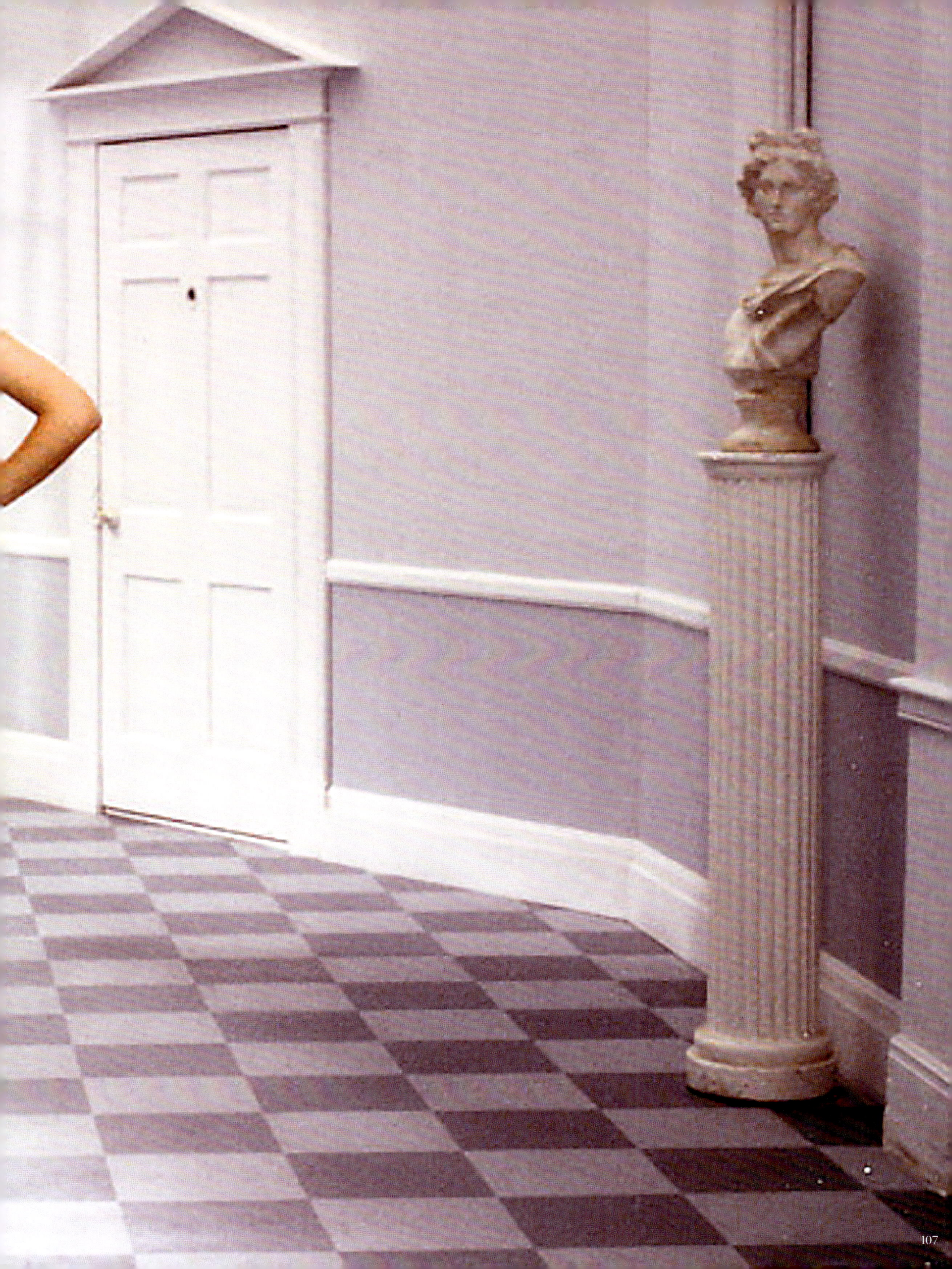

On a rare free afternoon, reading magazines on a sunny hot-tin roof in New York City. I think this might have been my first exposure to the heaven of sliced watermelon.

The novelty of a helicopter ride in New York…
Places to go to, people to meet, songs to sing!

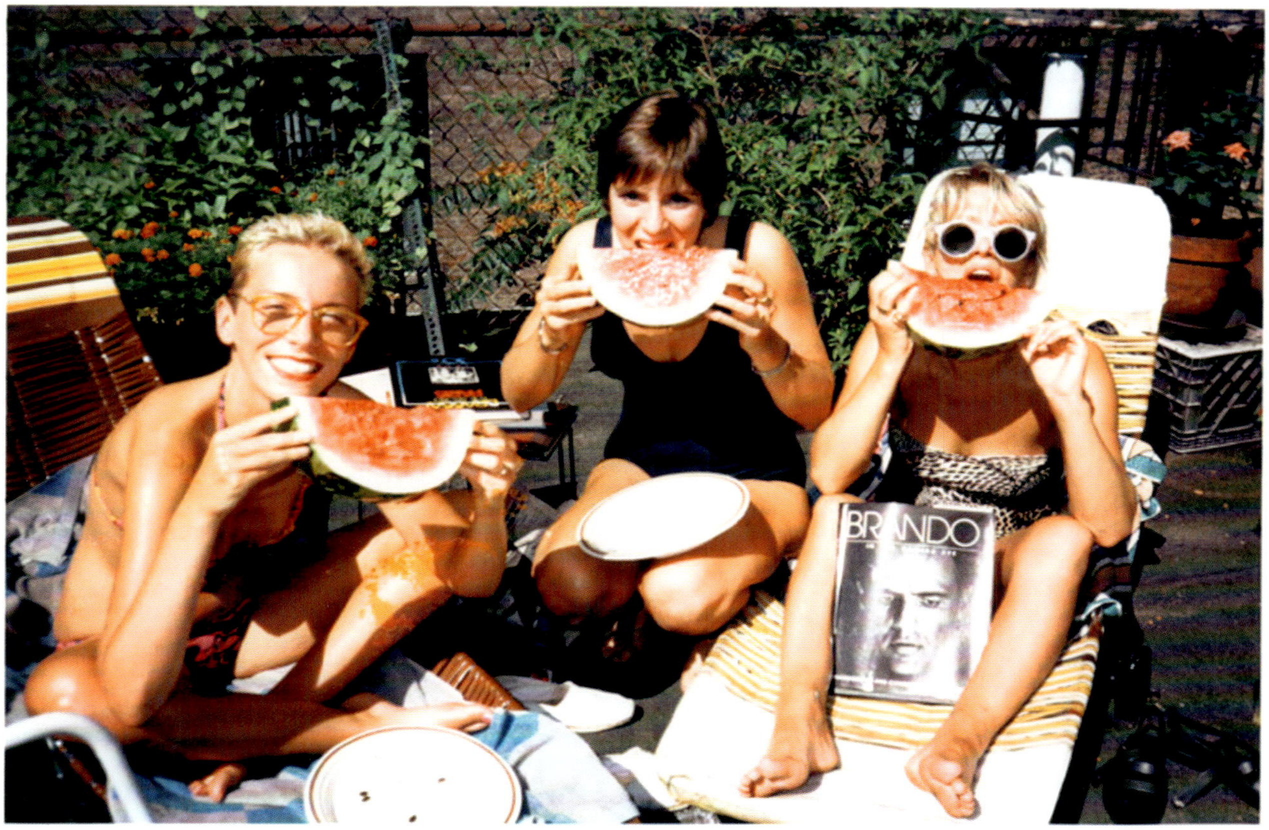
BRANDO

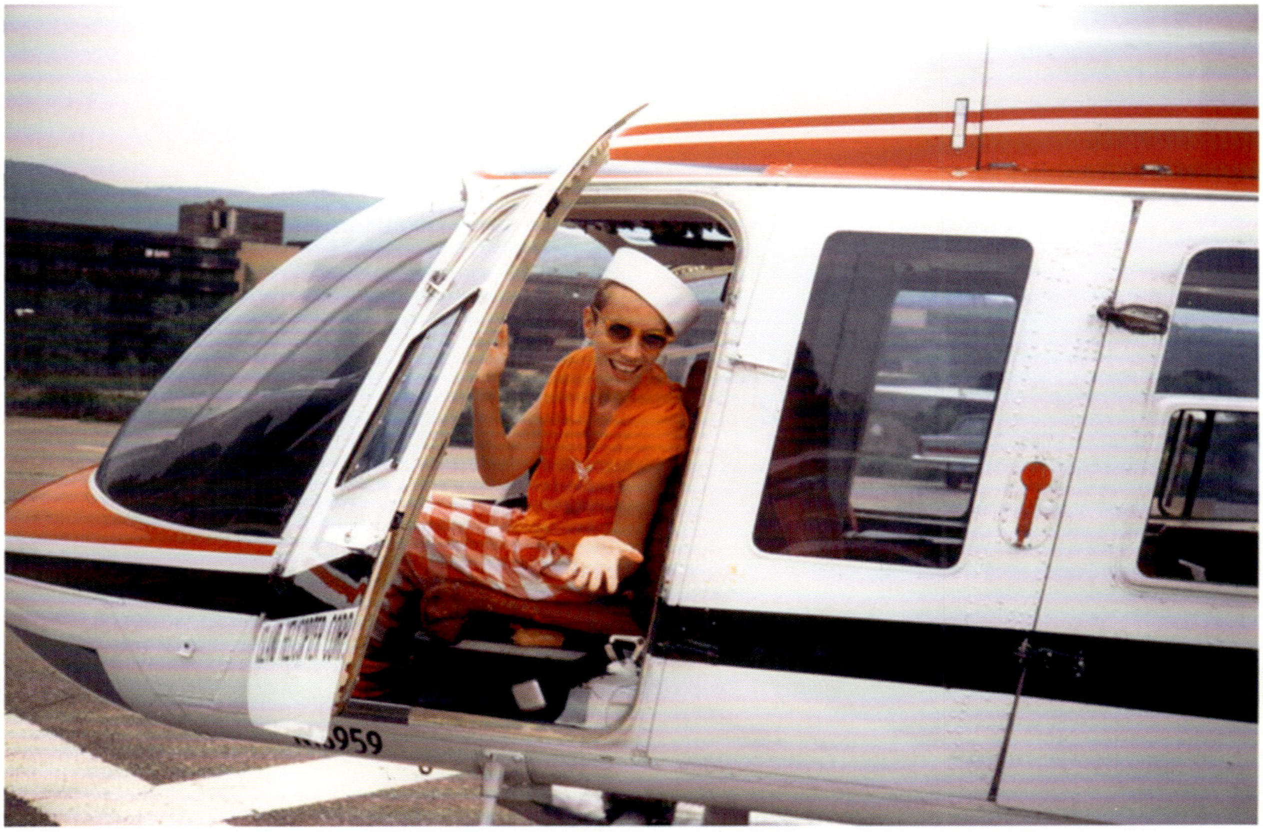

110

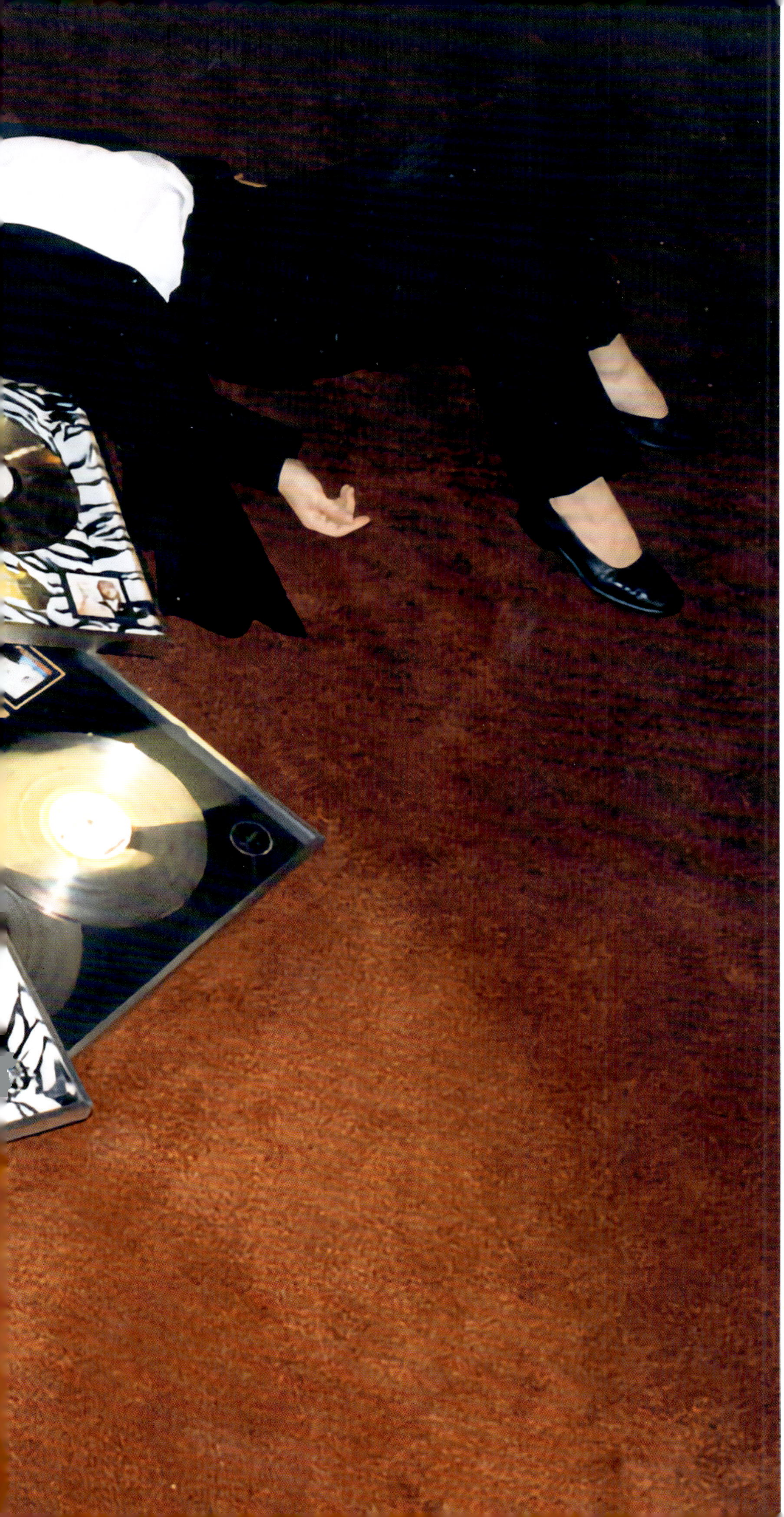

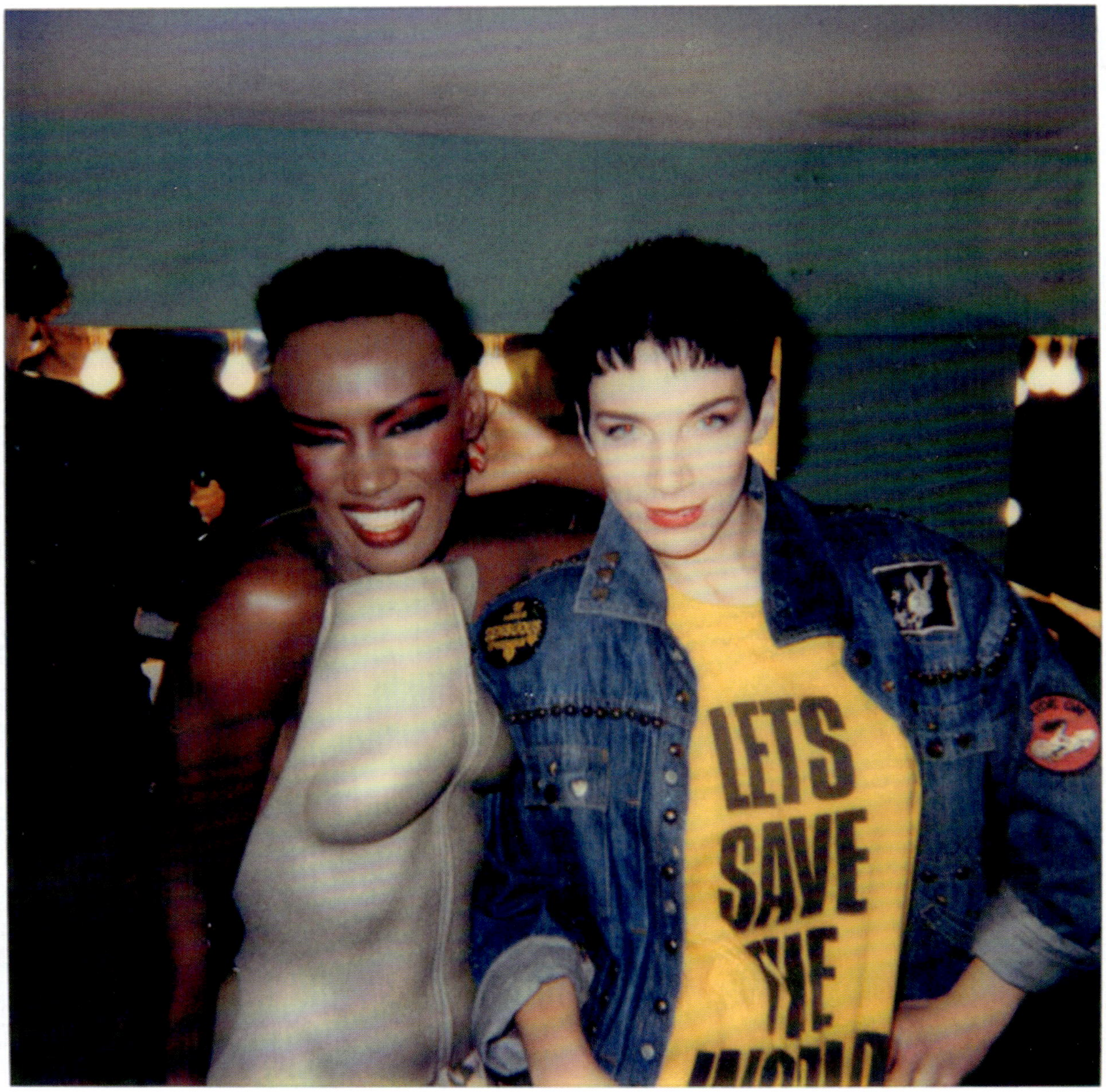
LETS
SAVE

Sometimes you happen to meet
musical spell-weavers on the road
Brief encounters
Sliding doors
Ships passing in the night…
The most outstanding artists
Encountered at different times
Grace Jones – Cindi Lauper – Chrissie Hynde.

Sweet little scenes in Paris, London, and New York...
I lived in and out of suitcases for decades.
Either about to be packed, or about to be unpacked.

115

I can't remember this photograph being taken.
In some ways, I don't recognize myself in it.
It reveals a fierce energy that usually
Only emerges through performance.
I know this feeling very well…
An almost a transcendent state.
Performance can be a special kind of 'portal'
To a powerful, almost transcendent experience.

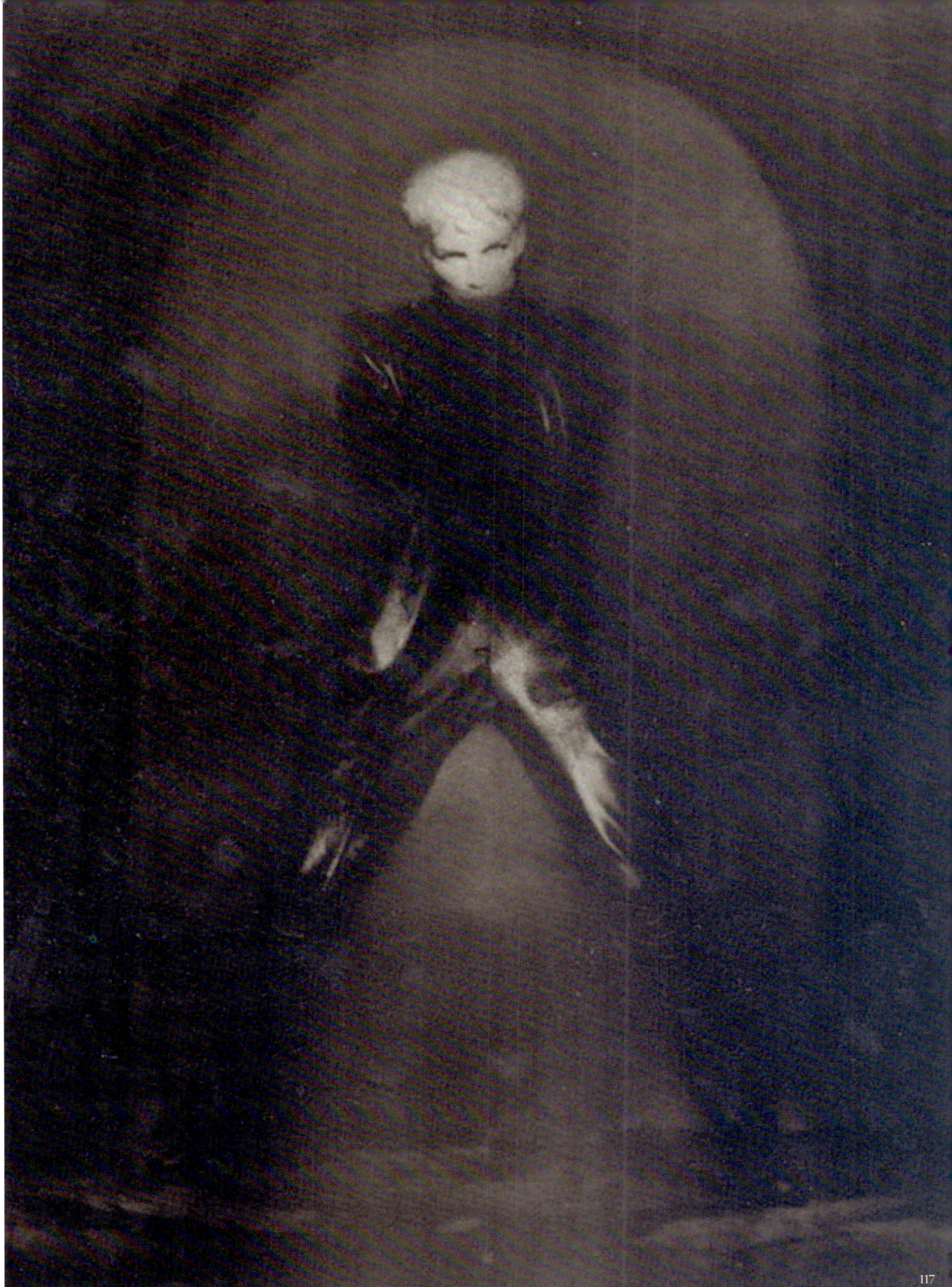

It's almost impossible to describe how much fun we had shooting the video for 'There Must be An Angel.' Having an opportunity to transform into different characters is an experience everyone should have, just once, whether you're an adult or a child. The whole world's a stage, after all. I became Ms Virginally Angelic, while Dave became Le Roi Soleil – as if we'd wandered into the realms of some dreamy high-camp Rococo Follies…

119

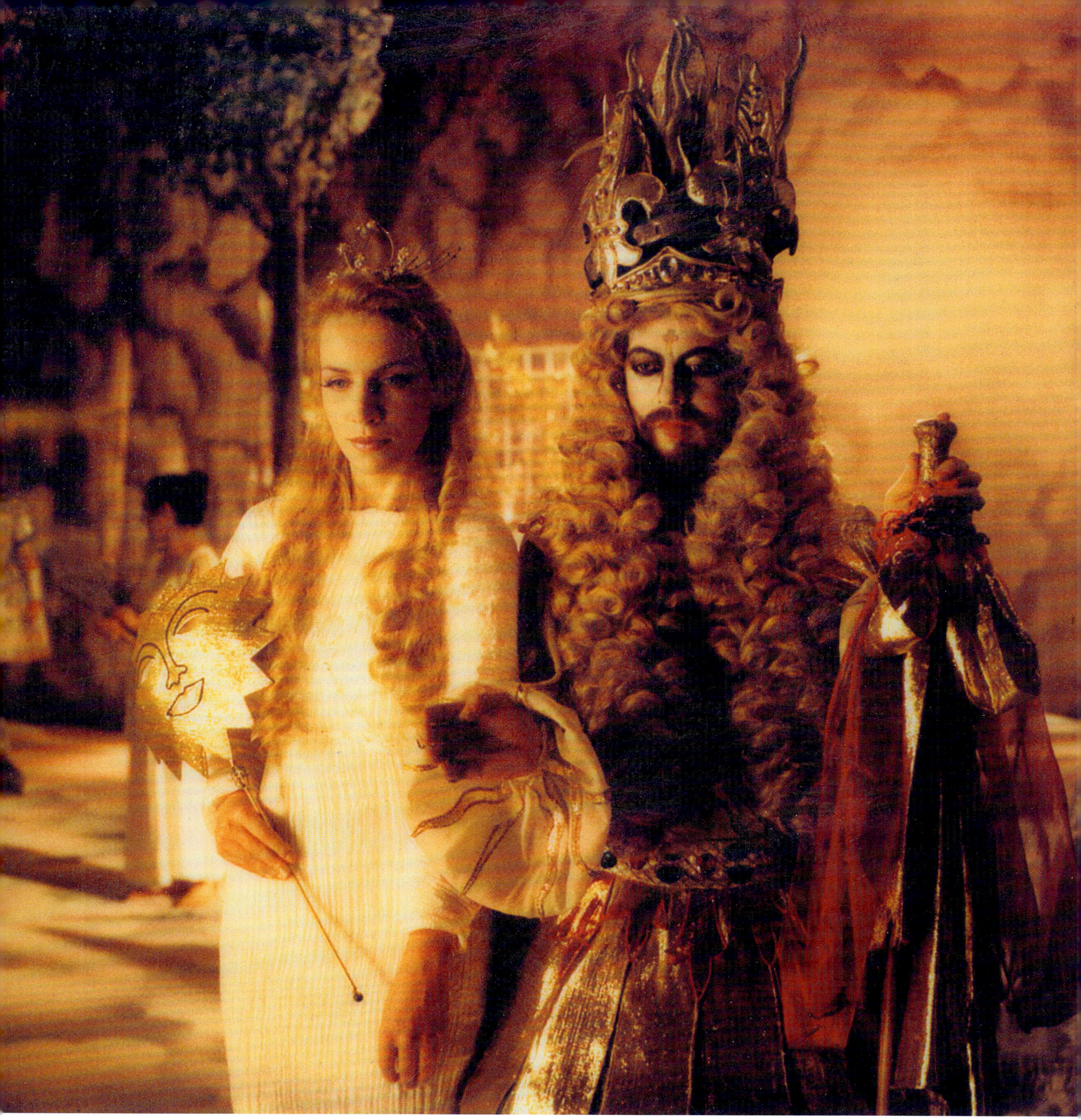

No one on Earth could feel like this
I'm thrown and overblown with bliss

There must be an Angel
Playing with my heart

I walk into an empty room
And suddenly my heart goes boom
It's an orchestra of Angels
And they're playing with my heart

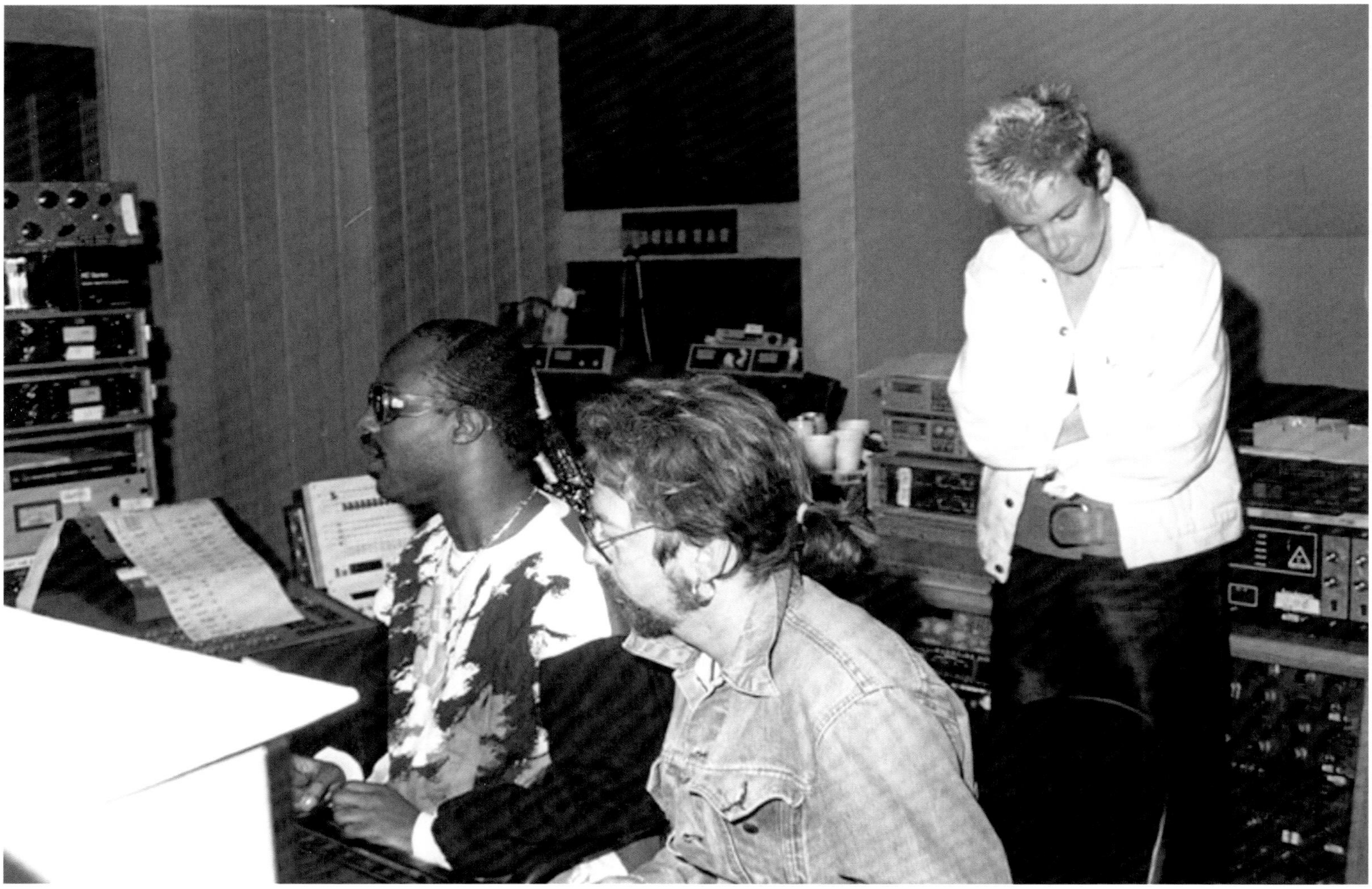

In the early hours of the morning in a Los Angeles studio with Stevie Wonder. We were told at short notice that Stevie would be ready to record harmonica on 'There Must Be an Angel.' I have adored Stevie Wonder ever since I first heard his voice and music.

Just before he was about to record, Stevie's assistant tenderly arranged and tied his beautiful beaded locks into a special pouch-bag, so the sound of the beads wouldn't interfere with the recording.

And I got to be there!

I still can hardly believe we had an opportunity to record
'Sisters Are Doing It For Themselves' with Aretha Franklin.
It still doesn't seem quite real.
I love Aretha's expression in this picture.
Her face looks beautiful – completely relaxed, at ease.

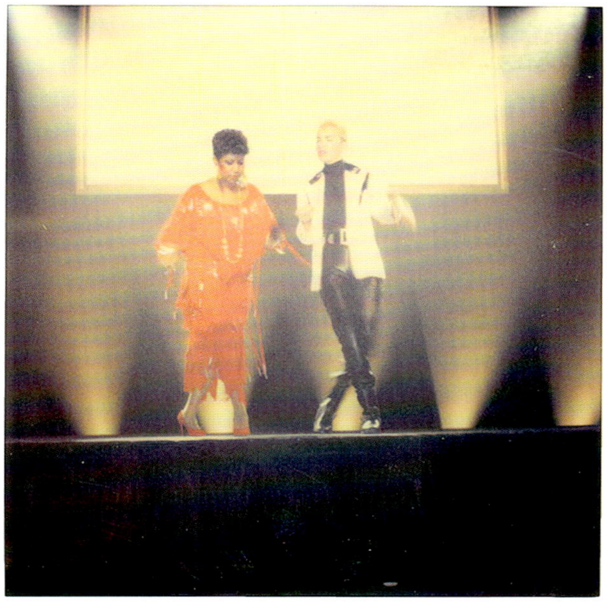

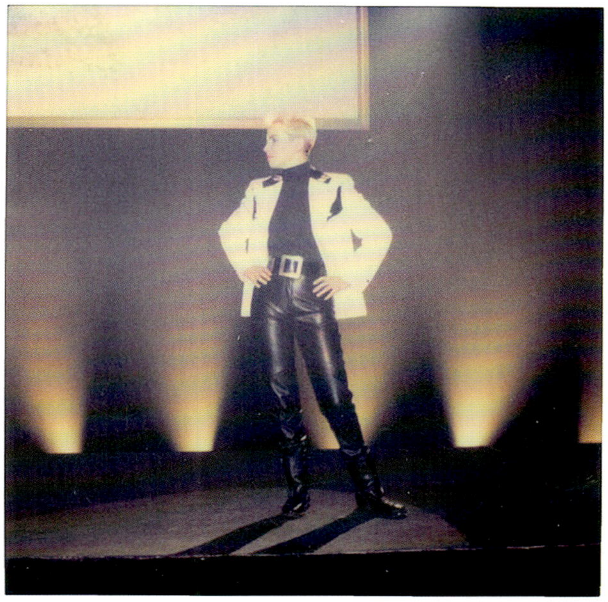

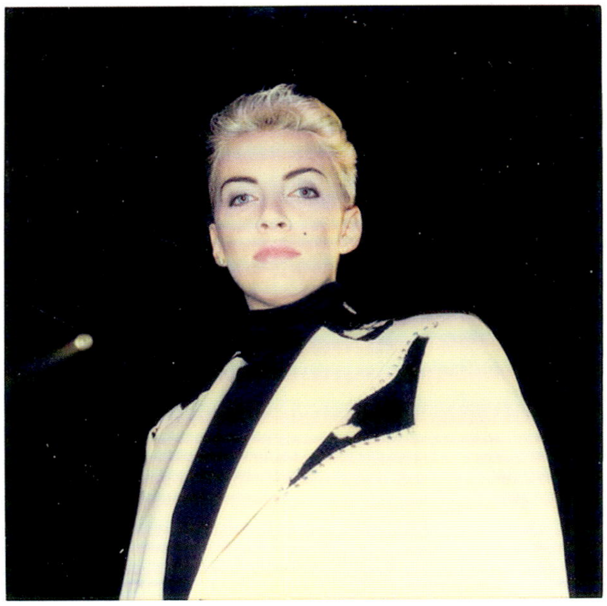

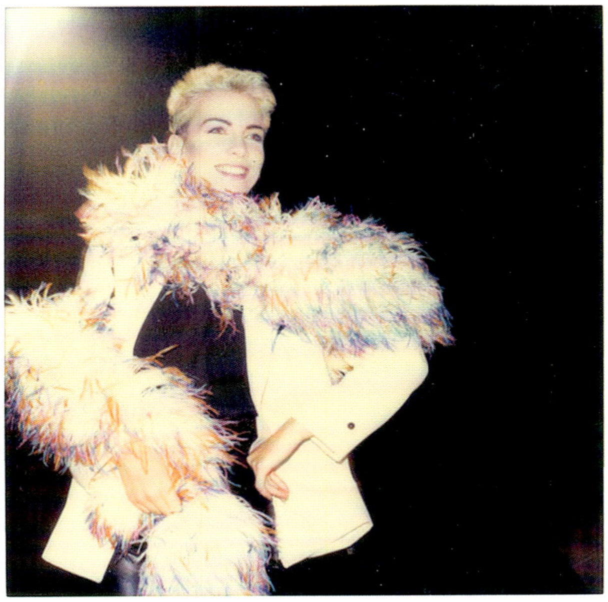

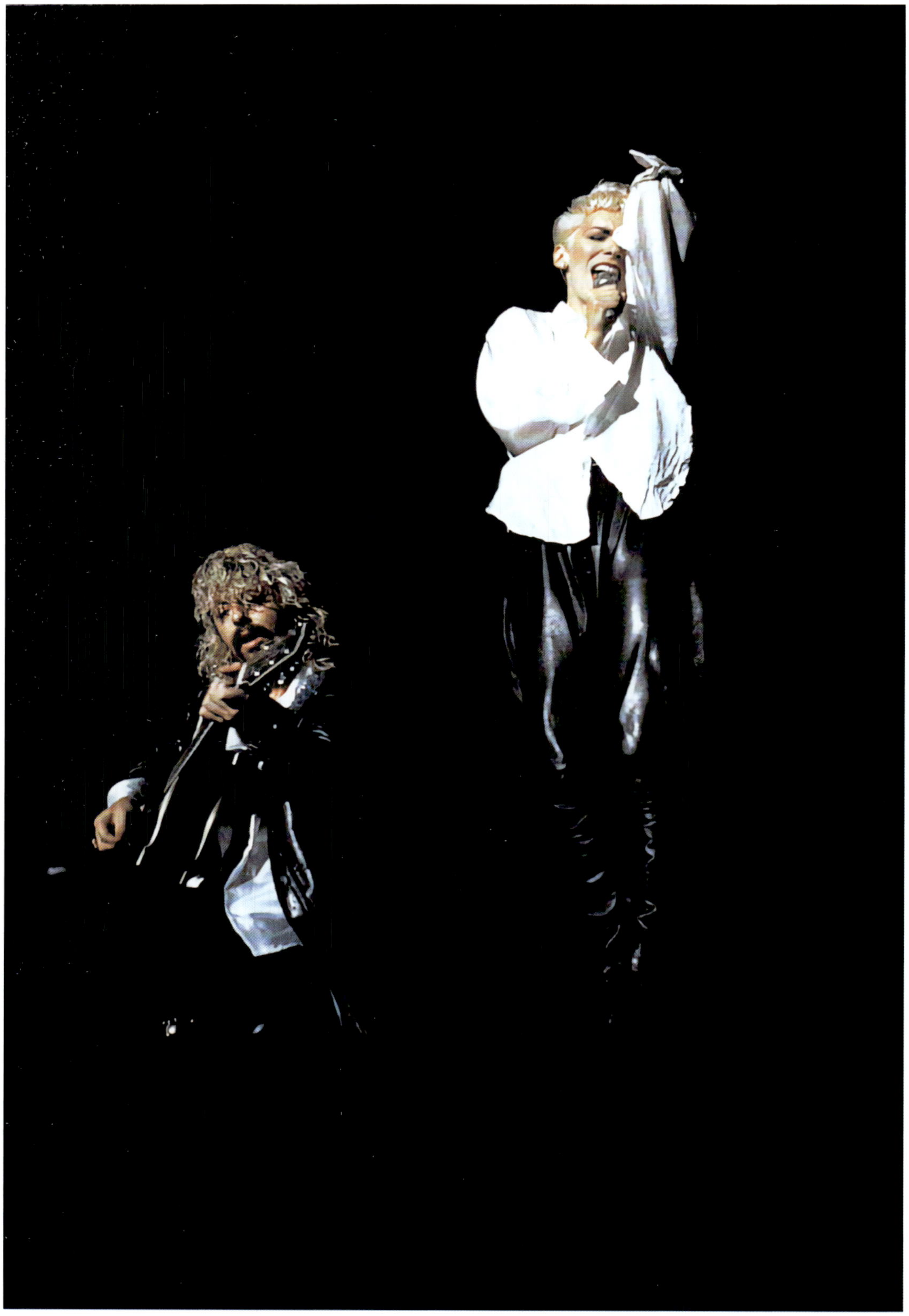

I have no idea how I came to levitate like this…

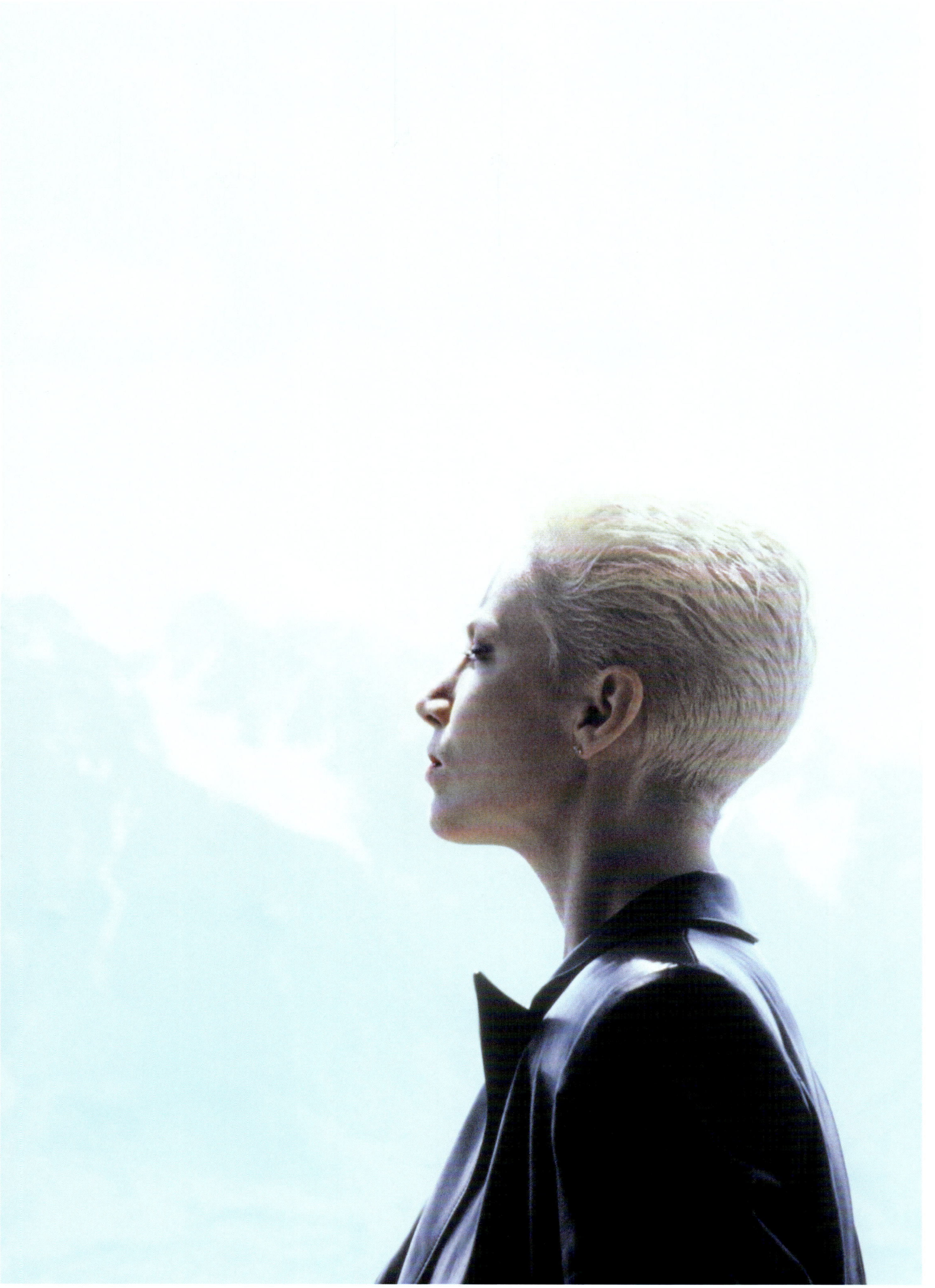

Dave and I in Montreux, where we headlined the Rock Festival in 1986… during the *Revenge* tour.

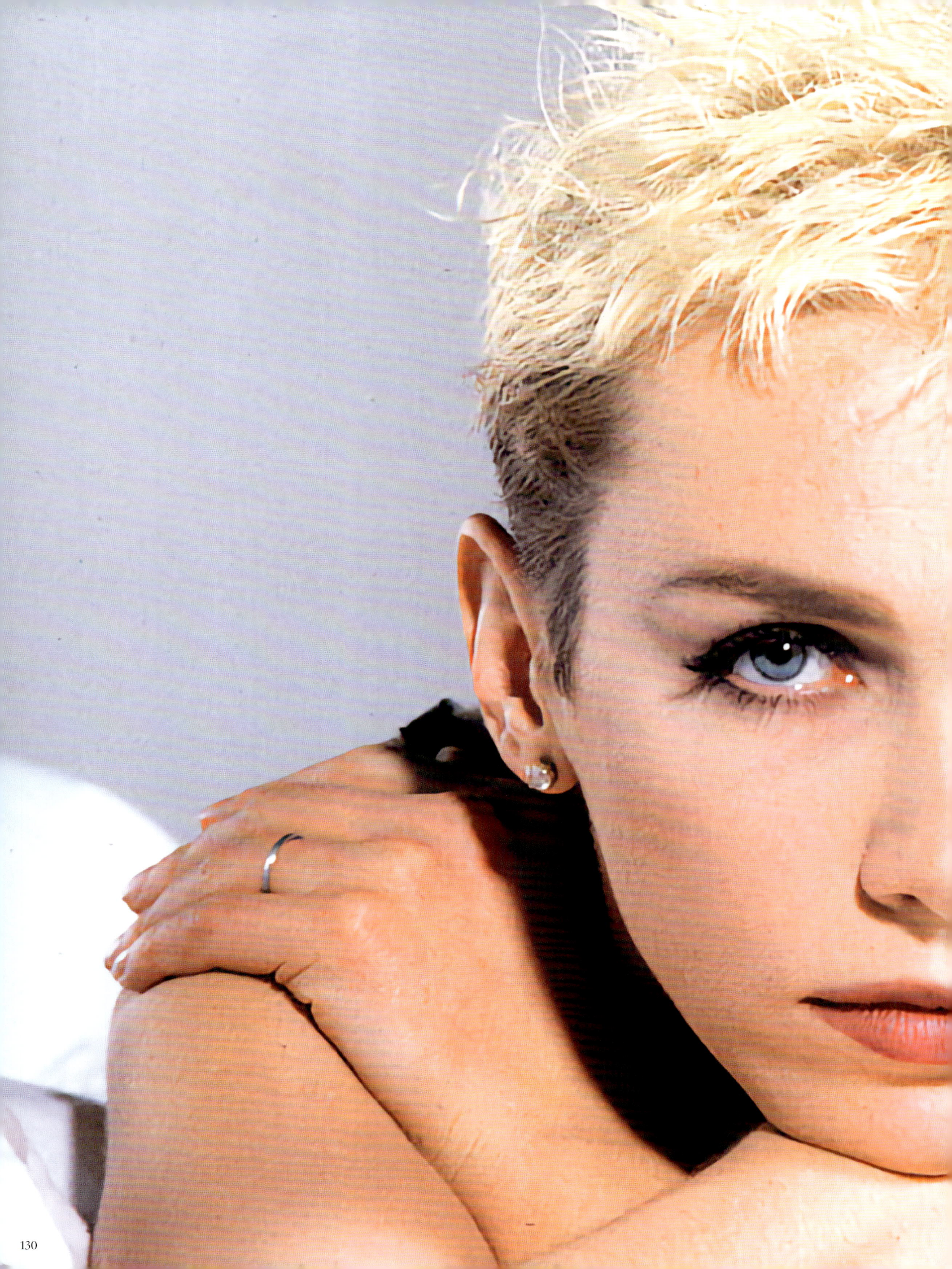

131

1987–89

Savage, 1987. The album cover photograph was taken by Alastair Thain. I presented the notion of a woman dressed as a man dressed as a woman; the male gaze and how many women think that's how men want them to look.

The woman dressed as a man dressed as a woman is raging-angry-defiant-rebellious-aggressive-dangerous-threatening-threatened-fragile-unstable-unhinged-needy-desperate-victimized-bruised-abused-violated-victim-seductive-manipulative-lost-addicted-traumatized…

135

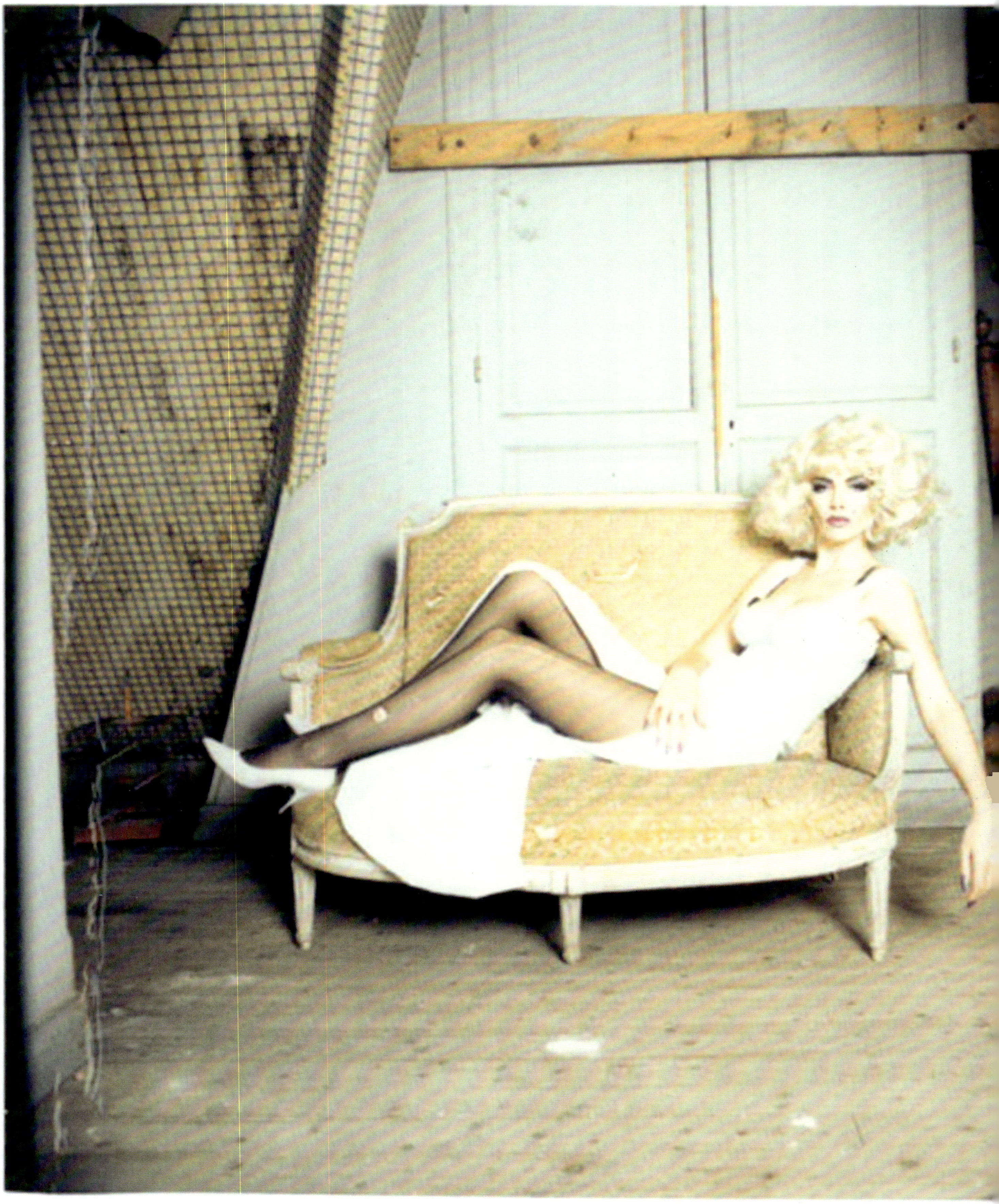

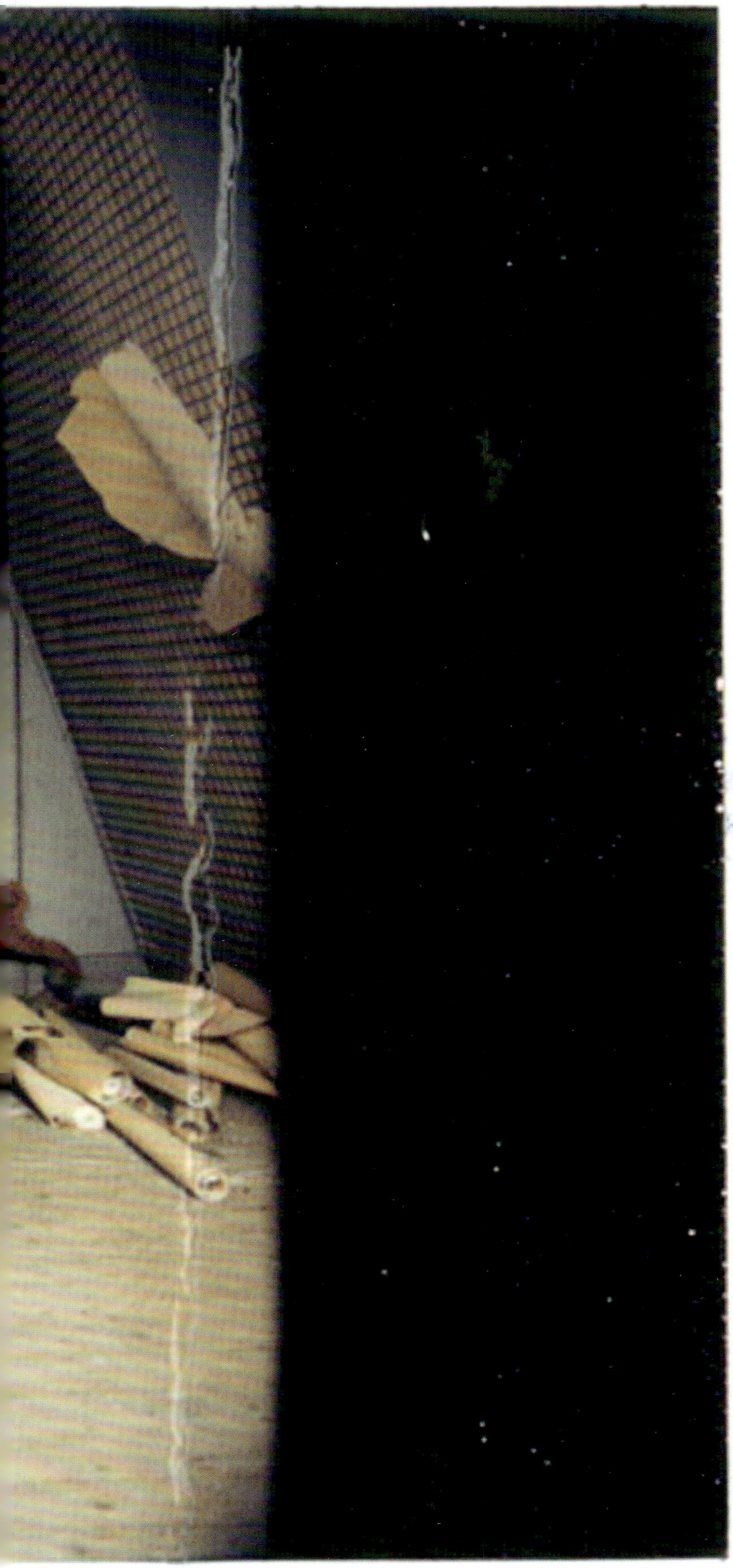

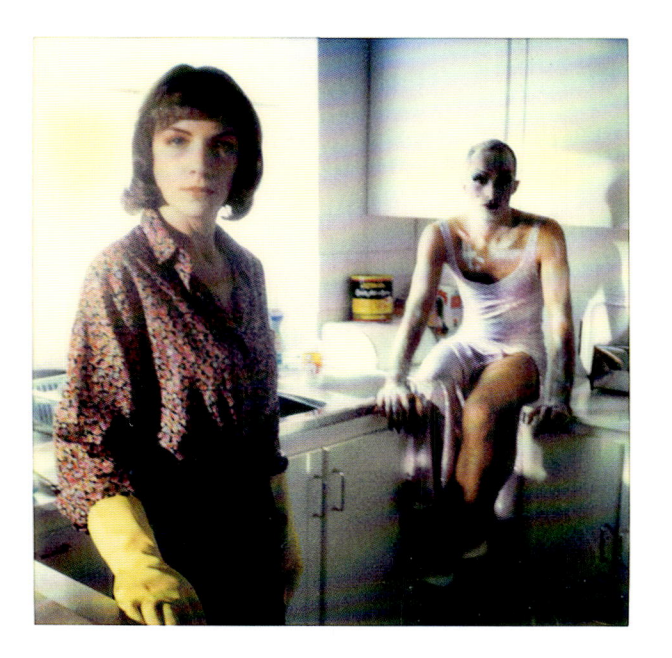

The Frump. The Housewife. The Plain Jane. The Spinster. The Neurotic. Exhausted. Frenetic. Overwhelmed. Psychotic. Enraged. Obsessive. Resentful. Bitter. Worried. Anxious. Depressed. Victim. Perfectionist.
Nasty. Plain.

139

Popping out from behind the columns
In the City of Light…
Every time I have the opportunity to spend time in Paris
I feel elevated and giddy with excitement.
This ancient city is an architectural miracle.
Centered around and spread out from the glorious River Seine, which has flowed from time immemorial, dividing both her right and left banks. Despite all the pressures of adapting to modernity, Parisians value certain aspects of tradition and culture in a way that makes me deeply appreciative.

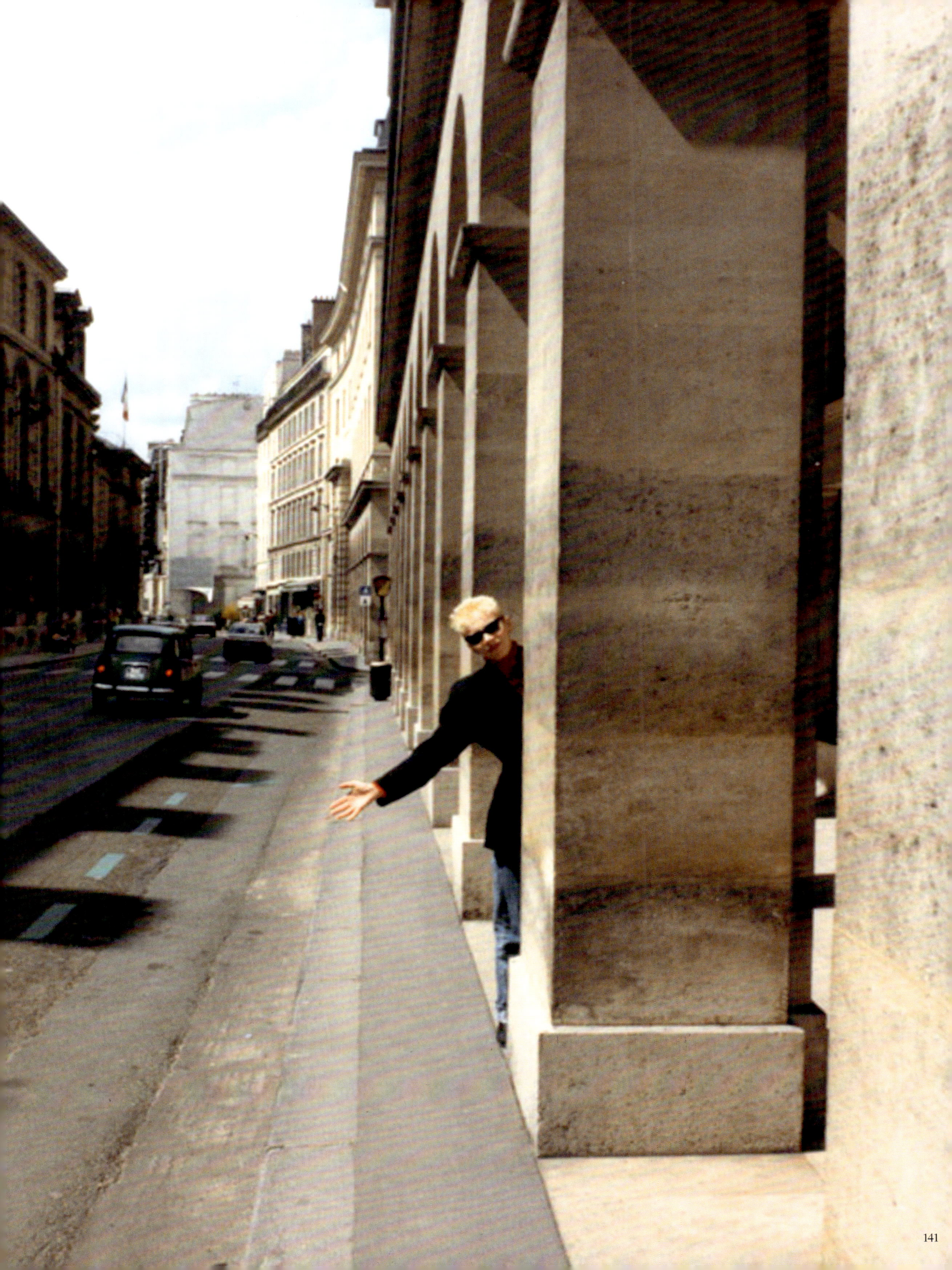

42

143

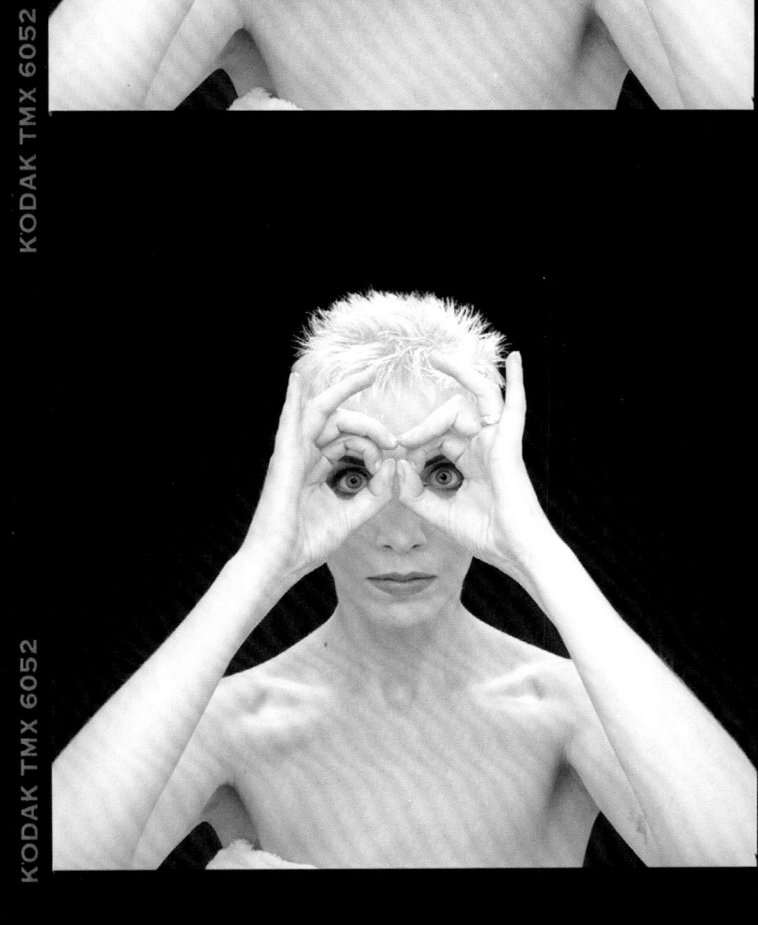

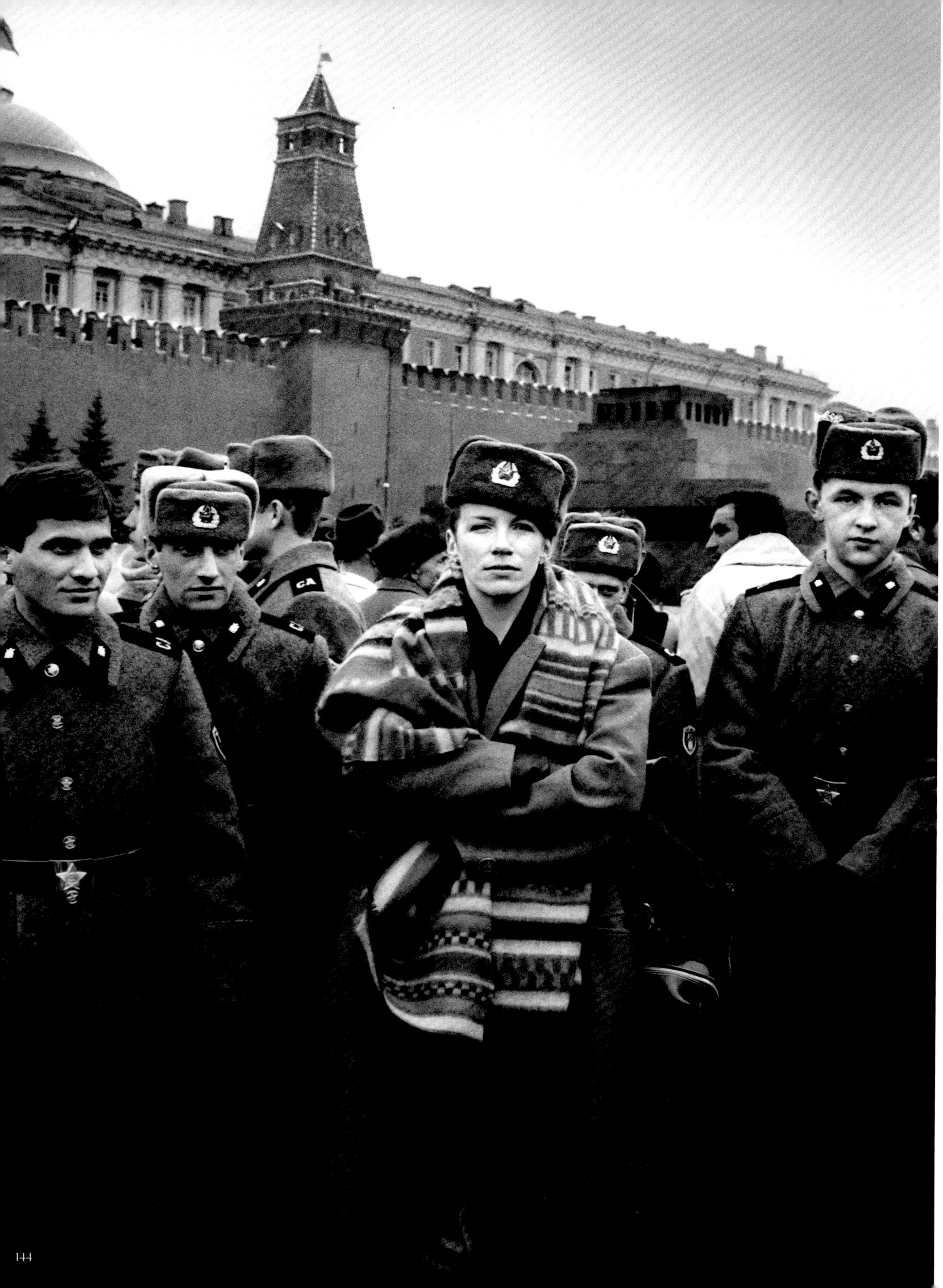

In Moscow's Red Square, just after the introduction of Perestroika in March, 1989.

I impulsively borrowed the hat of one of the Russian soldiers for the shot, while they looked on with discomforted bemusement.

Greenpeace had invited a group of musicians to help amplify the launch of the album *Breakthrough*, which helped finance the launch of their first office in the Soviet Union. Artists included Peter Gabriel, the Edge from U2, the Pretenders, Sting, Brian Adams, Talking Heads, the Thompson Twins, World Party, Howard Jones, and Belinda Carlisle.

Greenpeace Russia lasted for more than thirty years, until the authorities forced its closure in May 2023 for being 'undesirable' and 'critical of Russia's environmental issues.'

Jean-Baptiste Mondino, a French giant of image creation, took this pale-paler-palest portrait for the cover of the album, *We Too Are One* – the Yin and Yang of Eurythmics.

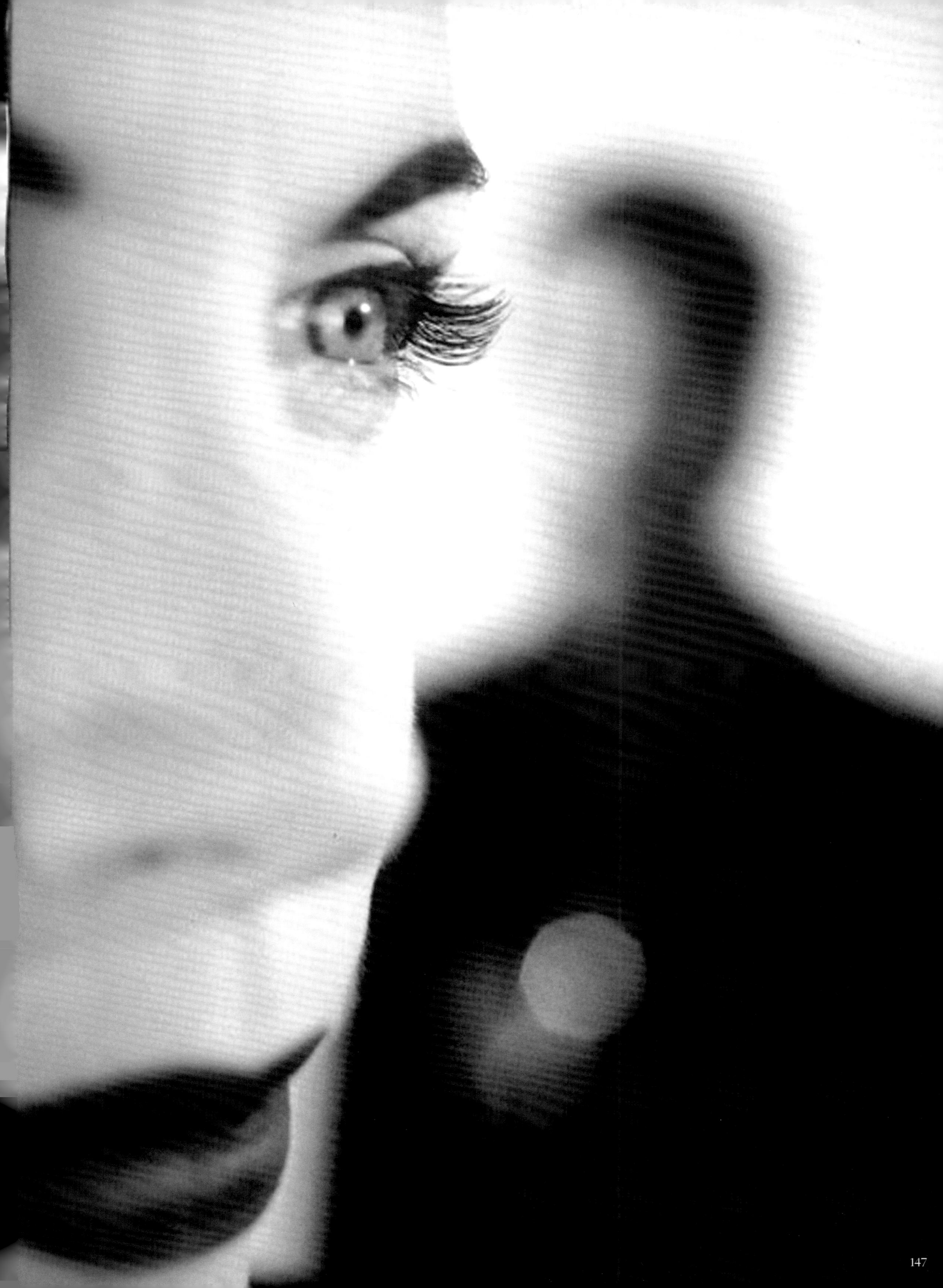

1990–94

I spent most of an afternoon working with the most remarkable Japanese photographer, Satoshi Saikusa… A quiet, gentle man with a unique visual eye, who sadly passed away in 2021. We took these photographs in an old theater in King's Cross, London. The atmosphere was redolent of a bygone era, with darkened Victorian balconies and walls of maroon damask flock wallpaper.

Come to me
Run to me
Do and be done with me
Cold cold cold
Don't I exist for you?
Don't I still live for you?
Cold cold cold

Everything I possess
Given with tenderness
Wrapped in a ribbon of glass
Time it may take us
But God only knows
How I've paid
For those things in the past

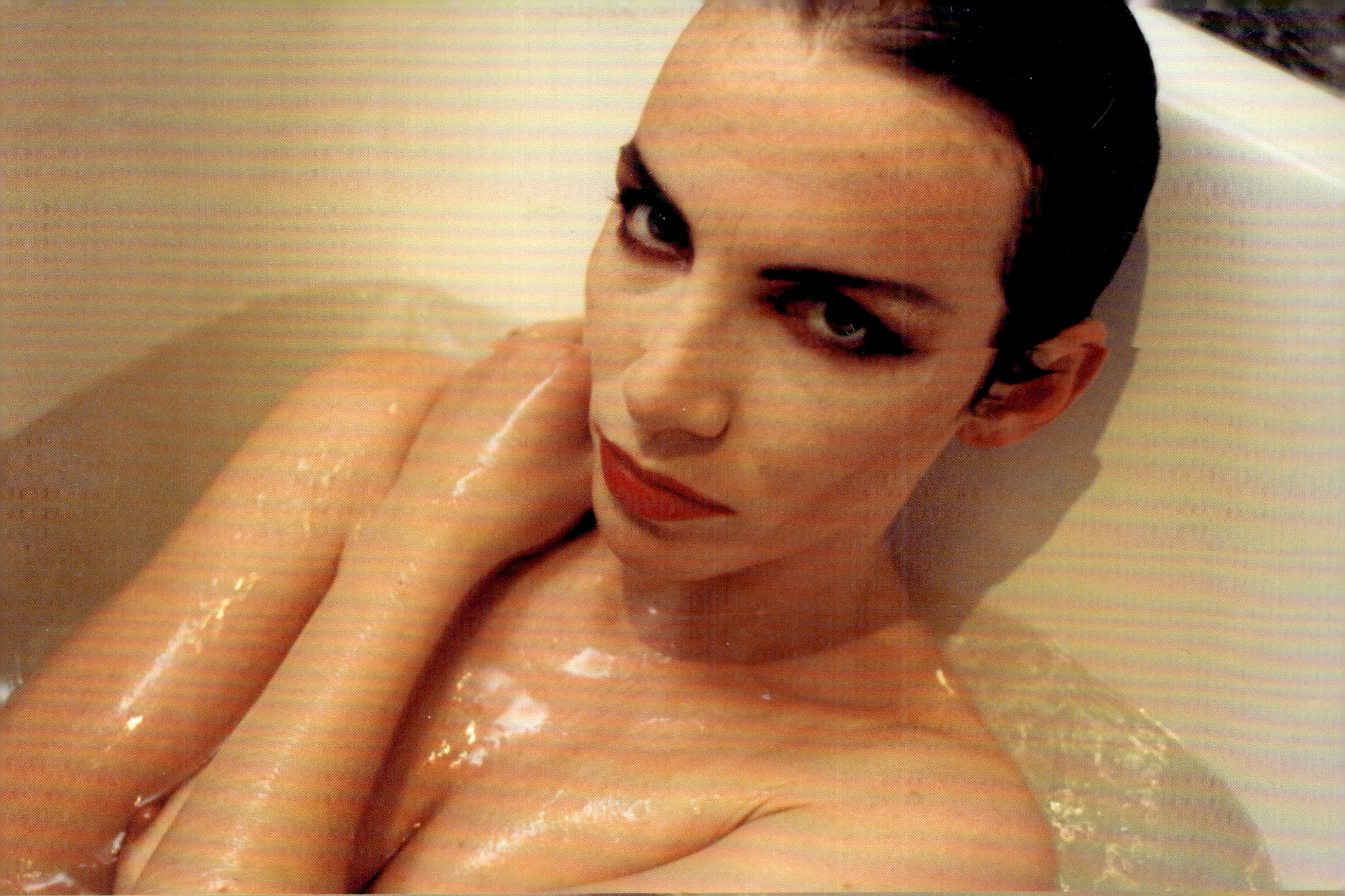

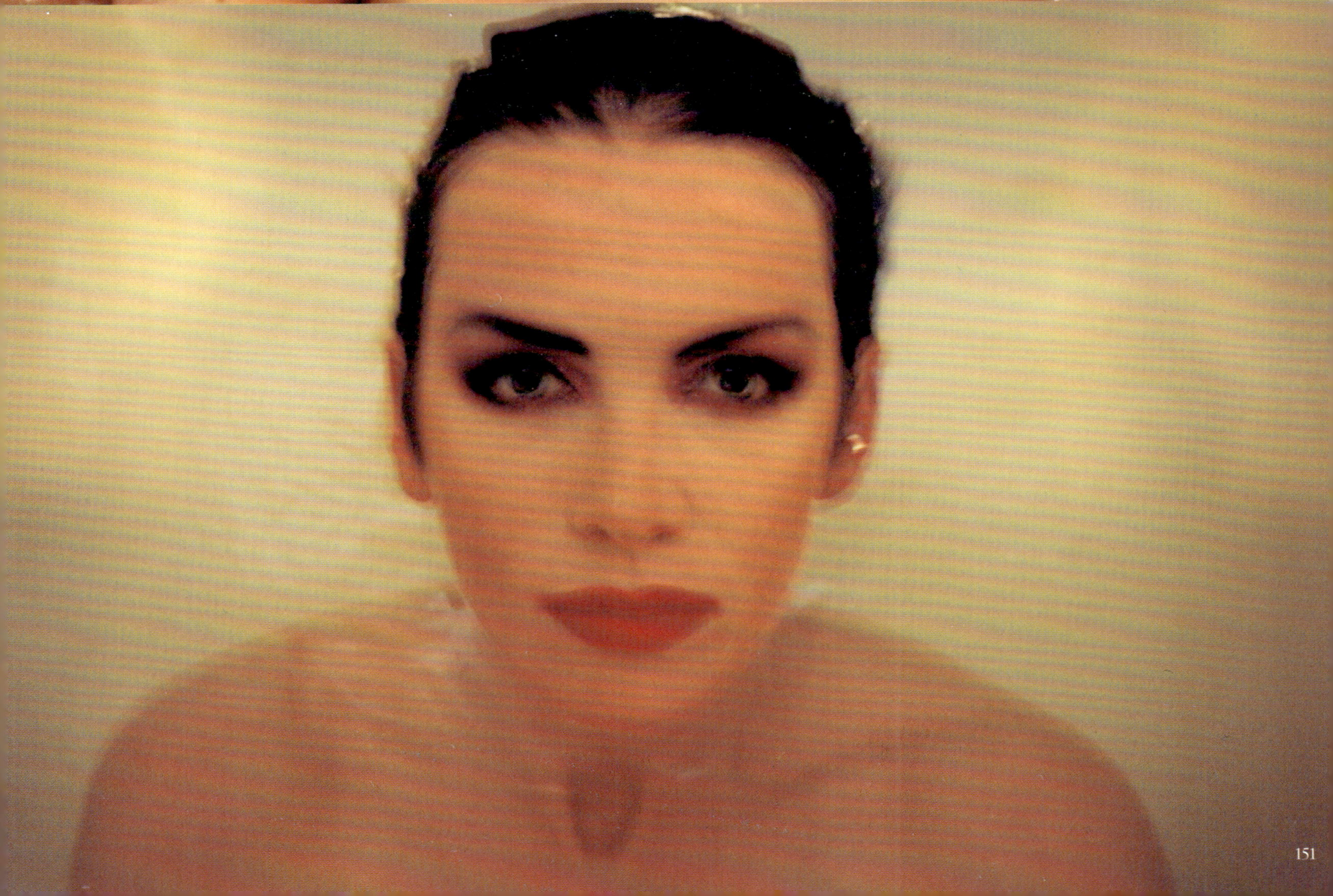

The tension between being a working artist and a mother is a conflicting situation I know a lot of women will relate to. I absolutely *loved* being a mother and I also didn't want to completely abandon being an artist. So I decided to try doing both, which also came with exhaustion, guilt, anxiety, and insecurity. I stopped touring completely and tried to be as balanced as possible with work time. It wasn't easy. I tried my level best and still do.

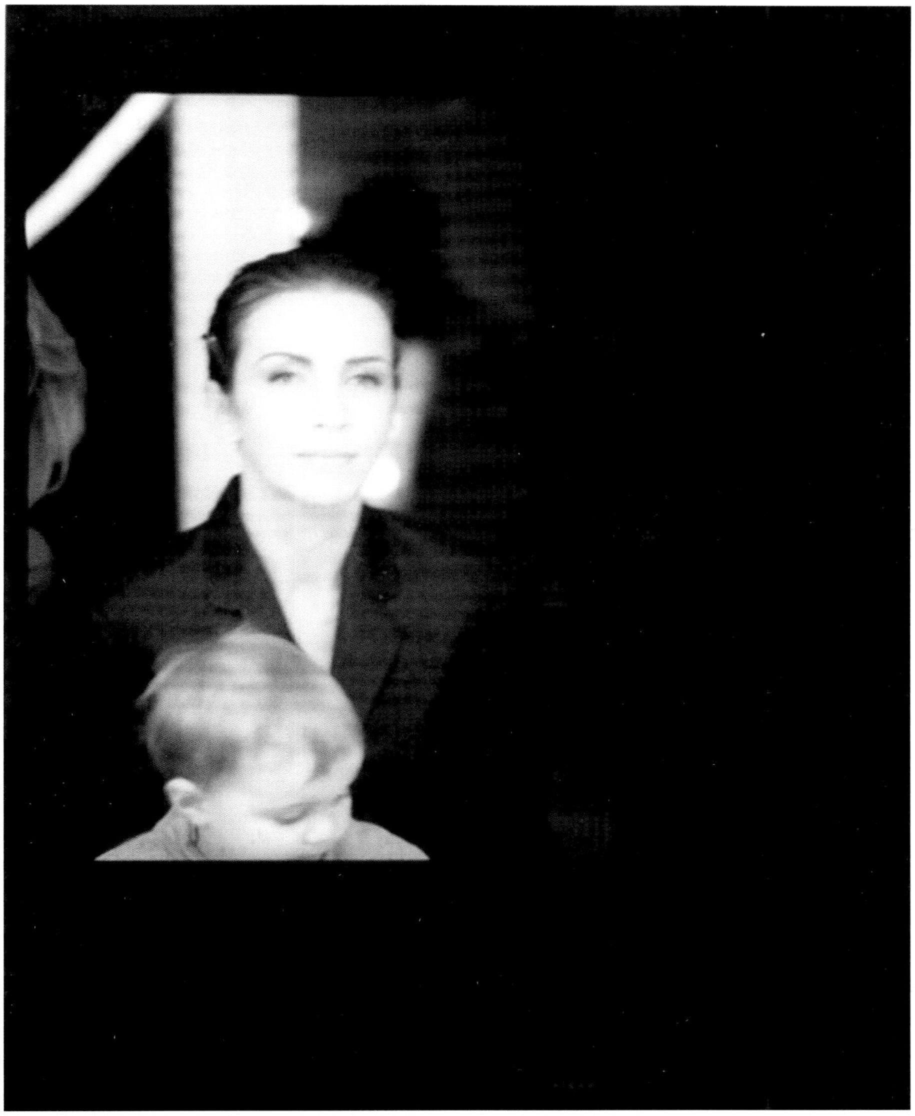

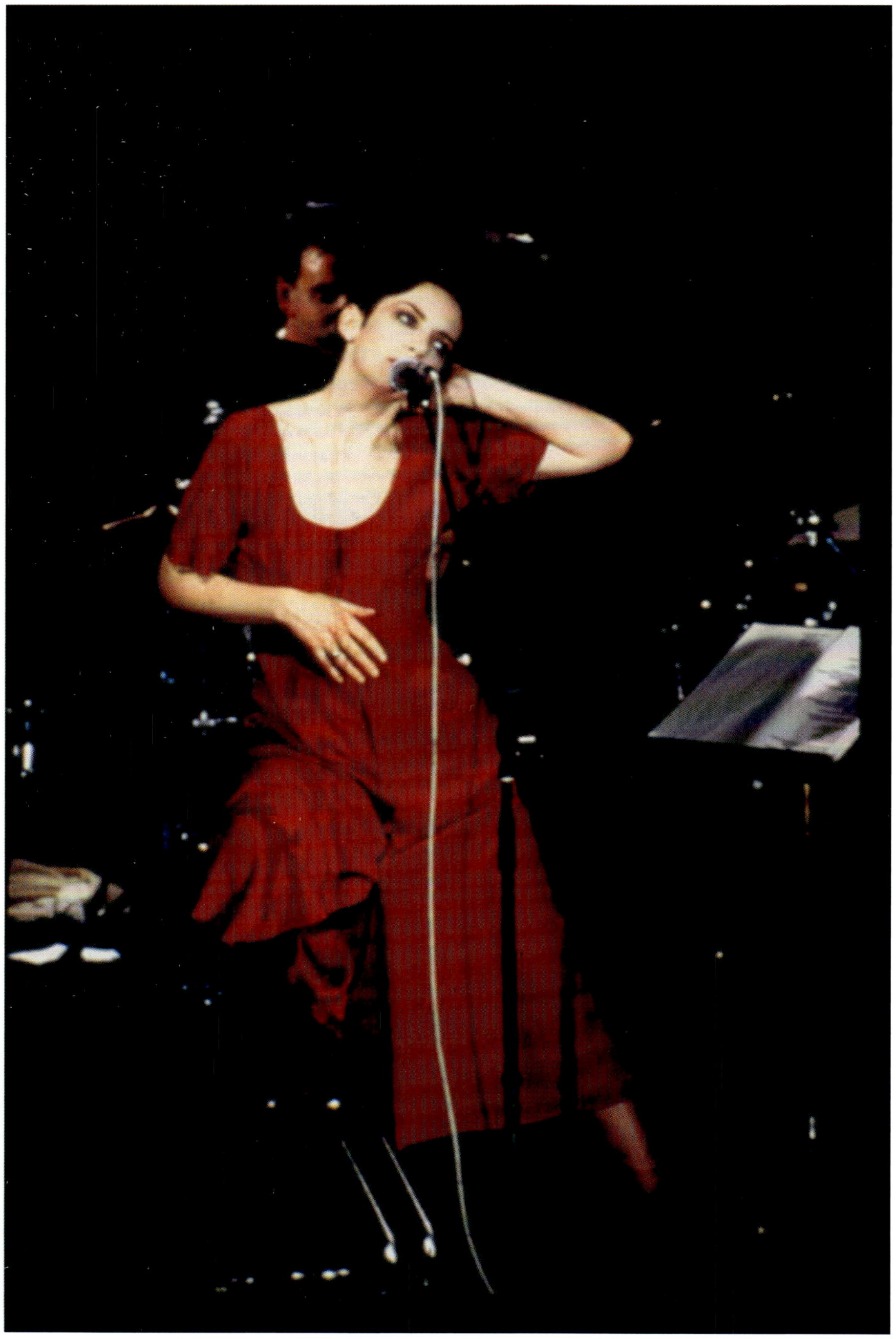

155

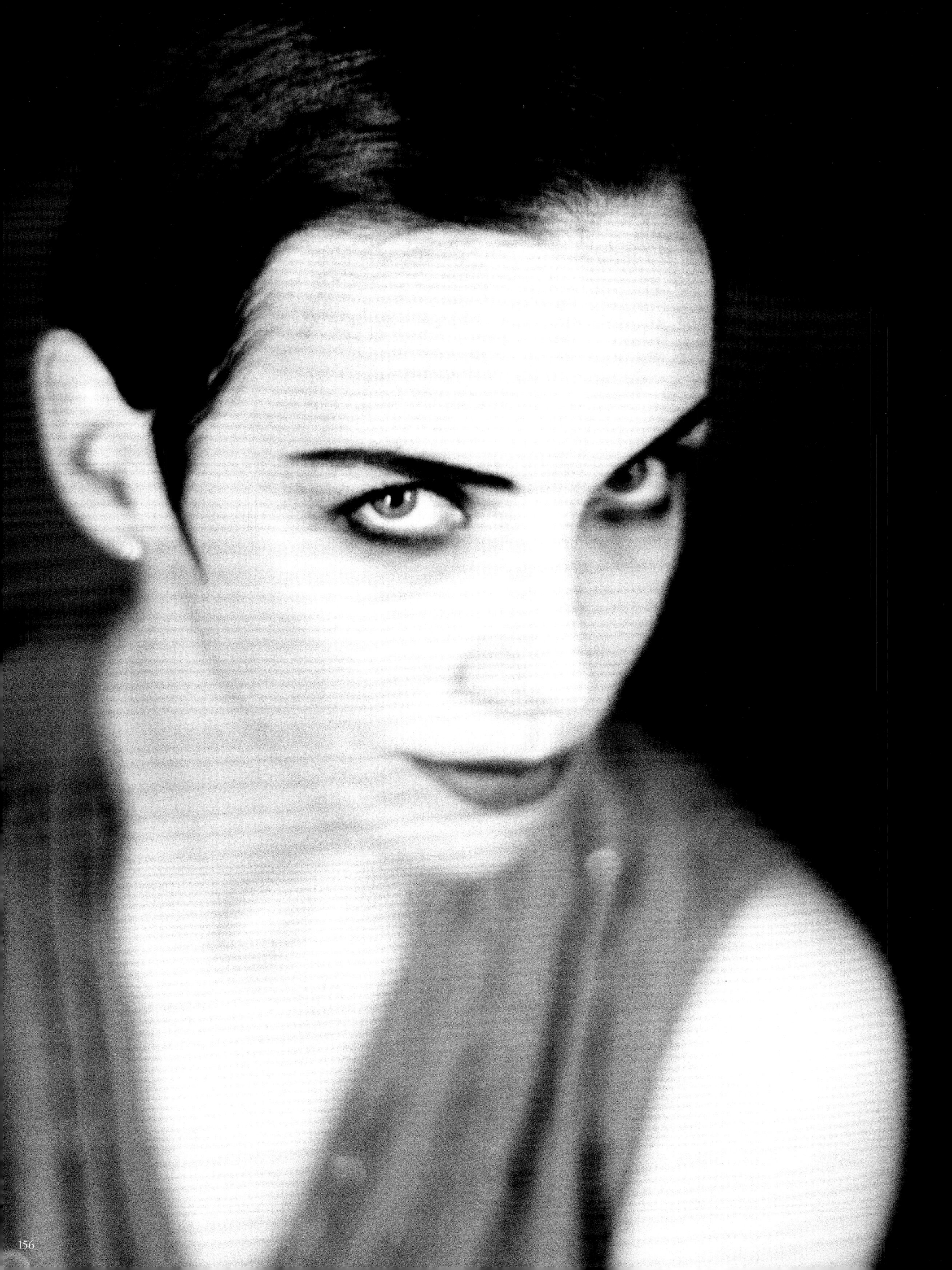

Ellen Von Unwerth has her own individual stamp, verve, and flair. She's a magical circus mistress, bringing out the lions and tigers and all the galloping ponies! A fearless image-maker... She knows what she wants and she *will* capture it!

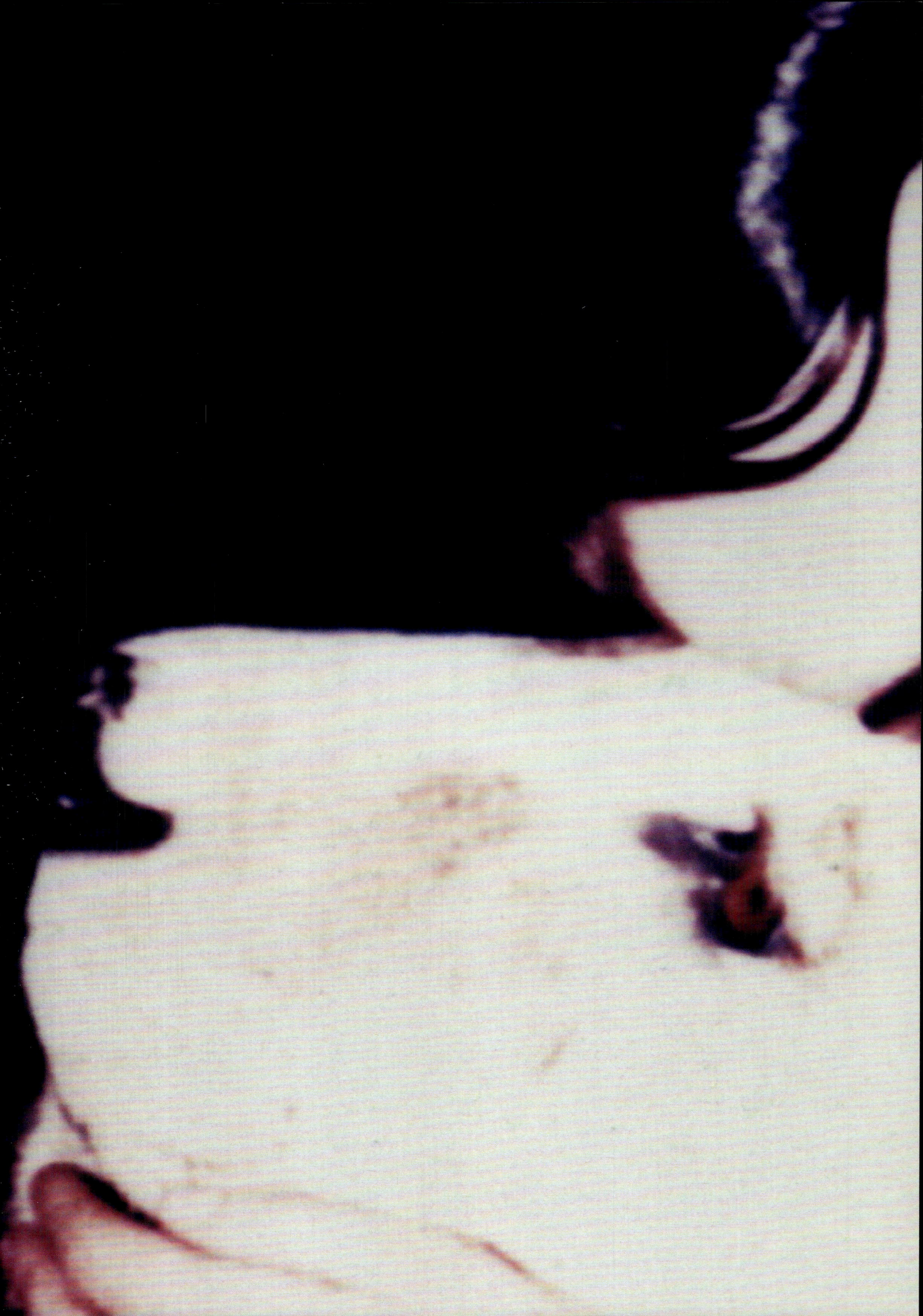

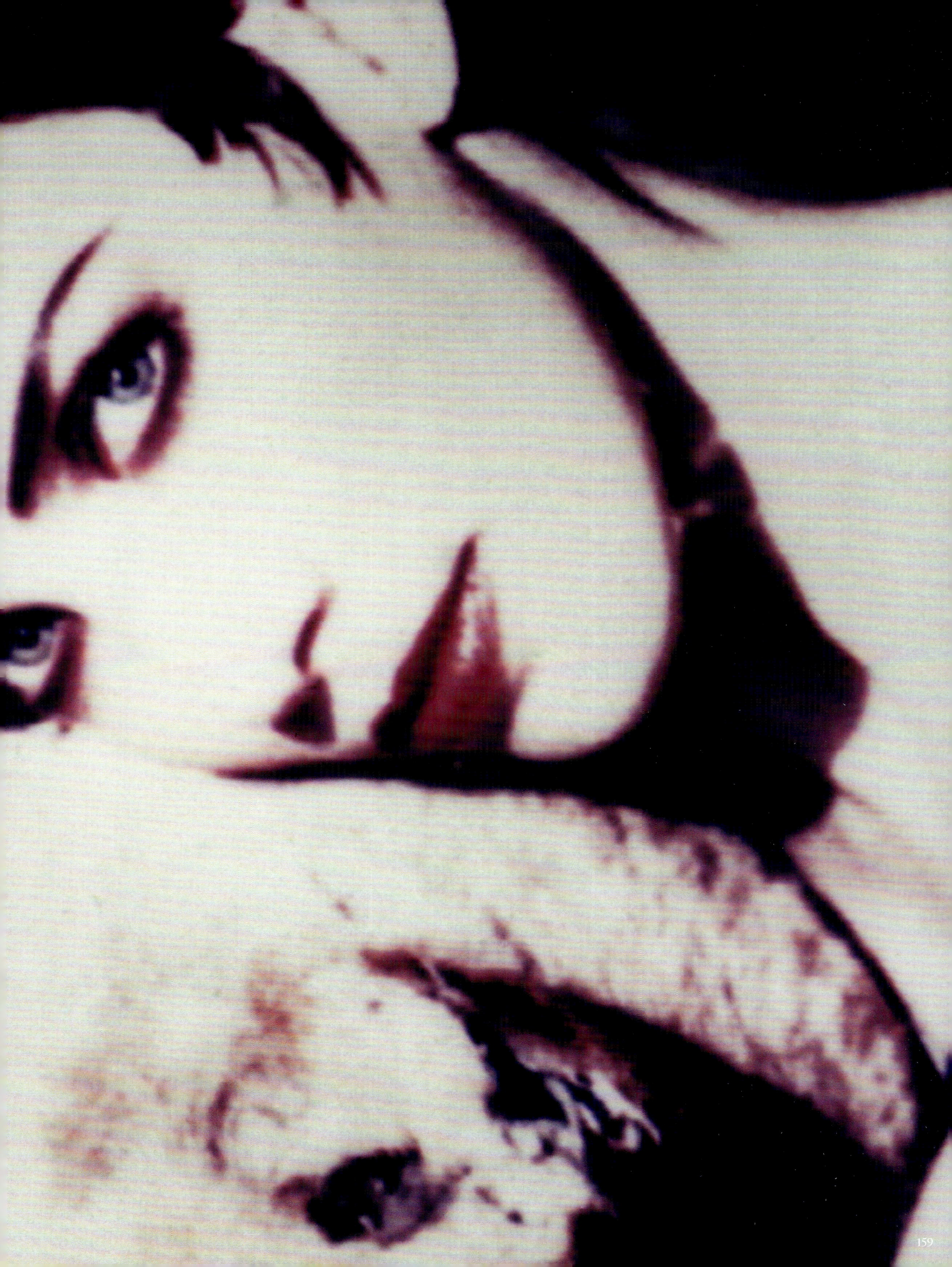

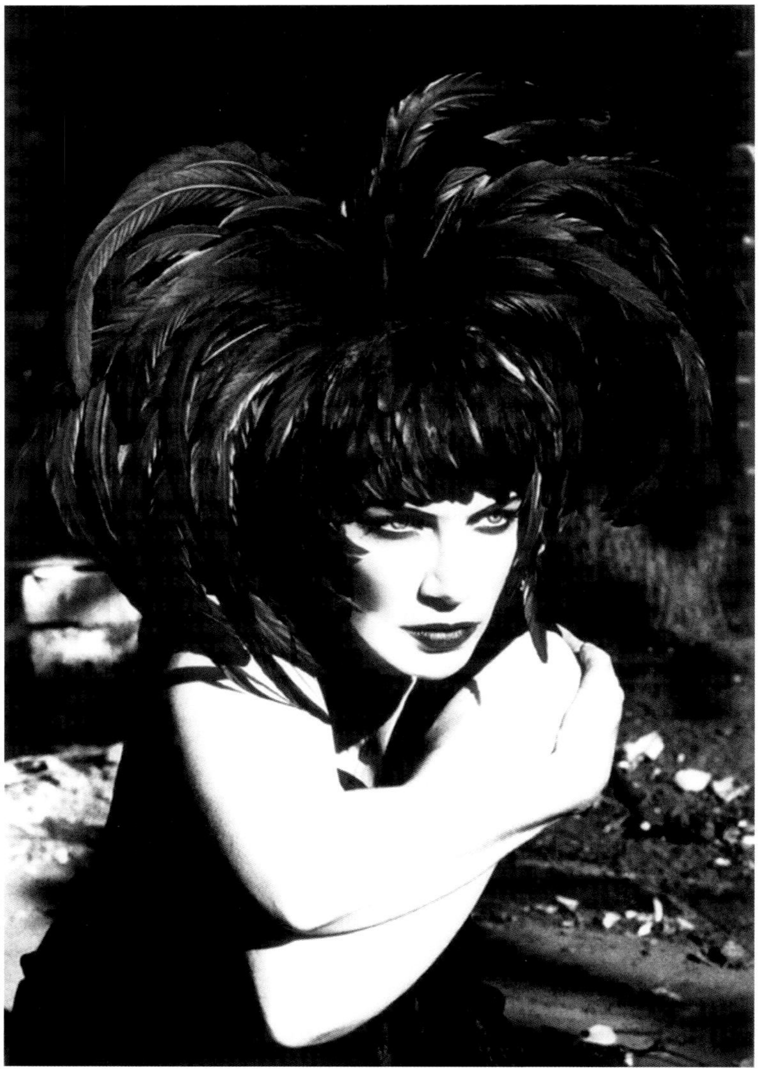

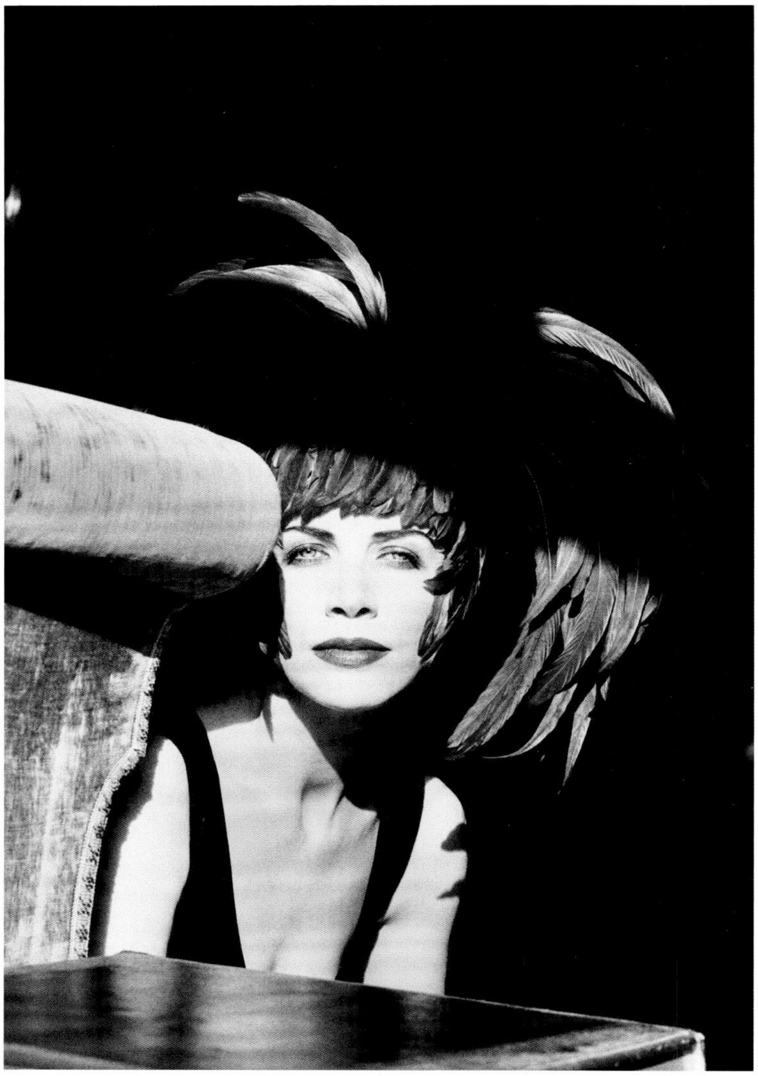

I look up to the little bird
That glides across the sky
He sings the clearest melody
It makes me want to cry
It makes me want to sit right down
and cry, cry, cry

I walk along the city streets
So dark with rage and fear
And I...
I wish that I could be that bird
And fly away from here
I wish I had the wings to fly
Away from here

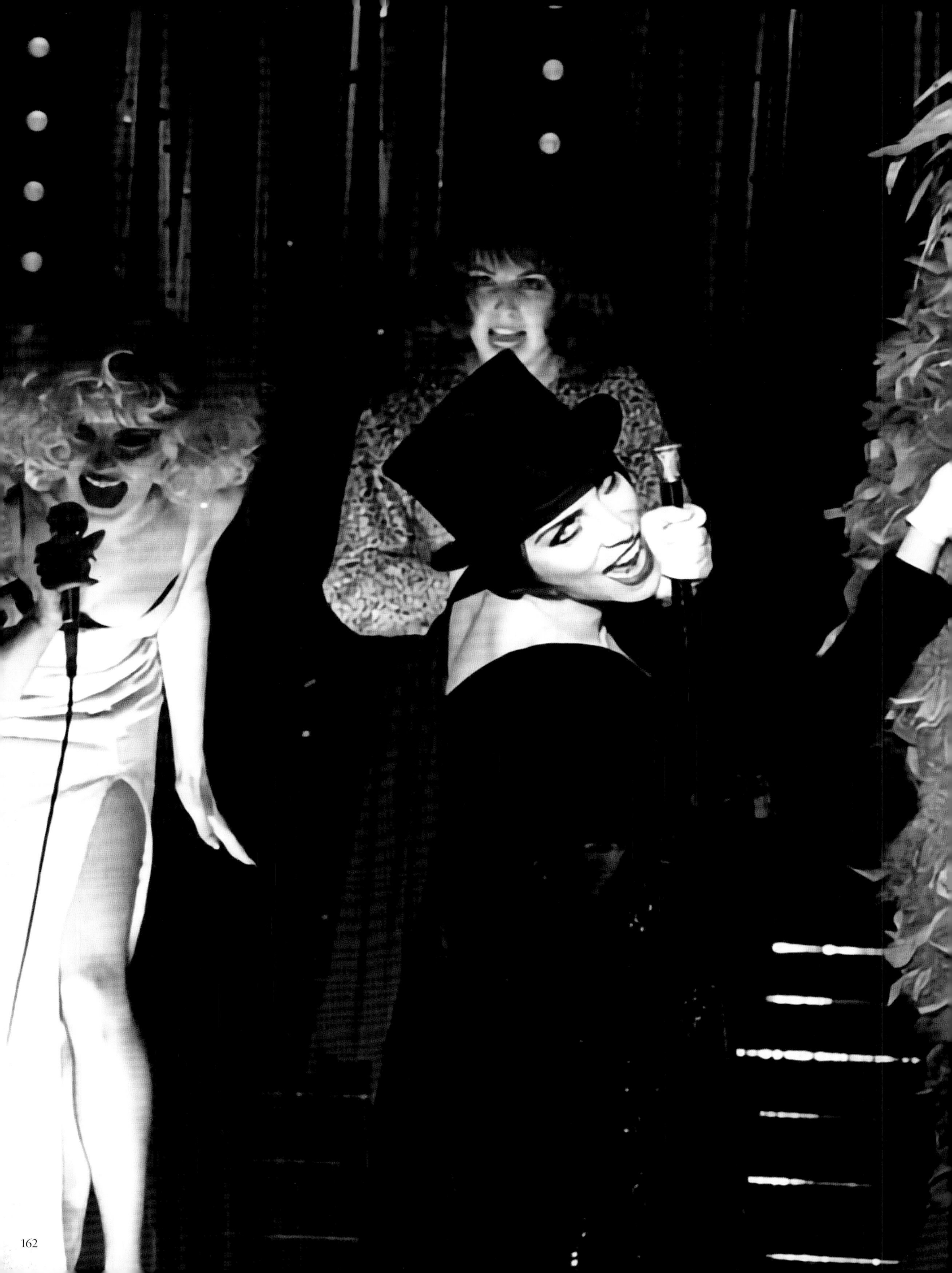

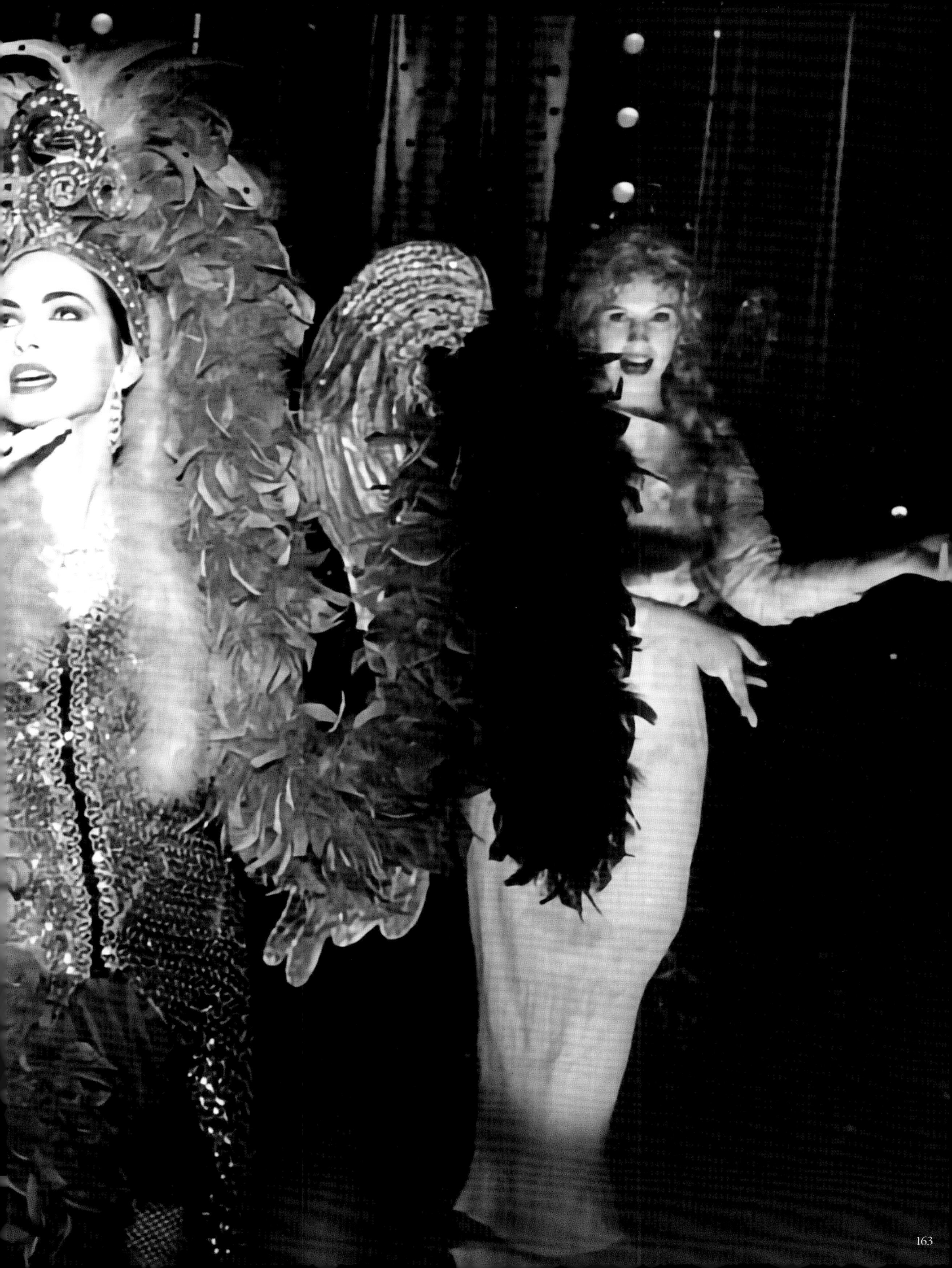

I tried to figure out a way to perform on the video for 'Little Bird' without exhausting myself, at seven months pregnant. I thought I'd probably have to sit down for most of the shoot. Then the idea came to have 'lookalikes,' who could literally replicate my performance.
An audition was held in a tiny theater near Charing Cross. We had to find eight different-looking 'Annie characters.' Sophie (Muller) and I sat in the darkness of the theater while the first of the 'Annies' arrived.
A young man stepped onto the stage wearing a floor-length brown fur coat, which gave him the appearance of an elderly grizzly bear.
The man-bear then started singing 'There Must be An Angel,' sounding more discordantly out of tune with each note.
Sorry to say, it was so bad that it almost sounded avant-garde. We could envisage the audition might last for hours.
More potential 'Annies' came, and it really wasn't looking too hopeful until, by some miracle, things started to improve as better 'Annies' started to arrive.
They were all spectacularly good on the day of the shoot! I only had to trip the light fantastic intermittently.
Best of all, I got to boss each one them about – for the camera only, dear reader!

On set for the filming of the 'Little Bird' video, directed by Sophie Muller. A collection of 'Annies'... or at least Annie's character projections, alter egos, or archetypes. Diva, Neurotic Housewife, Angel, Rockstar, Vamp, Fallen Angel, Gender Bender, Courtesan, Pregnant Ring Mistress...

Overleaf: Standing on the beautiful staircase of London's Home House during the filming of 'Walking on Broken Glass.' Two days of fantastic regalia, pomp, drama, and scandalous Baroque intrigue. Forever grateful to Hugh Laurie and John Malkovich for agreeing to take part in the madness of our method.

The sun's still shining
in the big blue sky
But it don't mean
nothing to me
Oh... let the rain
come down
Let the wind
blow through me

I'm living
in an empty room
With all the
windows smashed
And I've got so little
left to lose
That it feels just like
I'm walking on
broken glass

167

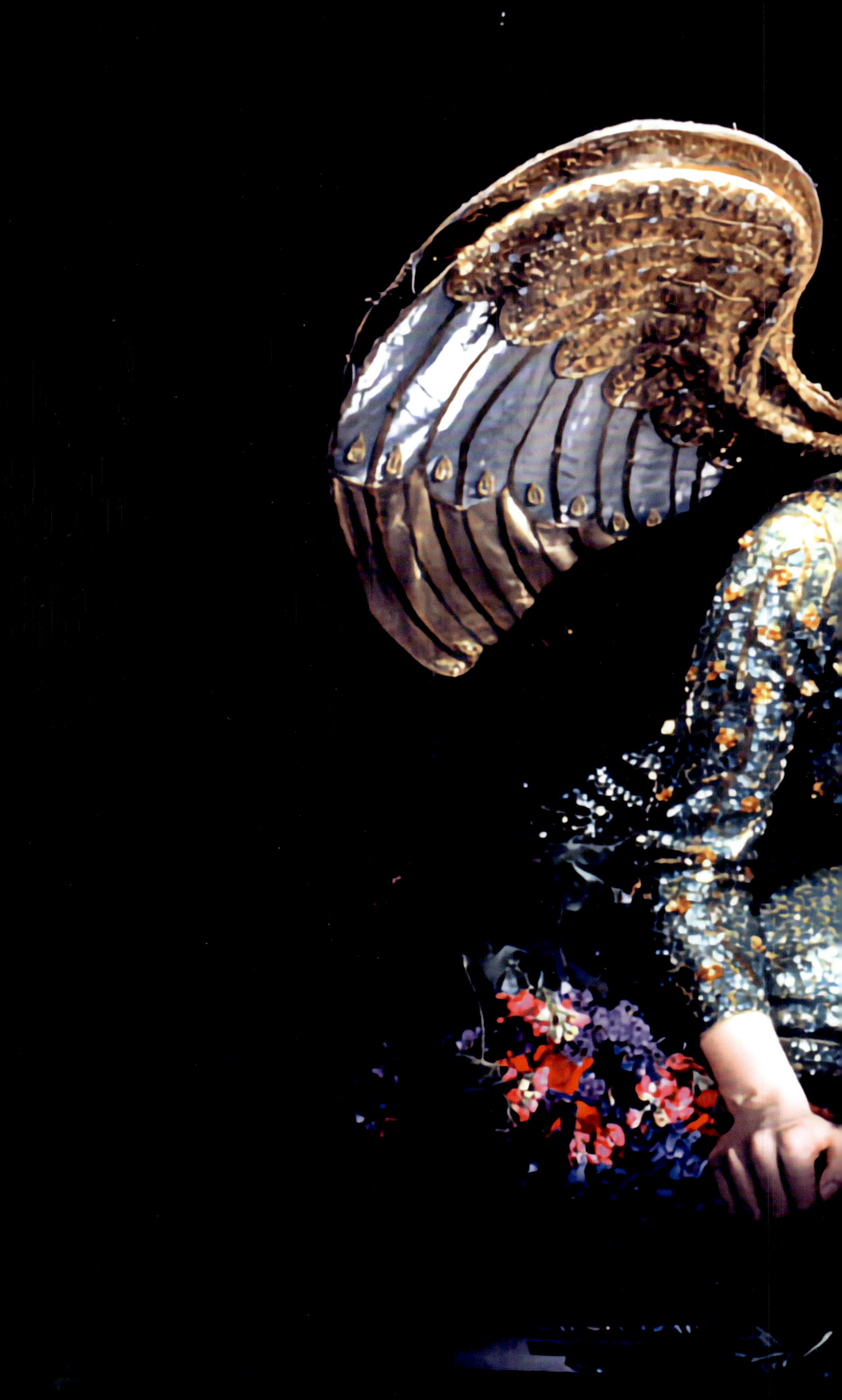

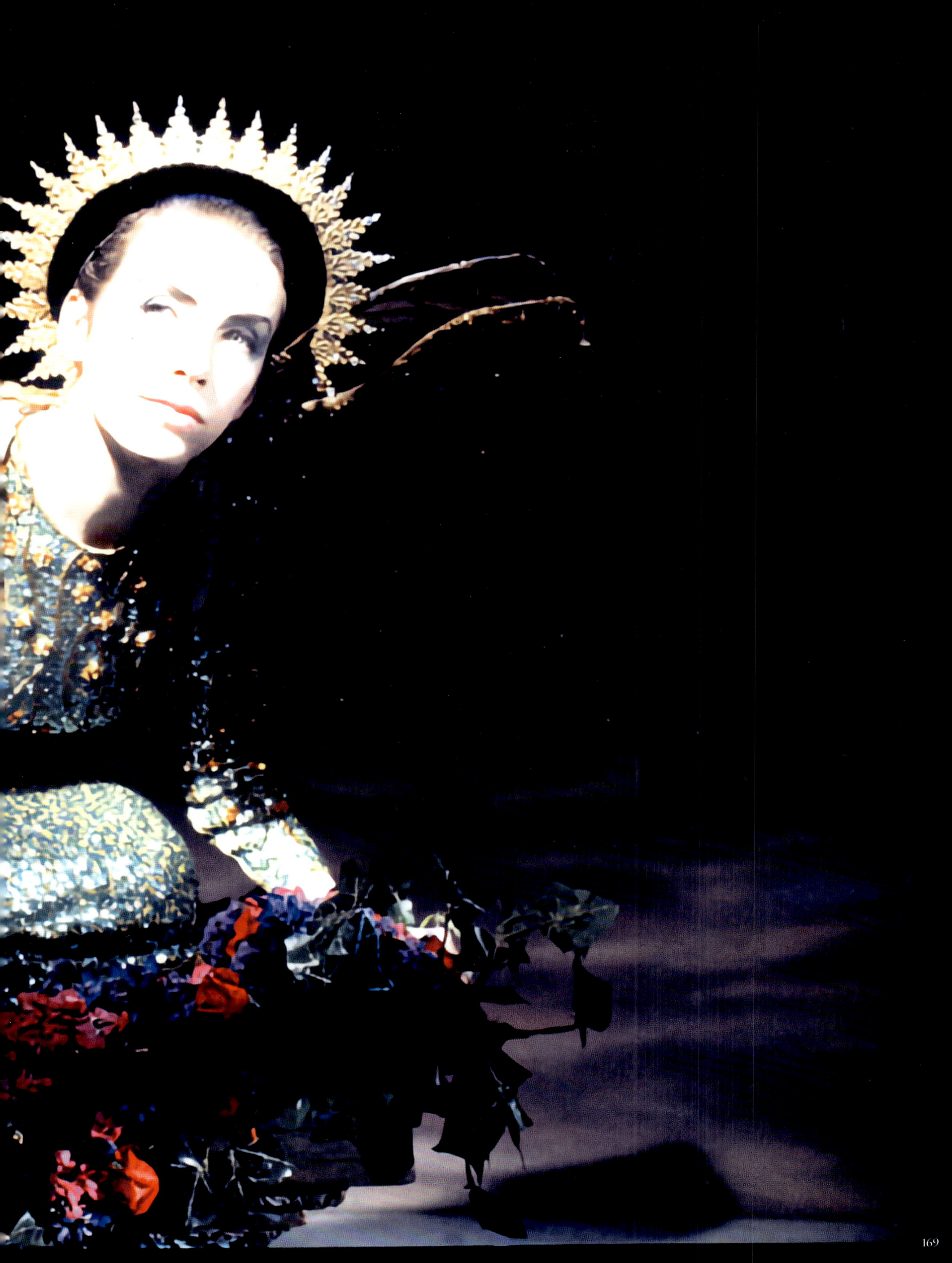

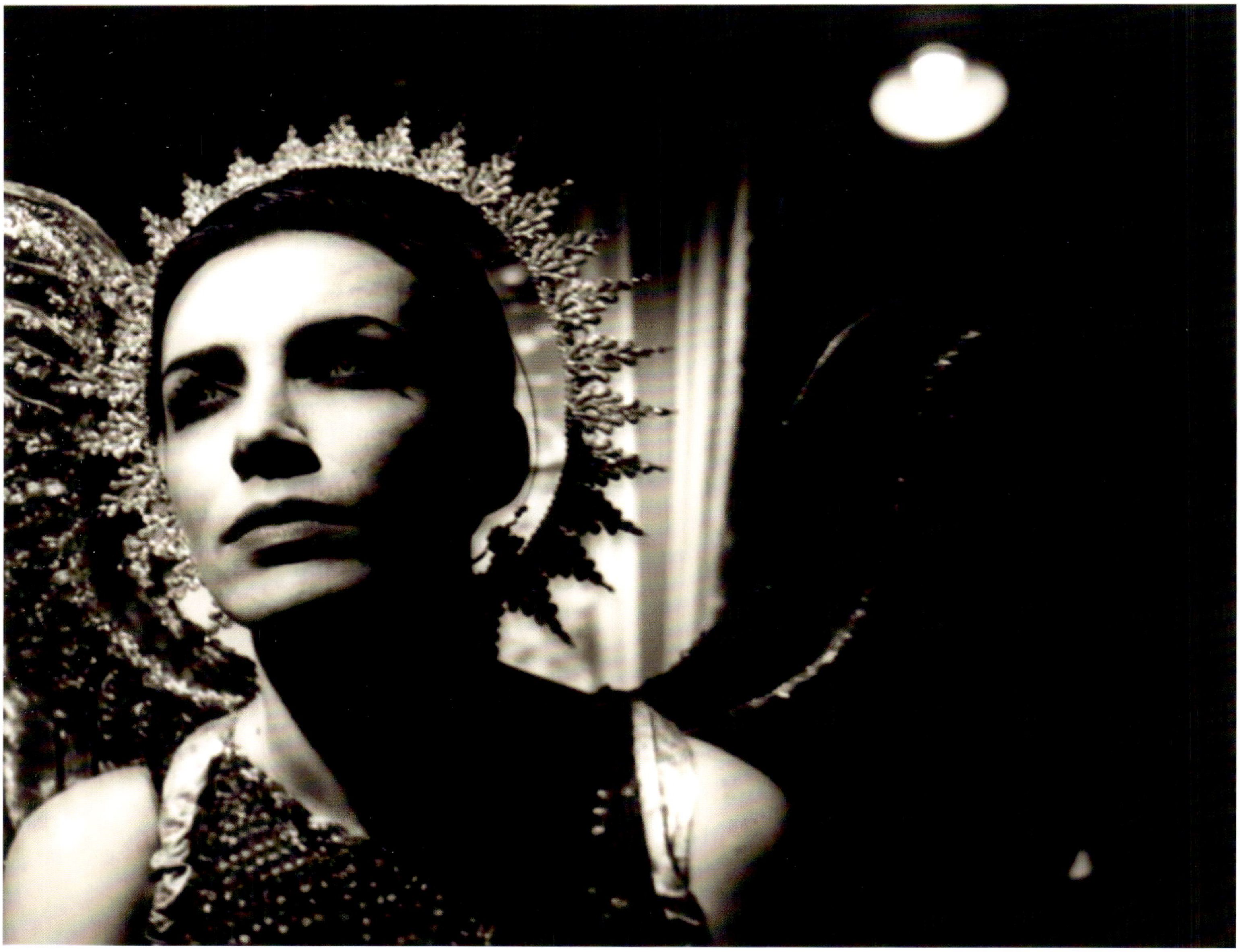

171

How many times do I have to try
To tell you that I'm sorry for the things I've done?
But when I start to try to tell you
That's when you have to tell me
"Hey...This kind of trouble's only just begun..."
I tell myself too many times
"Why don't you ever learn to keep your big mouth shut?"
That's why it hurts so bad to hear the words
That keep on falling from your mouth
Falling from your mouth
Falling from your mouth,
tell me
Why?...

I may be mad I may be blind
I may be viciously unkind
But I can still read what you're thinking
And I've heard it said too many times
That you'd be better off, besides
Why can't you see
This boat is sinking--this boat is sinking
Let's go down to the water's edge
And we can cast away those doubts
Some things are better left unsaid
But they still turn me inside out
Turning inside out
Turning inside out
Tell me
Why?

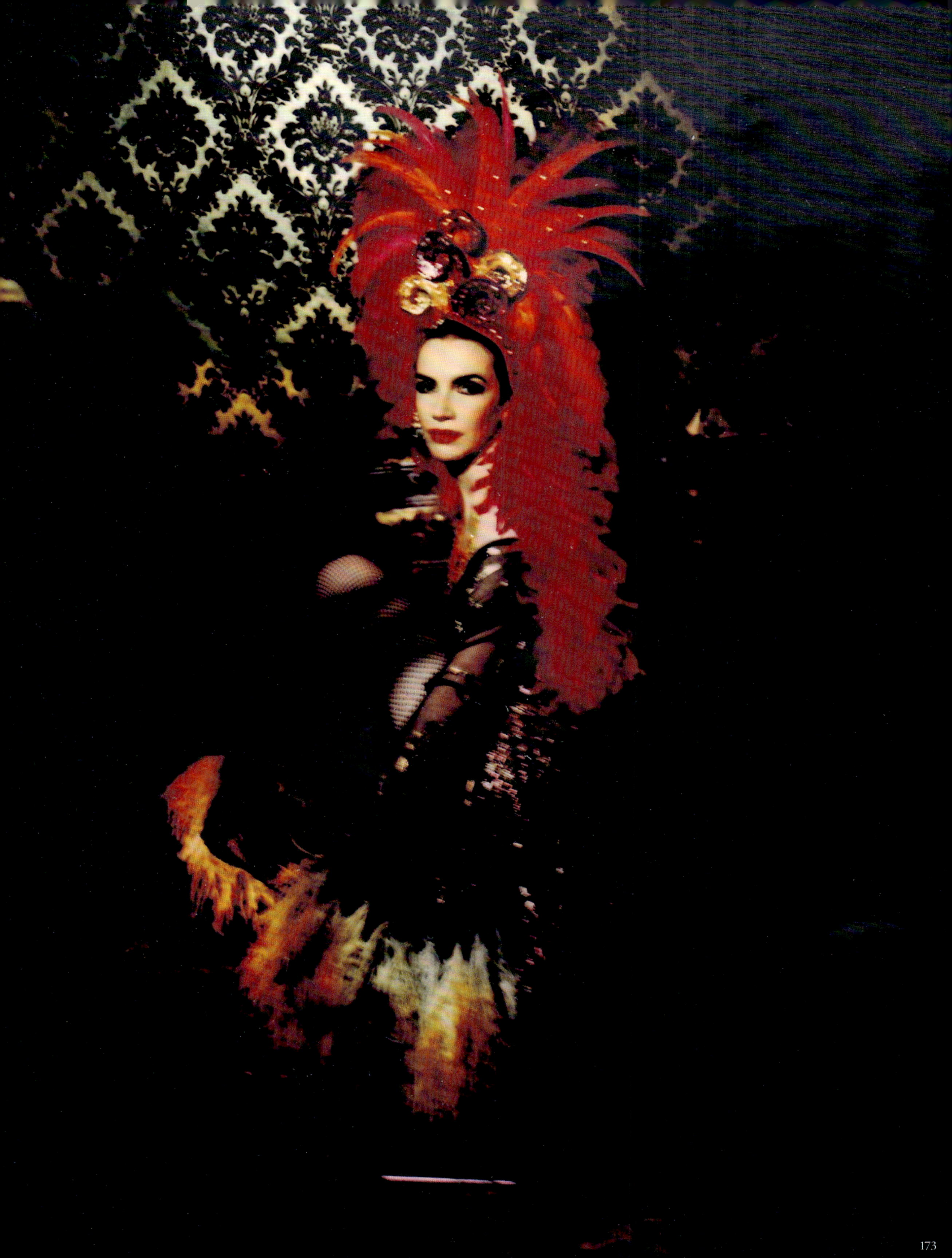

Performing 'Under Pressure' with David Bowie, at the Freddie Mercury Tribute Concert at Wembley Stadium in London, April 20, 1992. One of the most thrilling experiences I've ever had on stage.

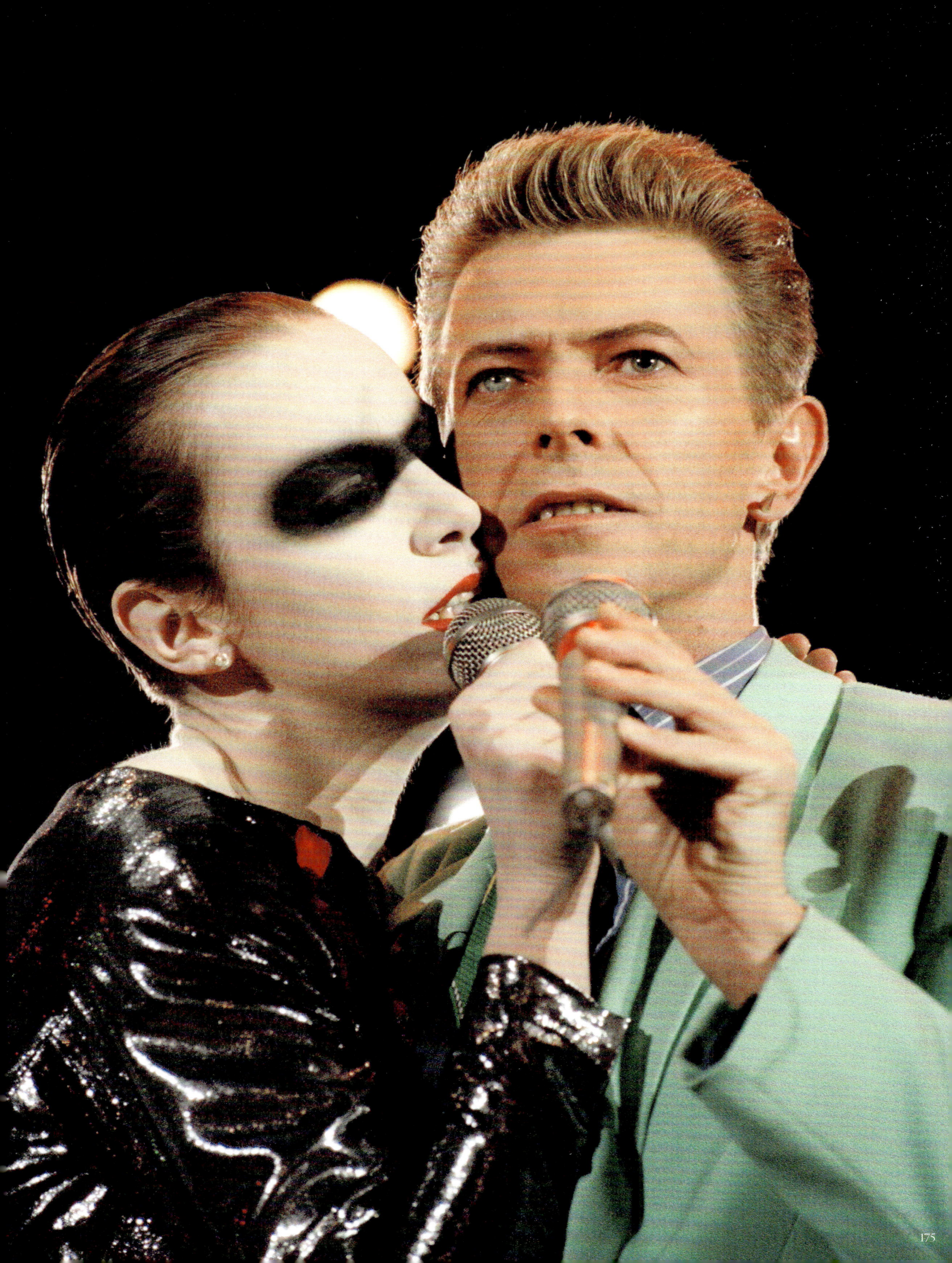

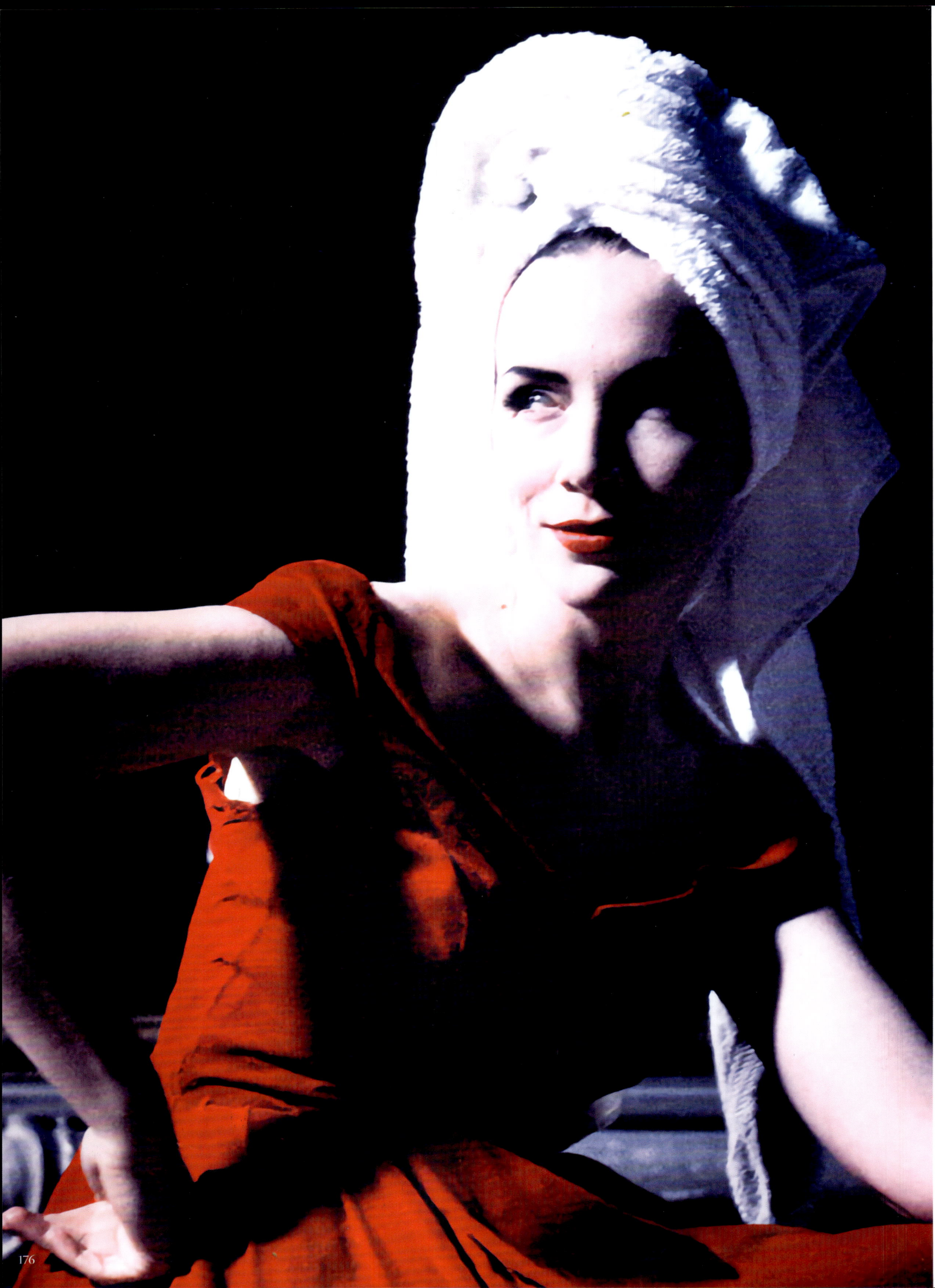

This picture was taken in one of Venice's grand historic palazzos, during the filming of a collection of videos directed by Sophie Muller over a period of several days.

Sophie was actually at the beginning of what was to become an outstanding career in the field of directing music videos.

Although we had a schedule and knew the scenes we wanted to capture, a fair bit of the process relied on improvisation and 'making things up as you go along.'

For some reason she thought it would great for me to wear a bathroom towel on my head. I was compliant, but I've often wondered what she was thinking.

1995–98

Cover shot for *Medusa* by Bettina Rheims, 1995. Of all the photographers I worked with, she was one that I'd really hoped I might have a chance to meet. She's a unique and exceptional person, whose photographic eye and perspective is hers ALONE.

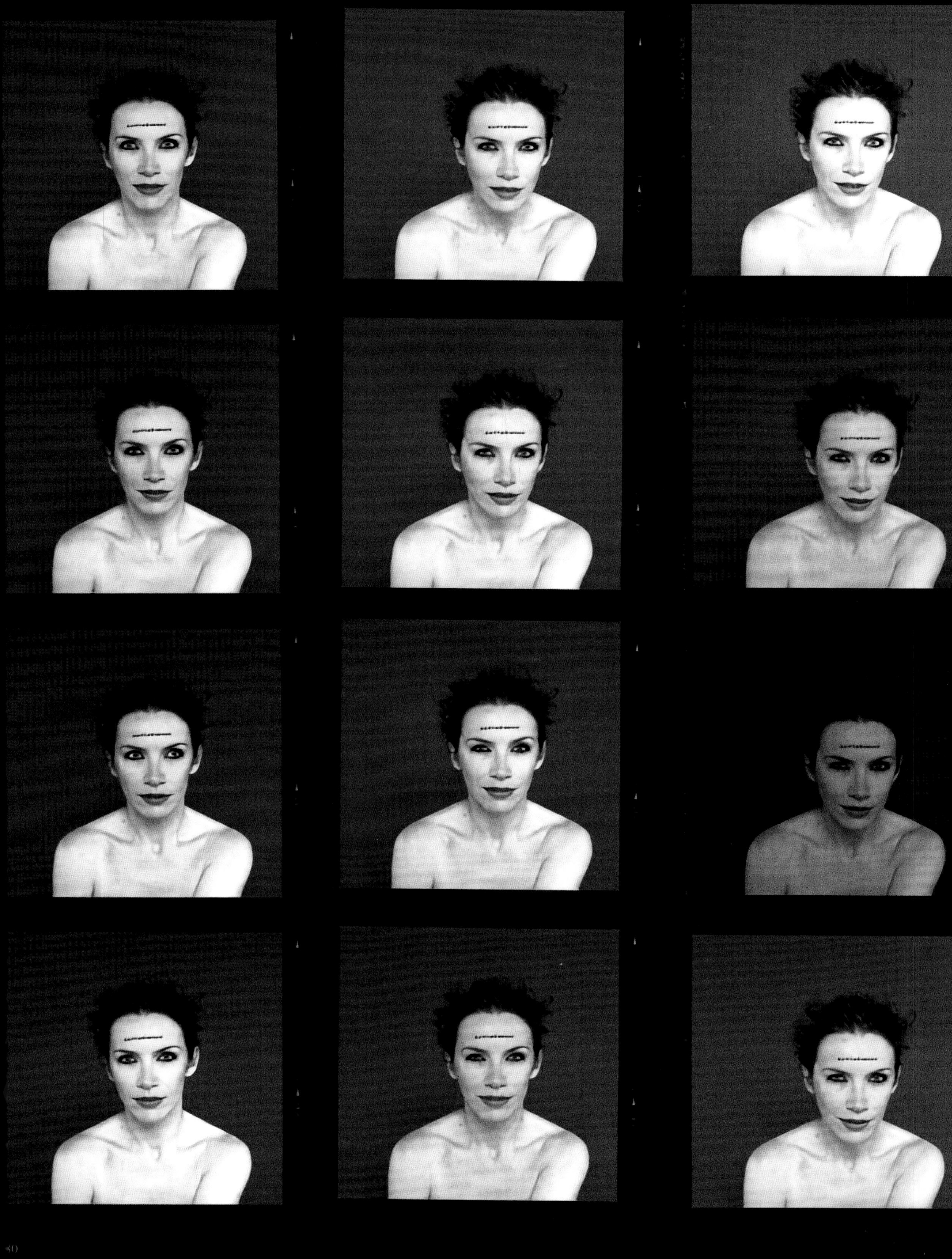

181

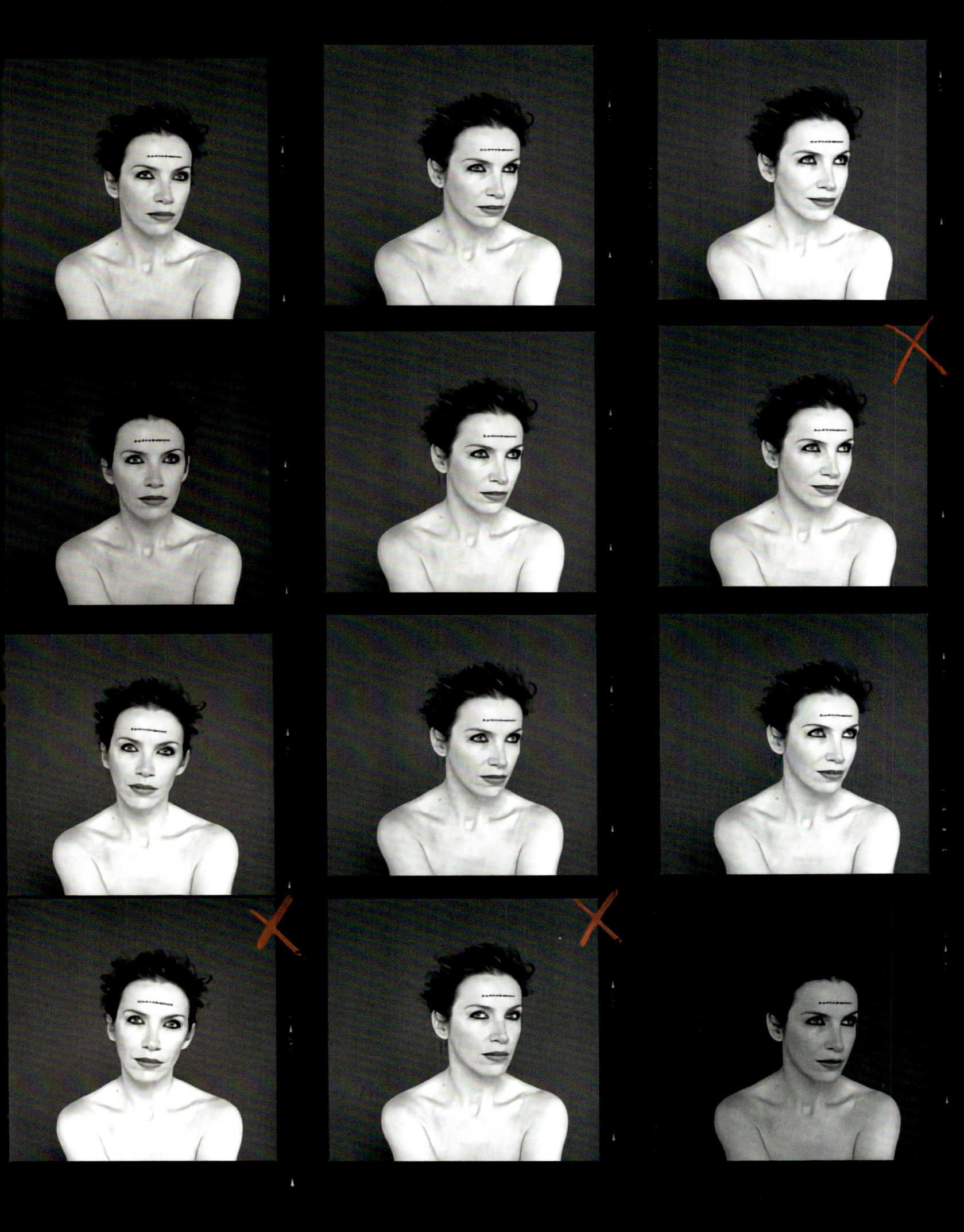

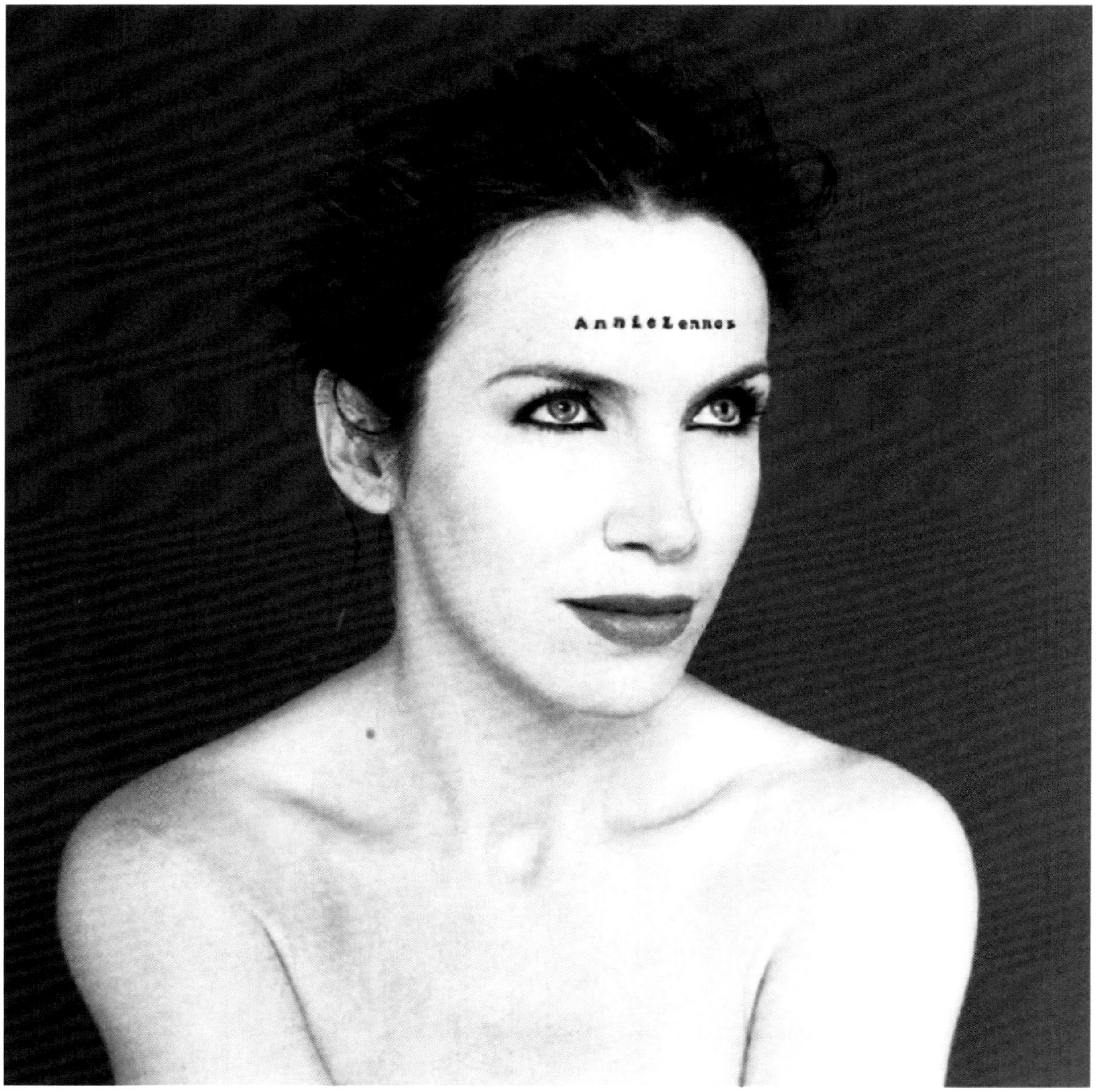
AnnieLennox

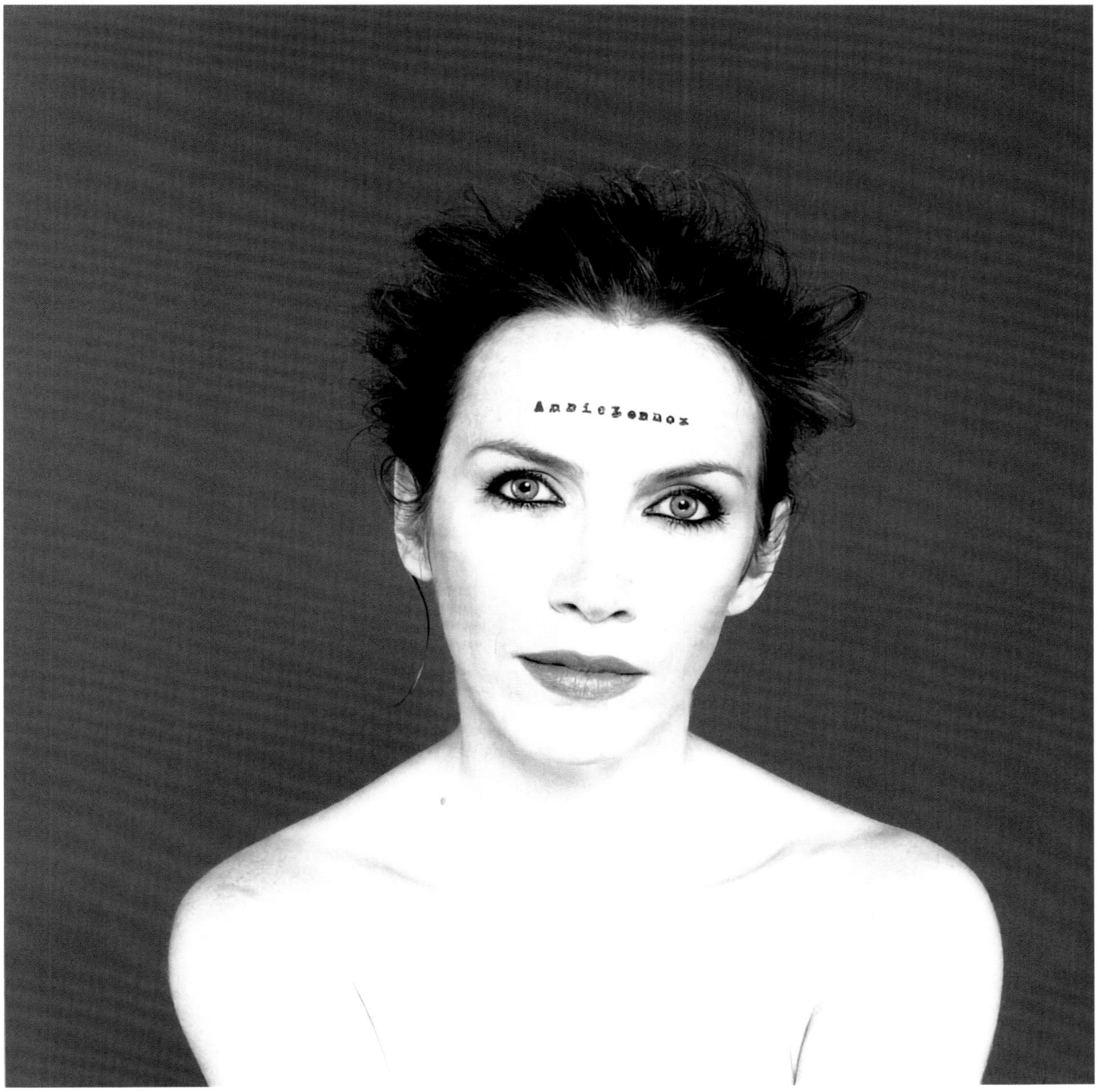
AnnieLennox

Loneliness
Is a place that I know well
It's the distance between us
And the space inside ourselves
And emptiness...
Is the chattering in your head
It's the call of the living
And the race from life to death
And I know
Yes and I know
What you feel...

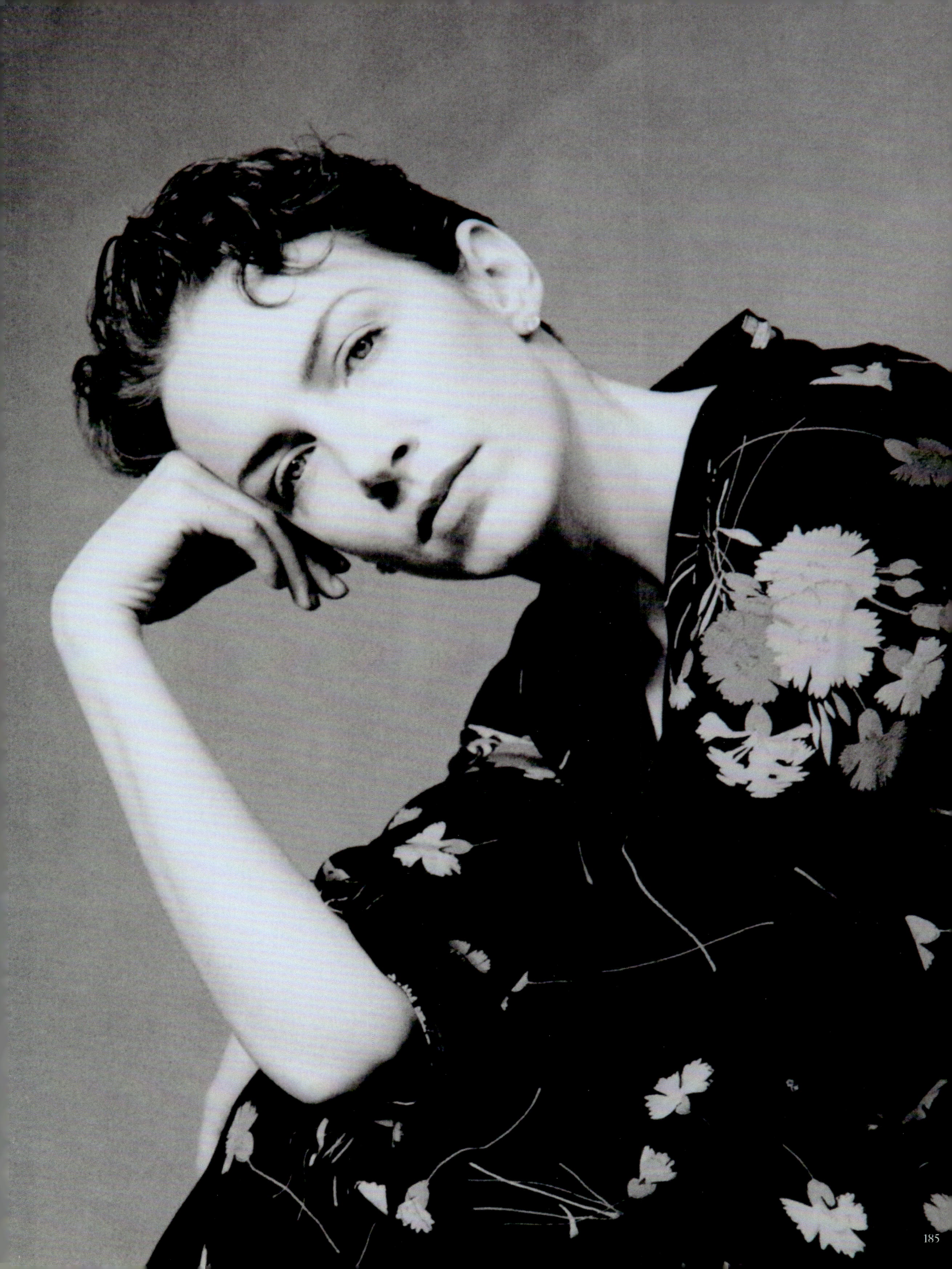

A colorful collection of wondrously curious characters.
Two days of intense work, costume, makeup, lashes, and hilarious joy!
Packed with the bygone-era magic of Wilton's Music Hall, a perfectly preserved Victorian theater in East London, where the video for 'No More "I Love You's"' was shot.
I had the notion of manifesting characters from the period of the French Impressionist painters of Montmartre, Paris.
A visual blend between Toulouse-Lautrec and Degas.

The production truly manifested the dream!
The most transcendent male dancers floated fawned and pirouetted in snow-white 'Swan Lake' tutus, drag, pointed ballet toes, and tiaras. .

Recreating the shadowy atmosphere of an underground world, in the cigar smoke-filled company of sexual fantasists – top-hatted gentlemen in formal evening wear, judges, lawyers, men of bourgeoise 'substance' and rank – appreciating the company of some disinterested drunken courtesans.
An evening with the outliers and deviants of the French Belle Epoch.

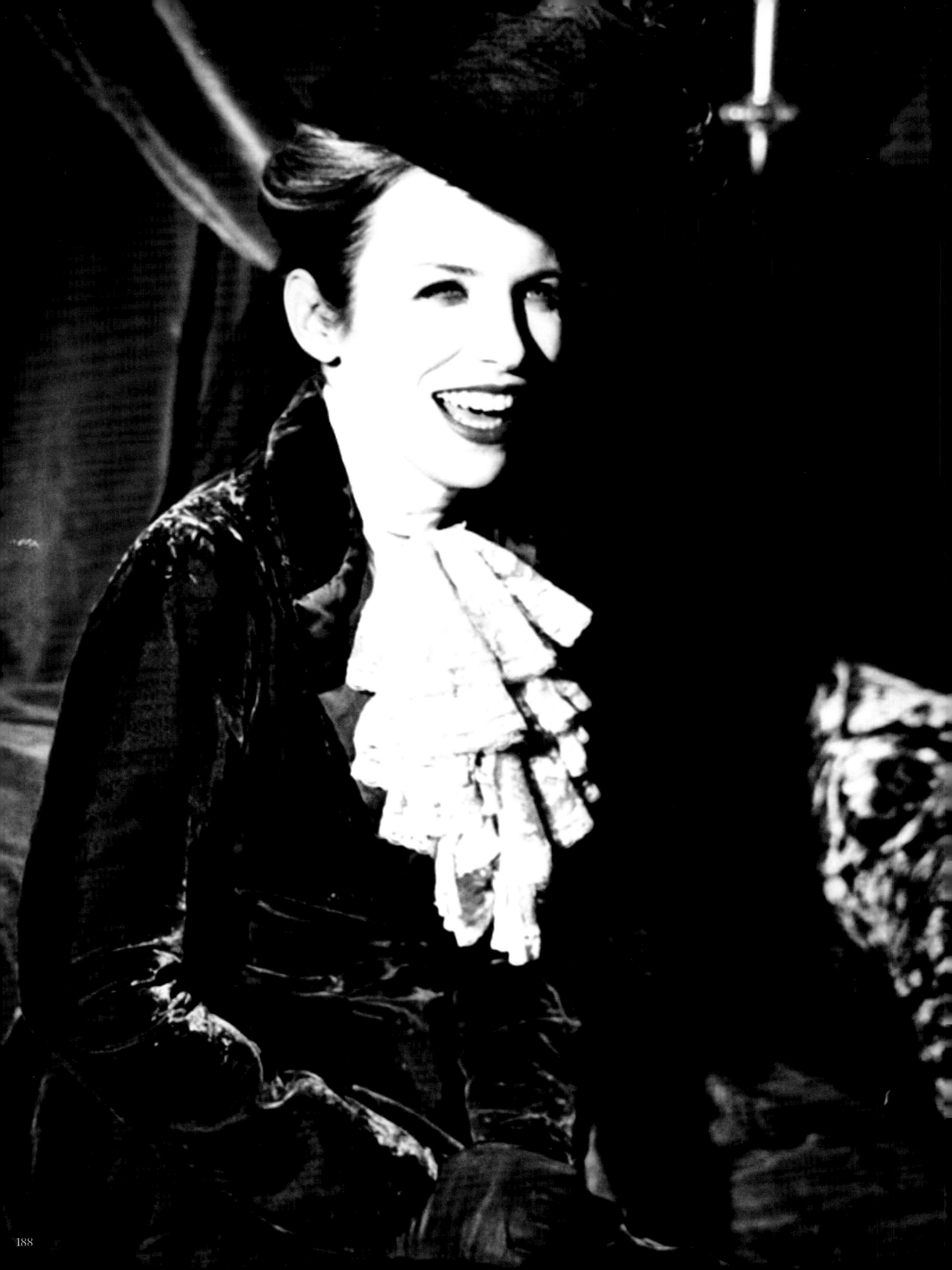

I've always wanted to time travel – to journey back to the places and environments of moments that will never return. Absolutely everything is temporary and evolving continuously.
The closest you can go is to recreate proximities, with costume and atmosphere.
I'm so grateful to have had so many experiences like these throughout my life.
There's a tremendous freedom in being a performer.

Overleaf: I was heavily pregnant underneath this big blue crushed-velvet 'tent.' Glad to be sitting down, matching the cobalt blue wallpaper on a wall in London's Home House, before it was purchased and renovated to become a private members club. The building holds a very significant personal memory for me, in that over two decades after this picture was taken, I married my husband there in September, 2012.

Dyin' is easy
It's livin' that scares me
to death...
I could be so content
Hearing the sound
of your breath

Cold is the color of crystal
The snow light that falls
from the heavenly skies
Catch me
And let me dive under
'Cause I want to
Swim in the pools
of your eyes

191

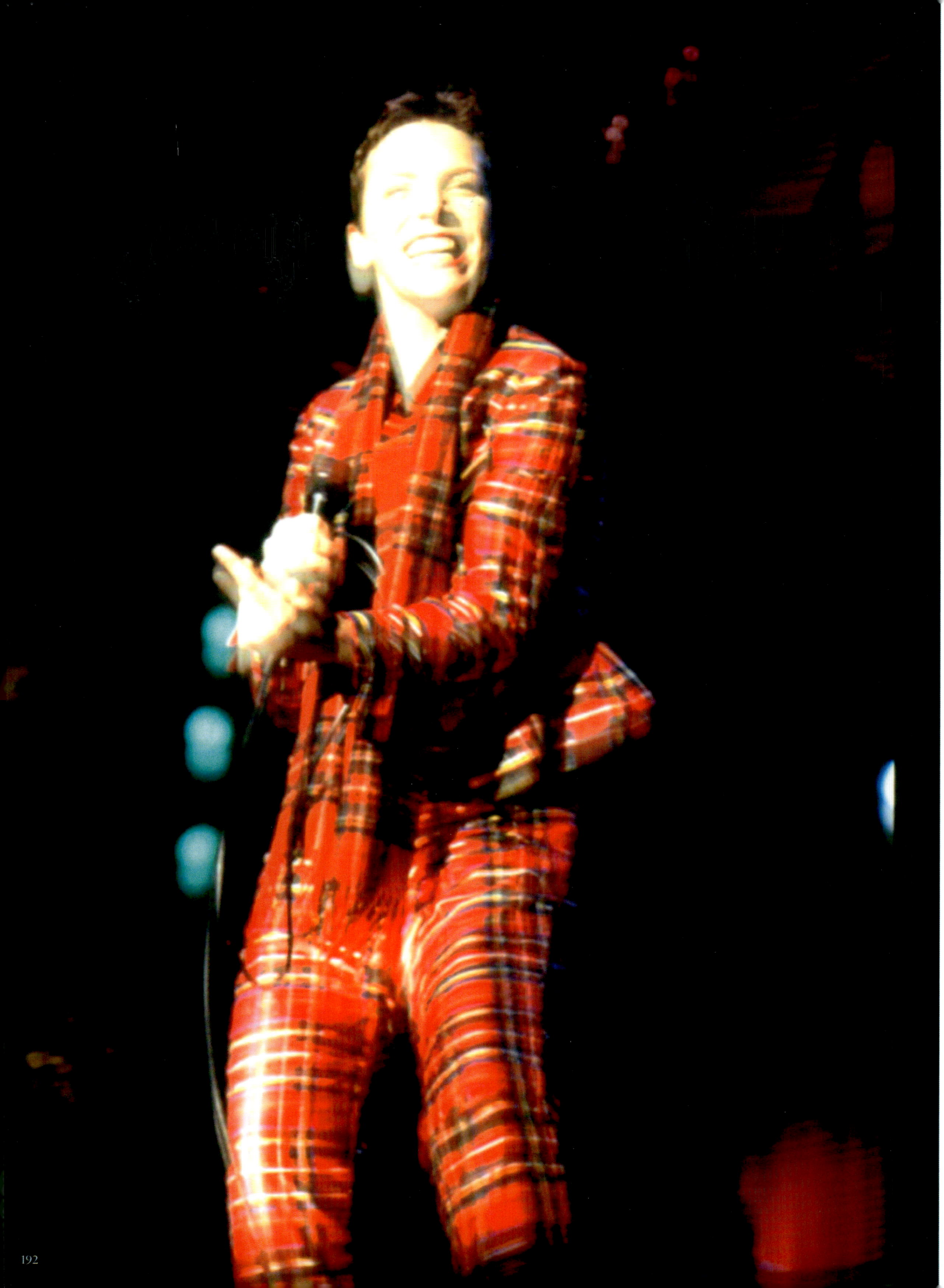

Performing is not for the faint of heart.
This photograph is taken literally 'Live From Central Park, New York,' in the Summer of 1995.
I had two sweet little cherubs of four and two at the time, so I wasn't going to head for a life on the road, but I did perform once or twice. This concert was a complete one-off: it was the only concert I gave with this wonderful lineup of musicians. We barely had time to rehearse… but we ended up playing a fantastic show that evening. It truly was a glorious event.
I came off stage and dropped right down like a prize boxer does after a match, with the greatest exhale of relief, triumph, and exhaustion.
Unless you're a performer, you cannot know or even understand what a performer goes through and the lives we live.

Behind the scenes.

In the studio. Practicing. In rehearsals. Taking voice classes. Practicing lines. Avoiding catching airborne diseases. Resting. Stretching and strengthening. Practicing again. Writing. Having meetings. Warming up the voice. Recording. Warming up the voice. Performing. Shooting videos. Preparing for shooting videos. Meetings. Resting. Putting makeup on. Giving interviews. Taking makeup off. Preparing for photographic sessions. Meetings. Putting makeup on. Having pictures taken. Taking makeup off. Meetings. Practicing. Travelling in cars, buses, and airplanes. Packing. Checking into hotels. Unpacking. Packing. Checking out of hotels. Unpacking…
On repeat cycle.

The glittering prizes... I'm holding a Grammy in my hand.

Feeling 'slightly' like a spare thumb in a gathering of all-American Superstar Female Artists at a Grammy event.

When I was just seventeen
I ran away from home
To be with all the pretty people
To be on my own
Bright lights and trains
And bedroom stains
And pavements paved with gold
And I believed in everything
That everybody told me
Have mercy
Have mercy on me

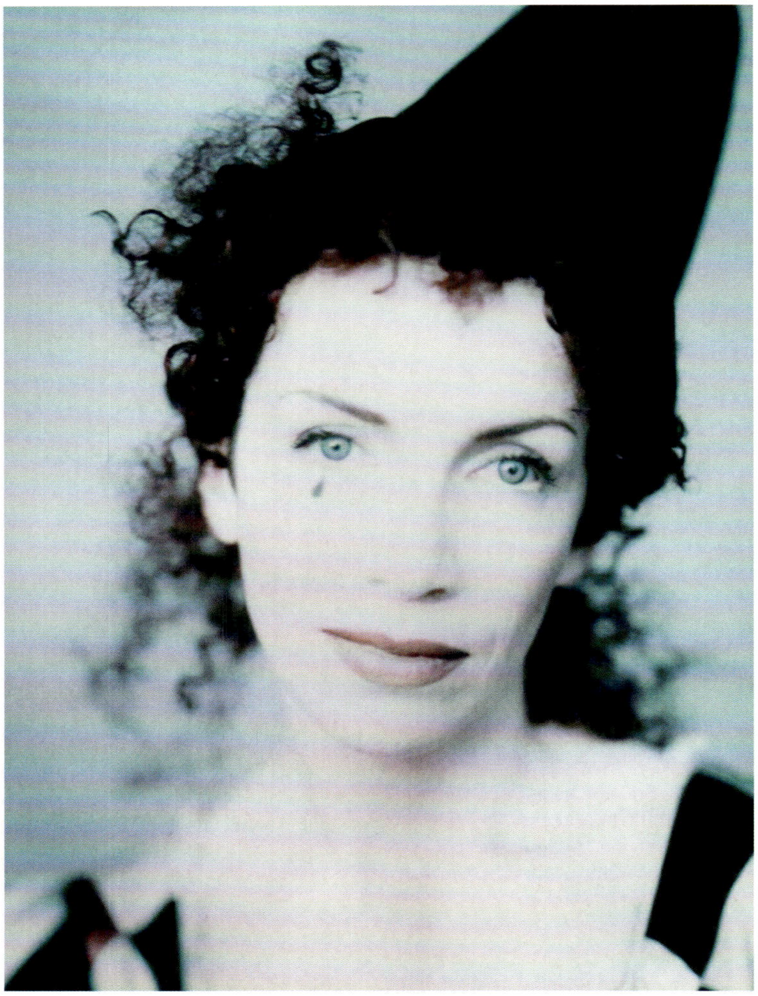

197

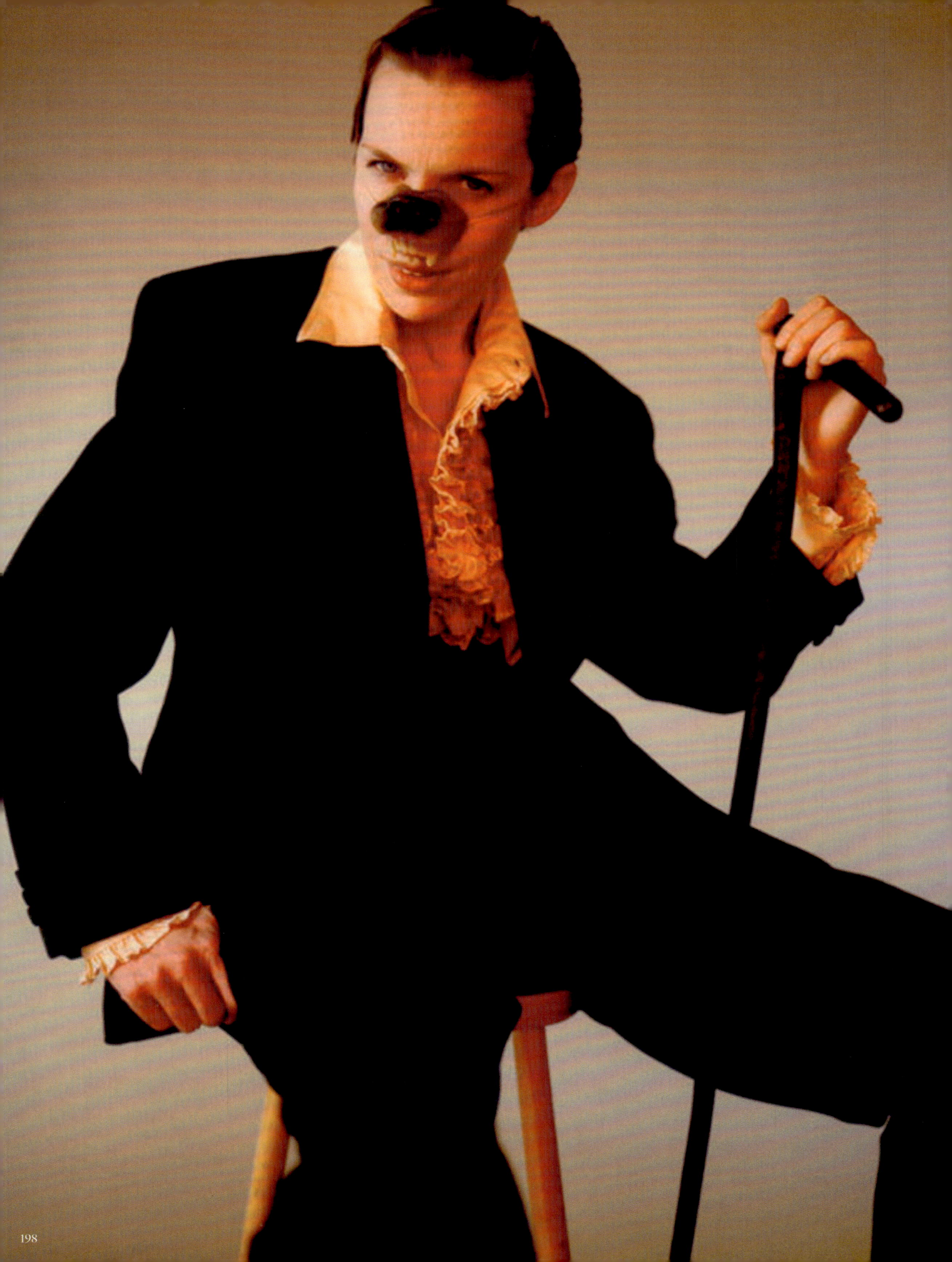

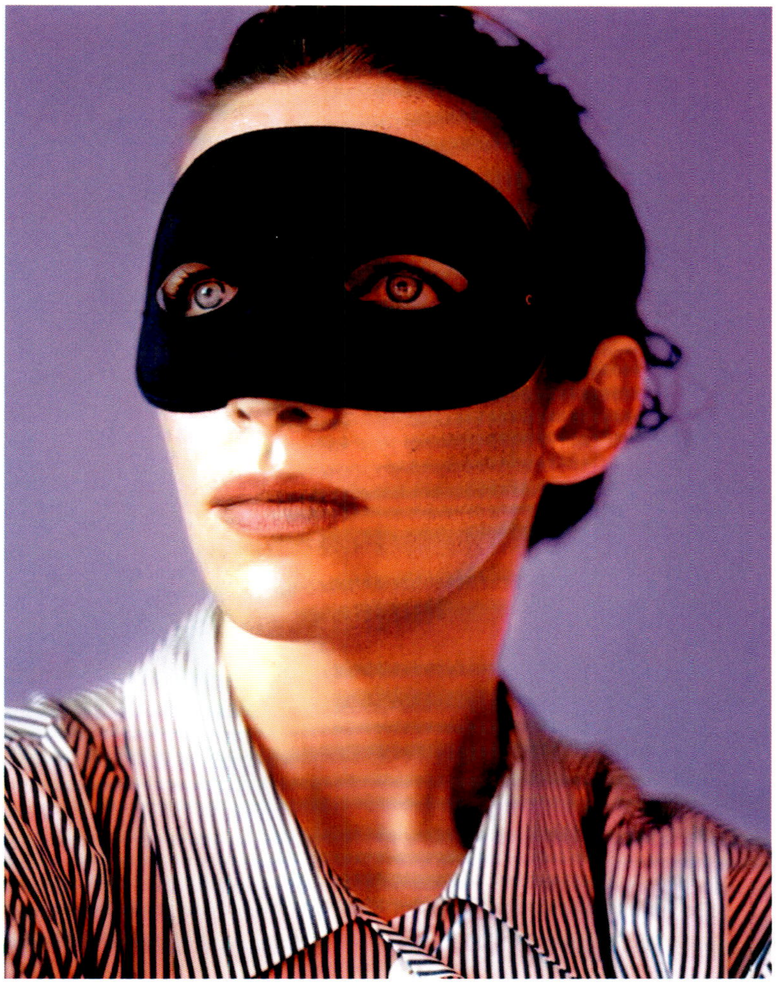

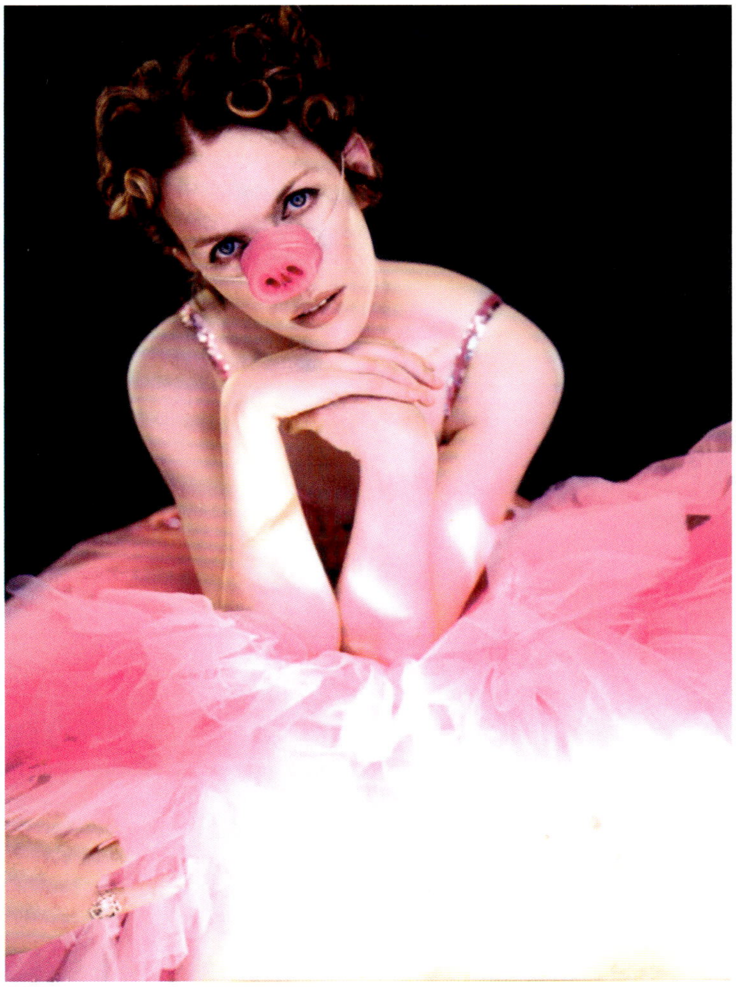

Three characters came out of this brilliant session with the acclaimed Spanish photographer Javier Vallhonrat, who I remember as a true gentleman who was great to work with. These shots were commissioned by the magazine Vanity Fair. I brought the little snout masks, the wolf and the pig, and most likely brought the black silk mask along, too. The wolf instantly became a louche, barfly, dandy, and pimp, while Miss Piggy was probably less complex… at least from the cheap seats!

201

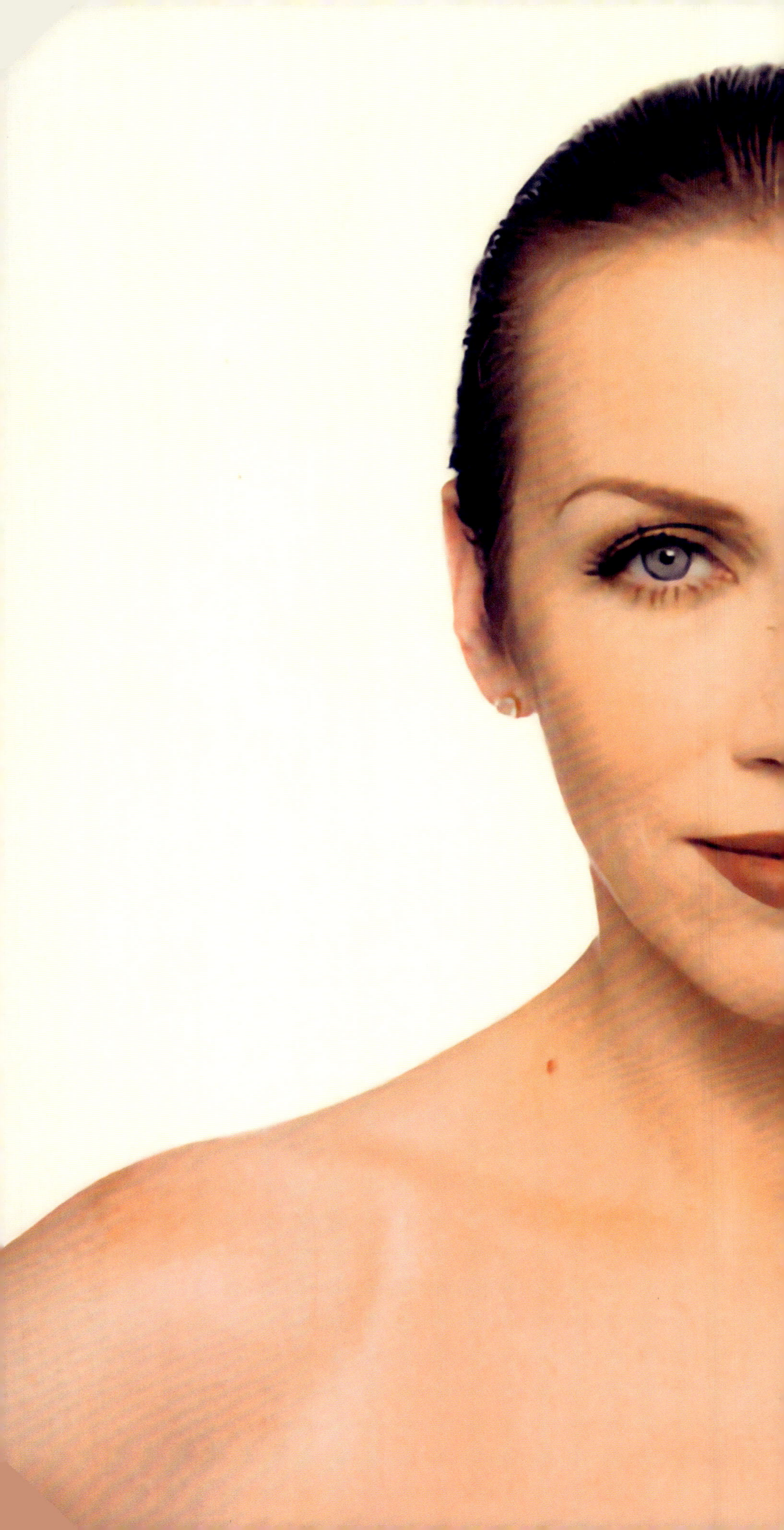

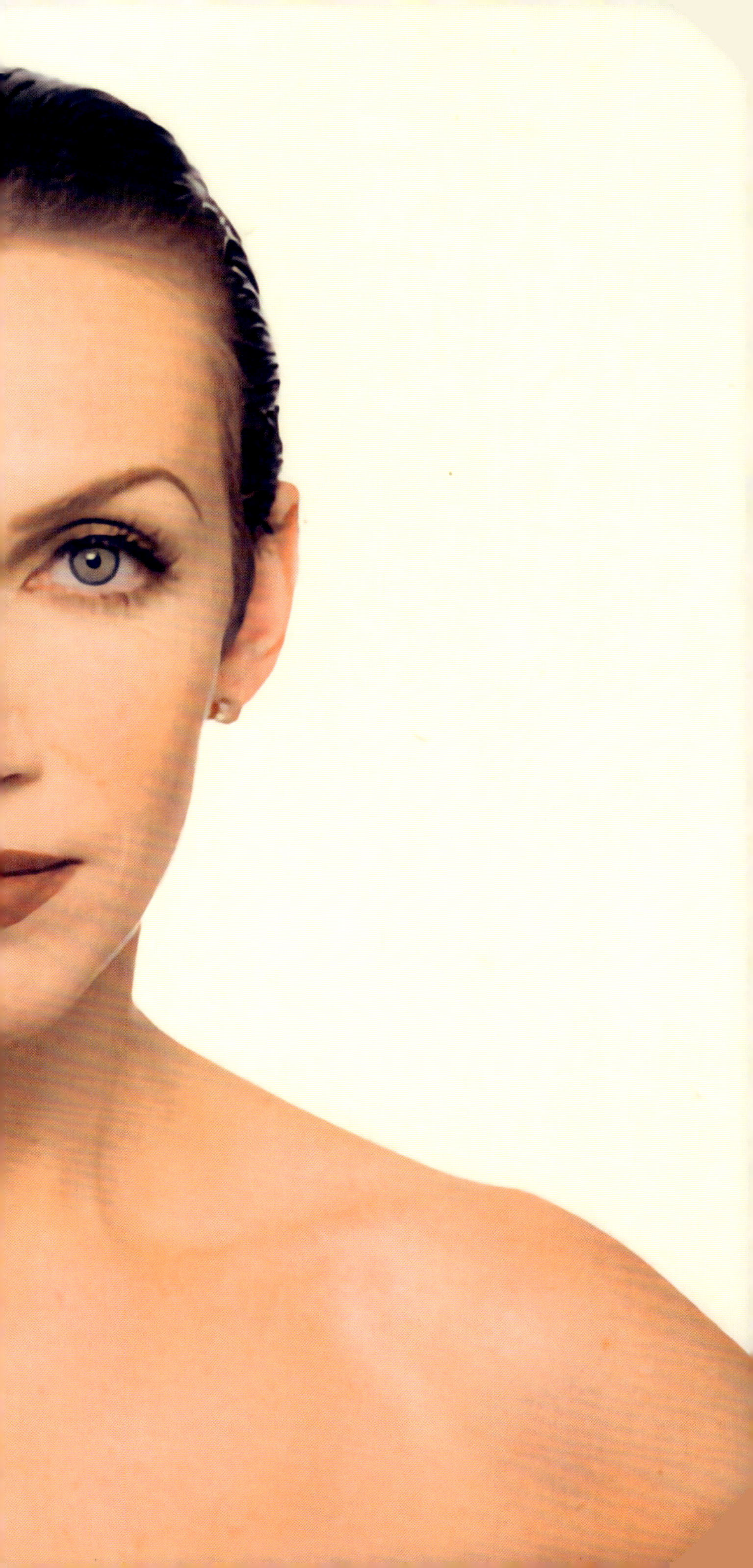

1999–

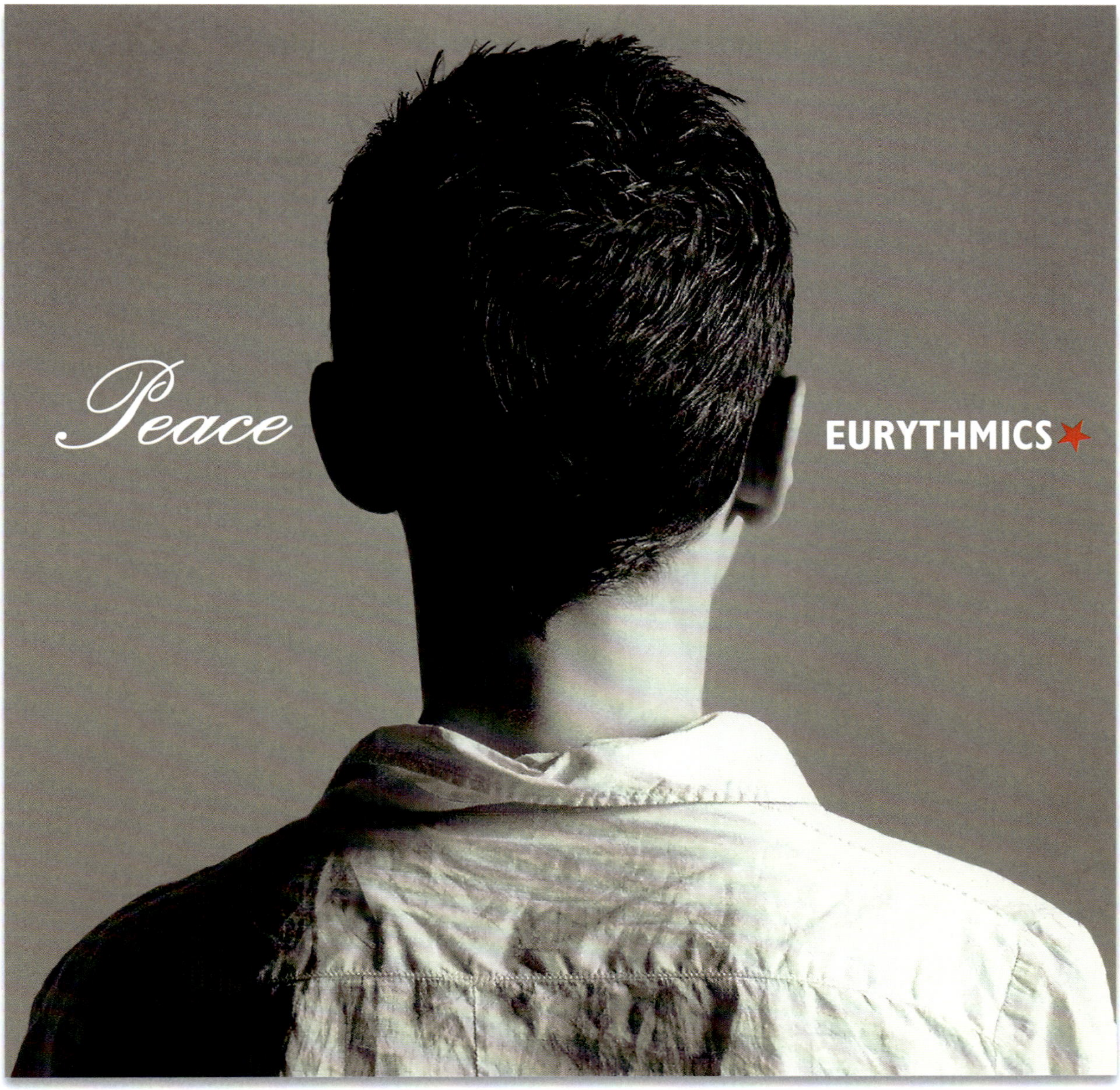
Peace
EURYTHMICS

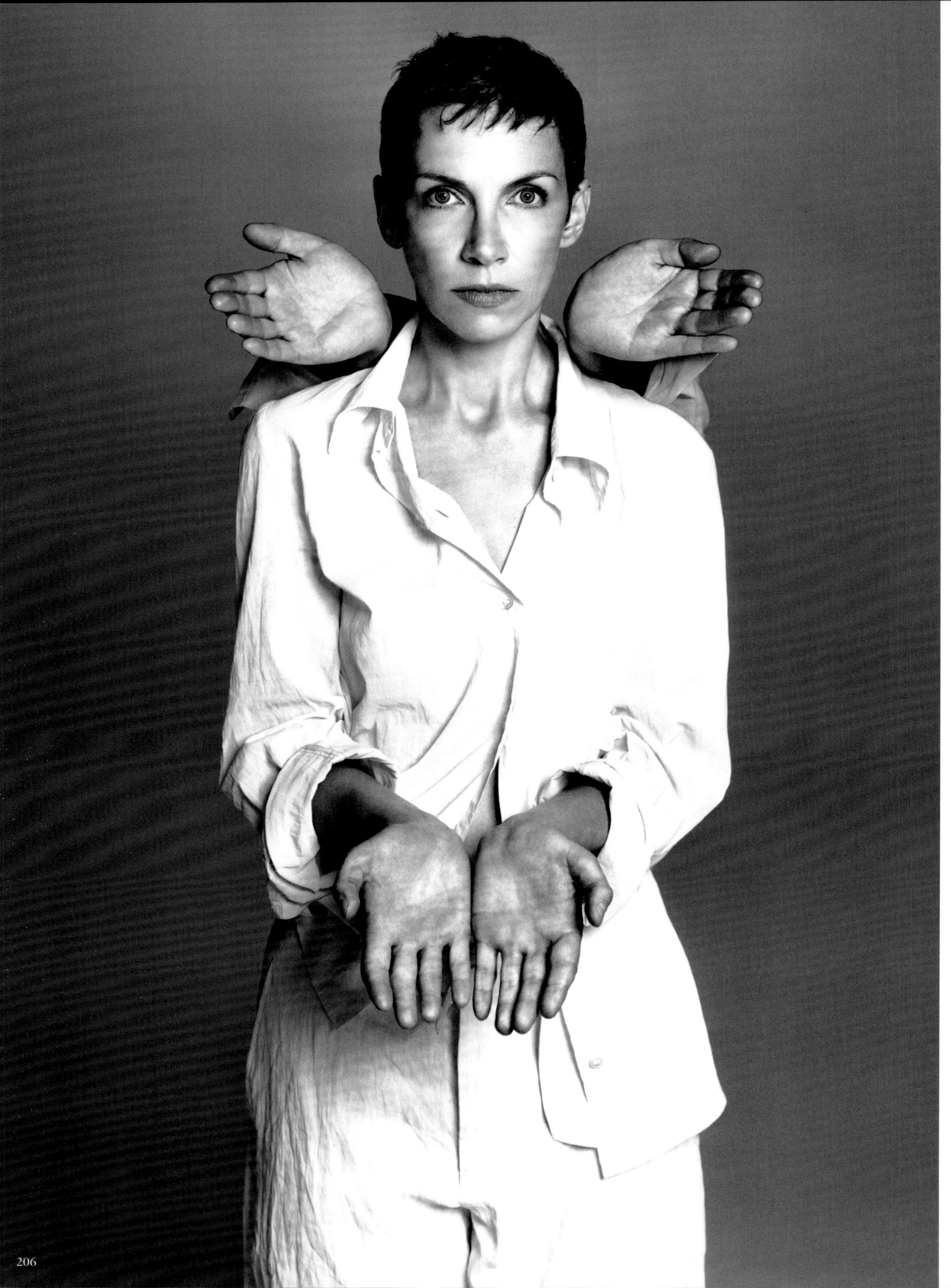

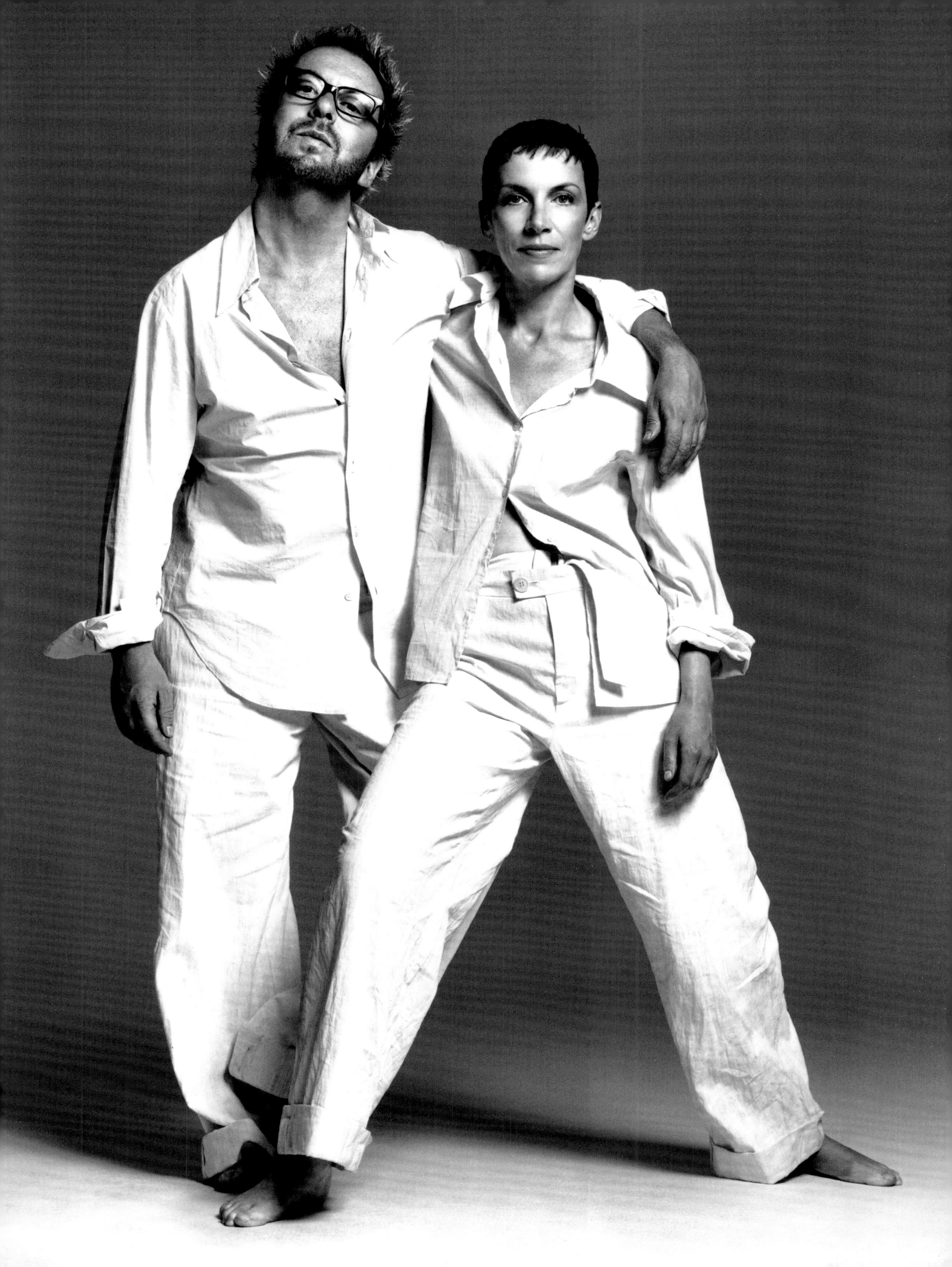

Working with Richard Avedon was like meeting the friend you've always known but have only just met. He was a genuinely wonderful man, with warmth, charm, humor, and humanity all rolled into one. Although we only spent a very short time together, the human connection was easy and instant. If we'd met earlier, I'm sure we would have become great friends, but he was based in New York, which wasn't my hometown.
Dave and I both agreed to turn our heads around to invisibly 'face' each other on both sides of the album. It wasn't a particularly commercial decision to take, but commercial decisions weren't something we were necessarily drawn towards.

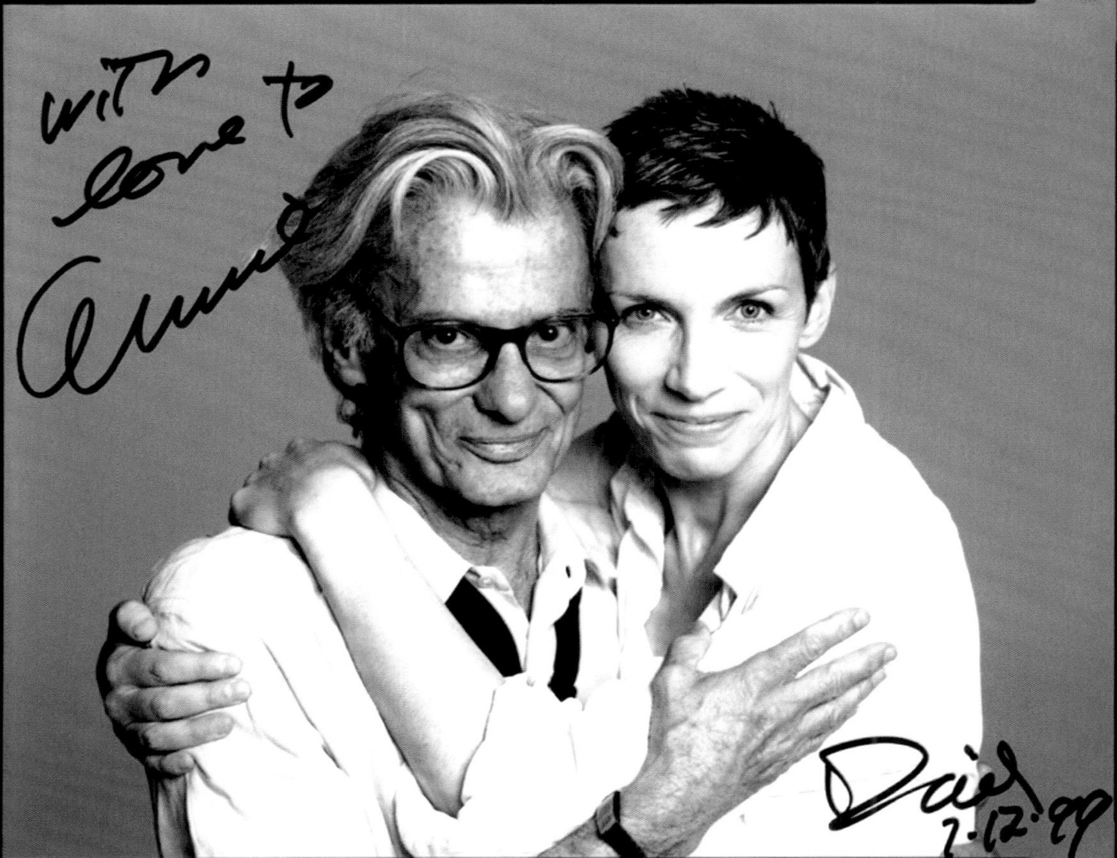
with love to

I bought a fantastic Hassleblad camera with a digital back and asked my friend Allan Martin if he'd like to collaborate on a photographic project with me. He set about learning how to use the camera and I came in with a concept.

I wanted to become a blank canvas with a surface of clay, so the form of my body could be transformed into something 'other' than its usual presentation. A mud person... or an ancient statue.

I brought my old red tartan dressing gown to the shoot. While I was thinking of something to put around my neck, I noticed the tie hanging around the dressing gown and thought it would help to make a powerful statement. Nationalism, History, Identity, Belonging... All or none of these things.

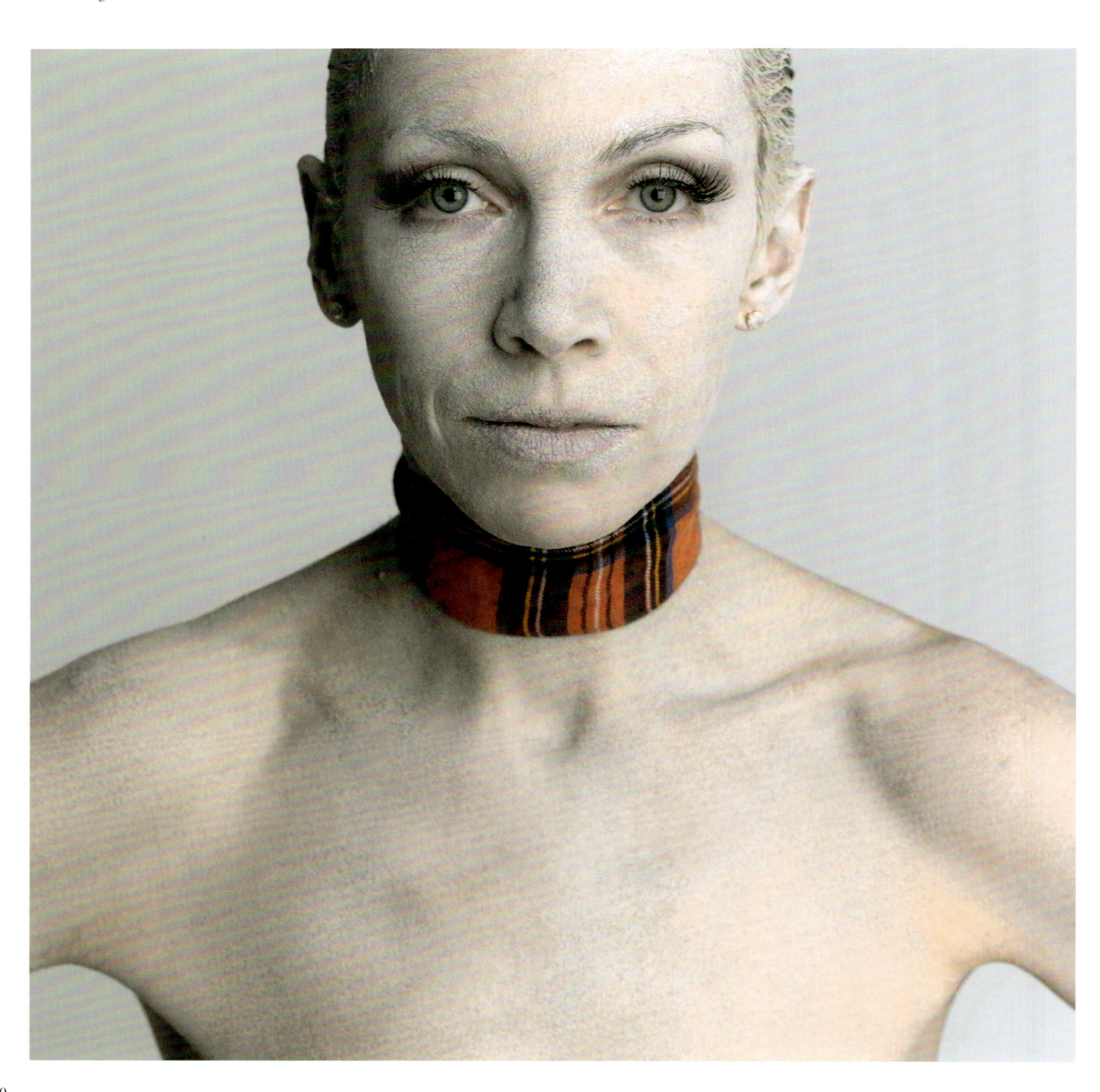

One of these photographs is housed in the Scottish National Portrait Gallery in Edinburgh.

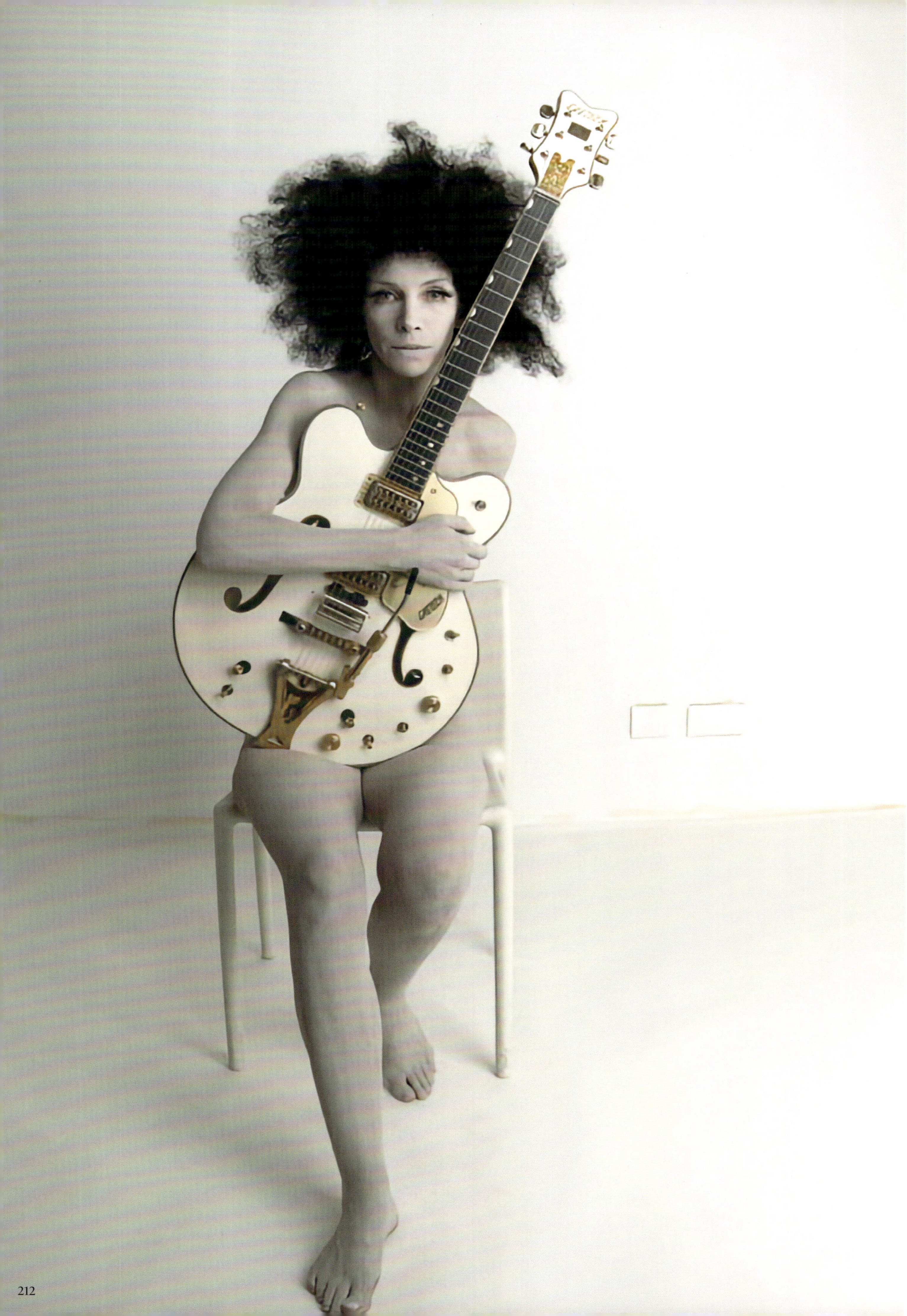

ALL THE NEGATIVE THOUGHTS TURNING INTO THICK PLUMES OF BLACK SMOKE RISING ABOVE HER HEAD.

It's a dark road
And a dark way that leads to my house
And the word says
That you're never
Gonna find me there
Oh no...
I've got an open door
It didn't get there
By itself
It didn't get there by itself

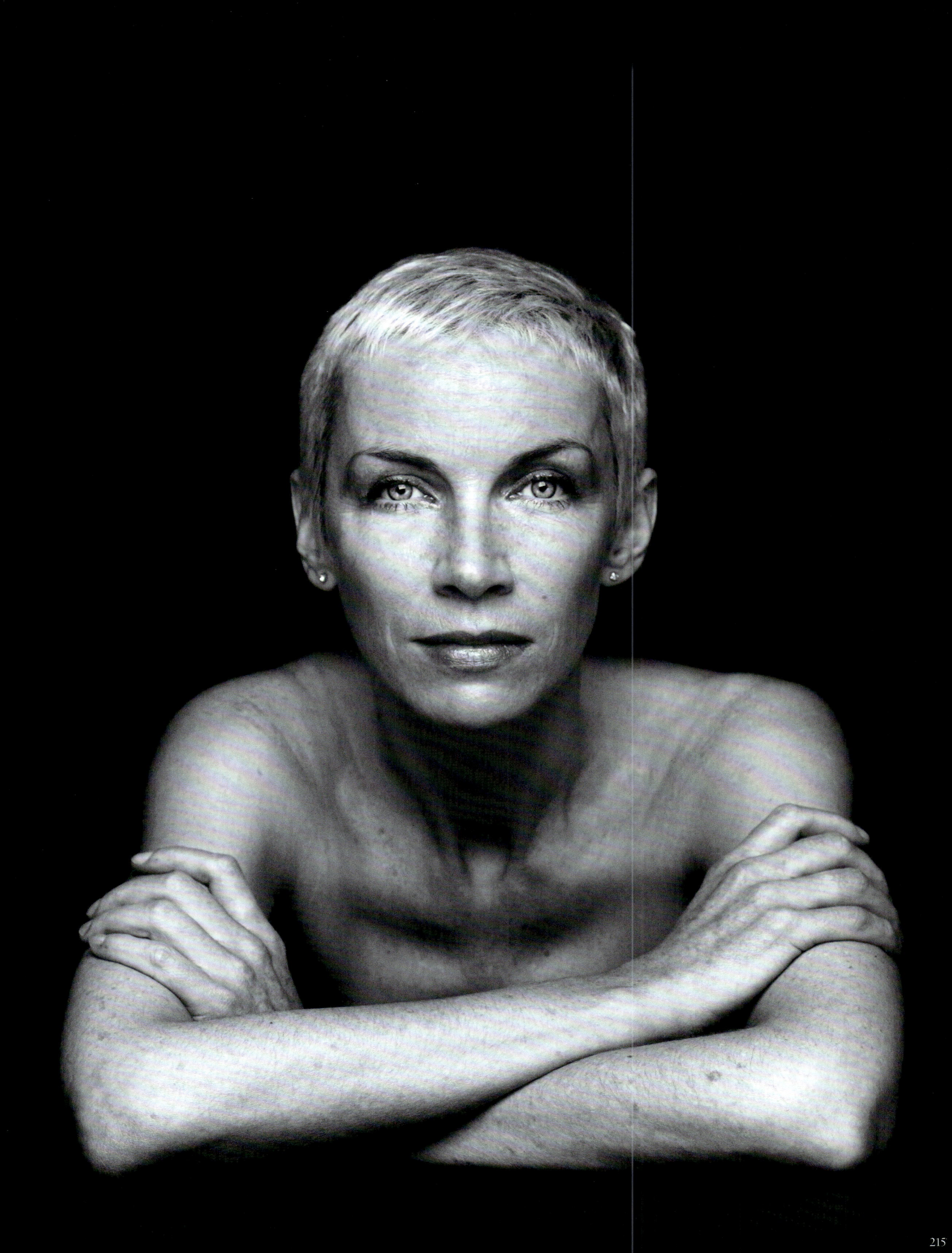

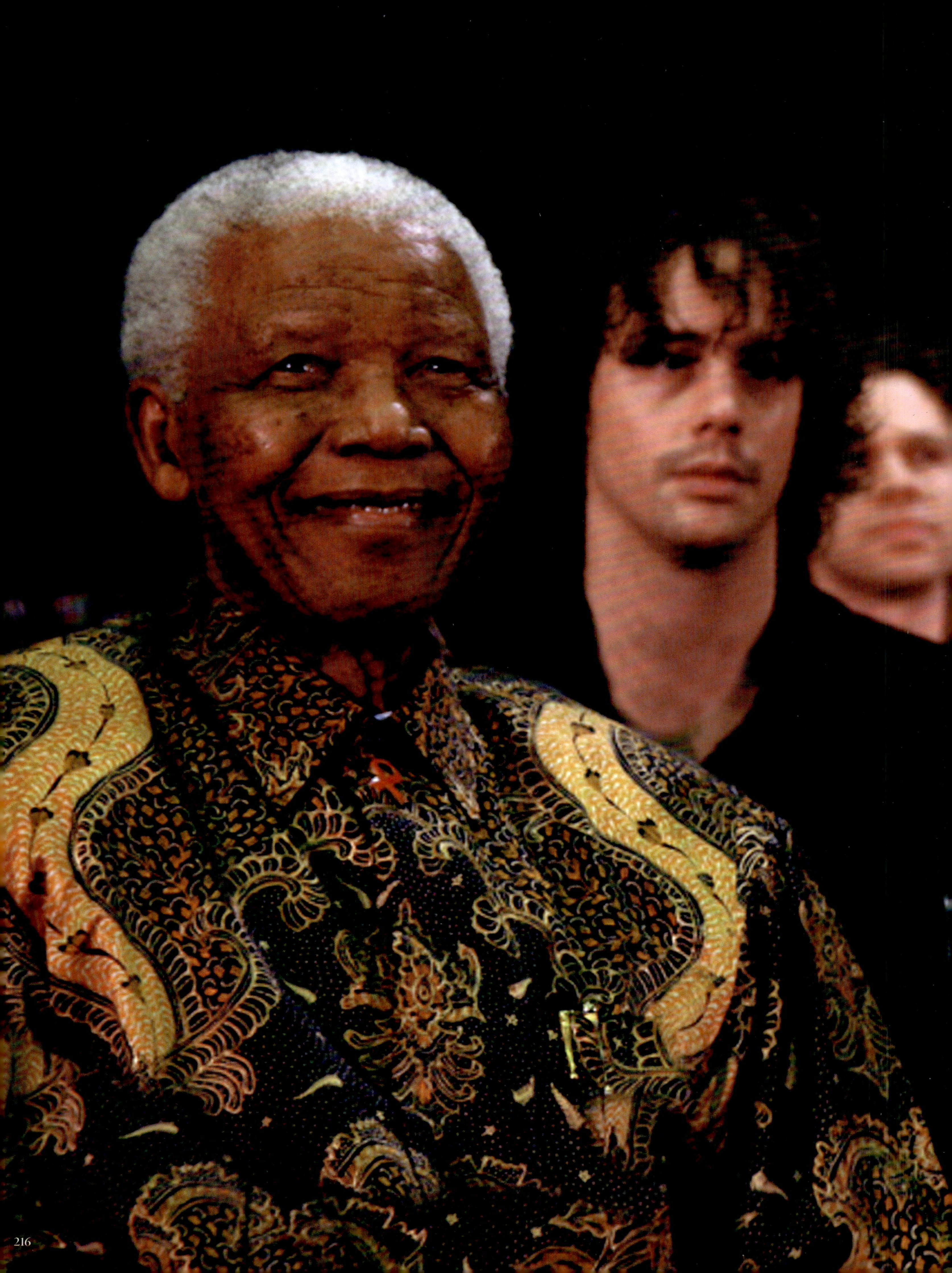

World AIDS Day: December 1 2007, in Johannesburg, South Africa.
Sitting adjacent to President Mandela in a fugue state between 'bliss' and 'I'm not worthy' during the third concert for 46664, Mandela's HIV/AIDS foundation.

I became a committed HIV/AIDS activist after the first 46664 concert in Cape Town in 2003, when I was educated about the scale of the pandemic as it was affecting millions of men, women, and children – essentially the entire fabric of every country in Sub-Saharan Africa.

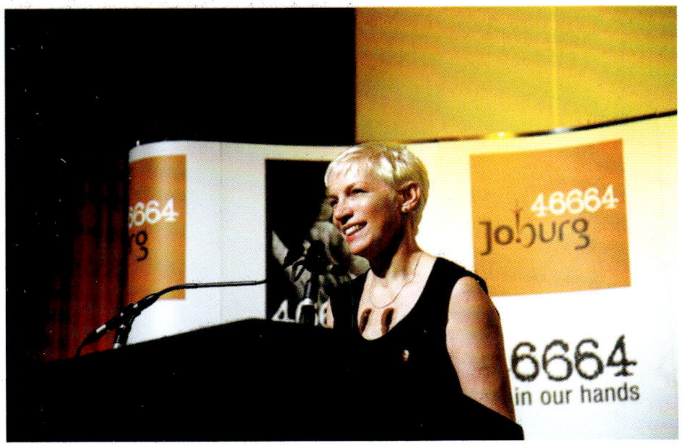
46664
Joburg
6664
in our hands

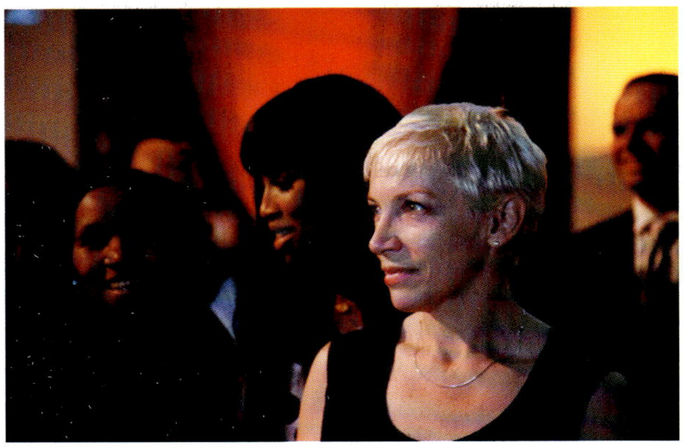

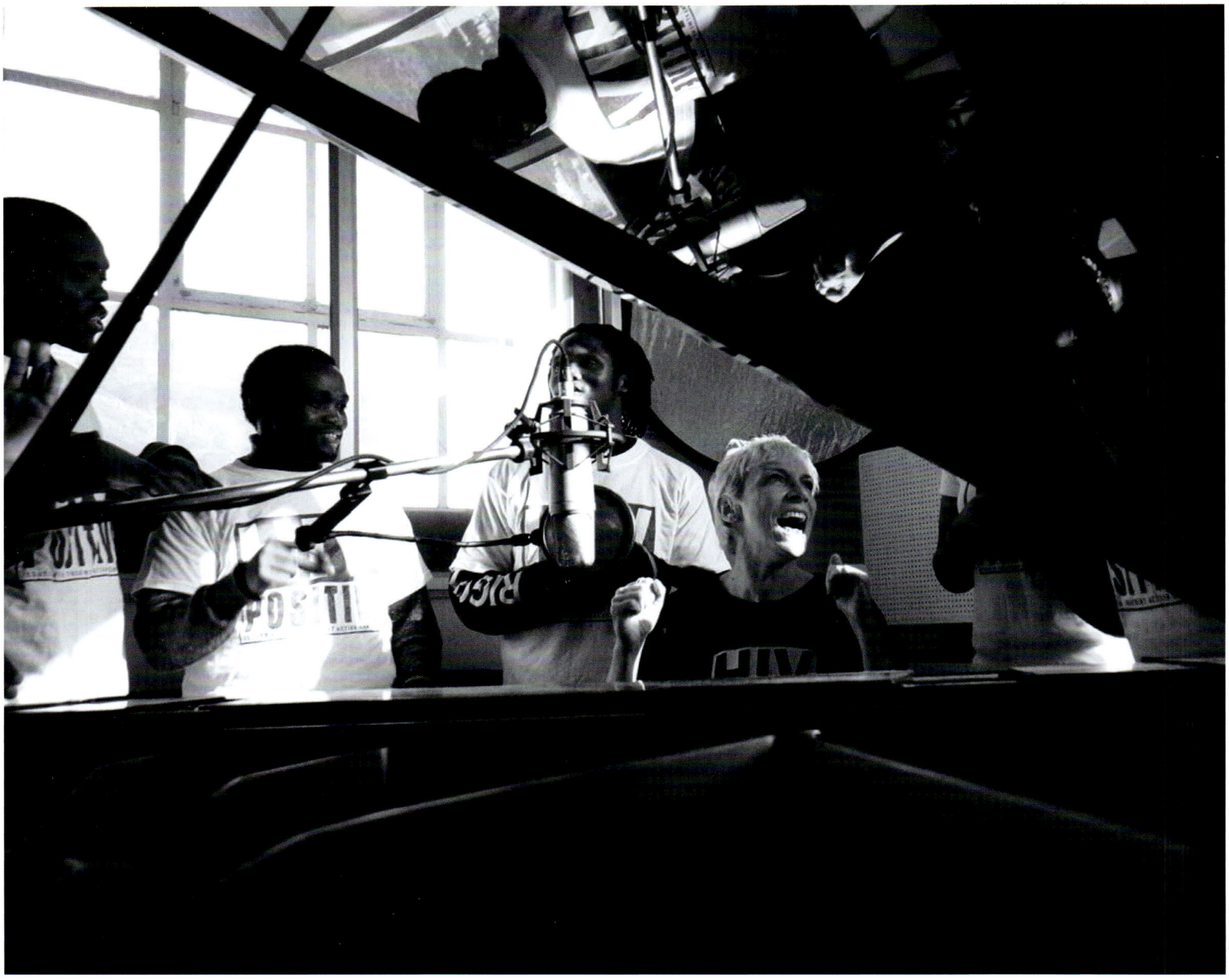
POSITI
HIV

I went on to form the SING Campaign, to support and contribute to organizations such as the Treatment Action Campaign.

With as many as one in five people living with the virus across Sub-Saharan Africa at that time, the population was being decimated across every level of society.

Lifesaving anti-retroviral treatment was neither accessible nor affordable.

The situation was dire, yet appeared to be completely ignored by Western media.

Things have changed greatly since then.

With the tremendous work of EVERY AIDS ACTIVIST, LOBBYIST AND CAMPAIGNER, eventually treatment became far more readily available and mortality rates came down.

This was no small achievement and took a massive collective effort from individuals and organizations over many hard-earned years.

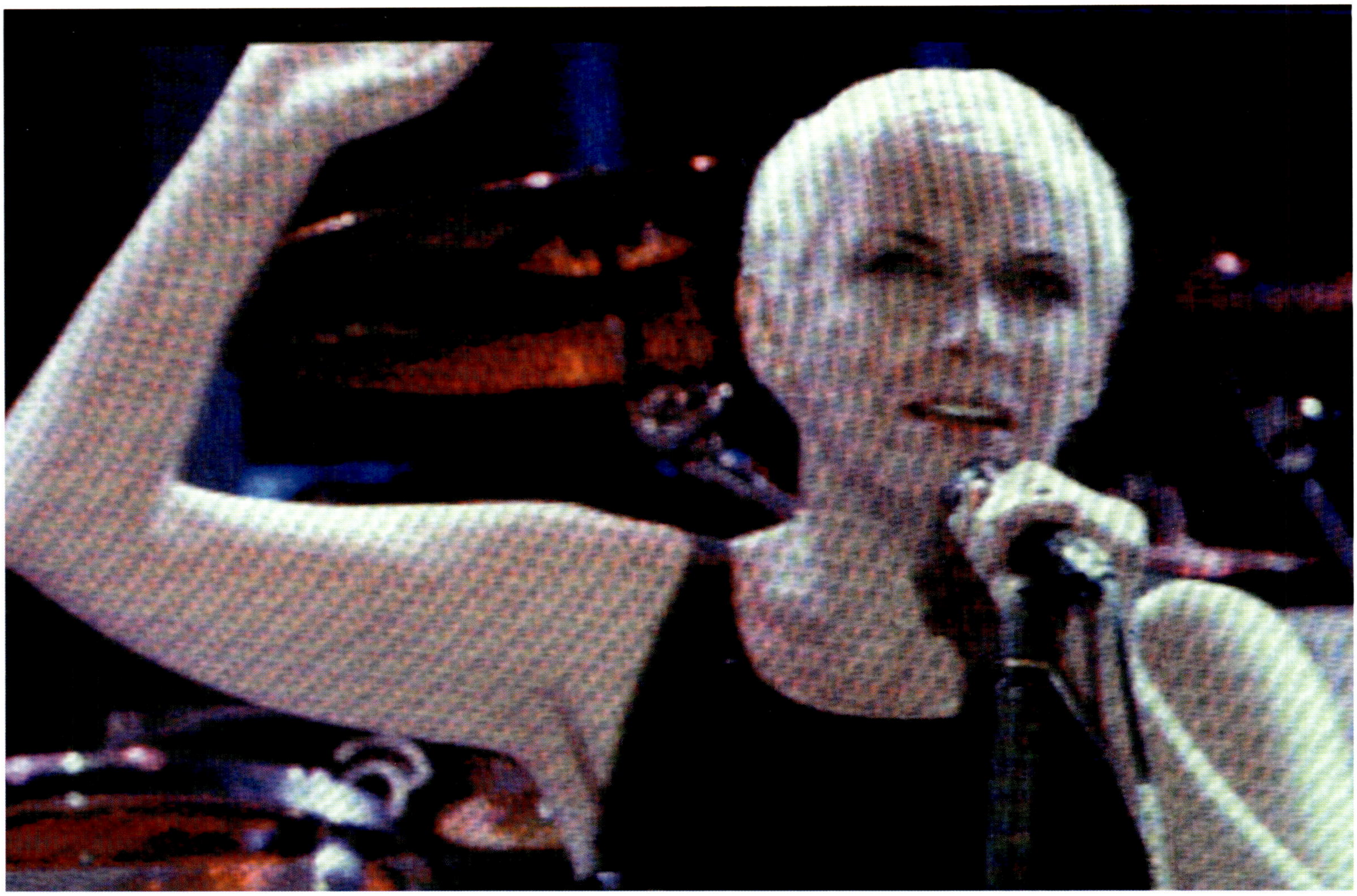

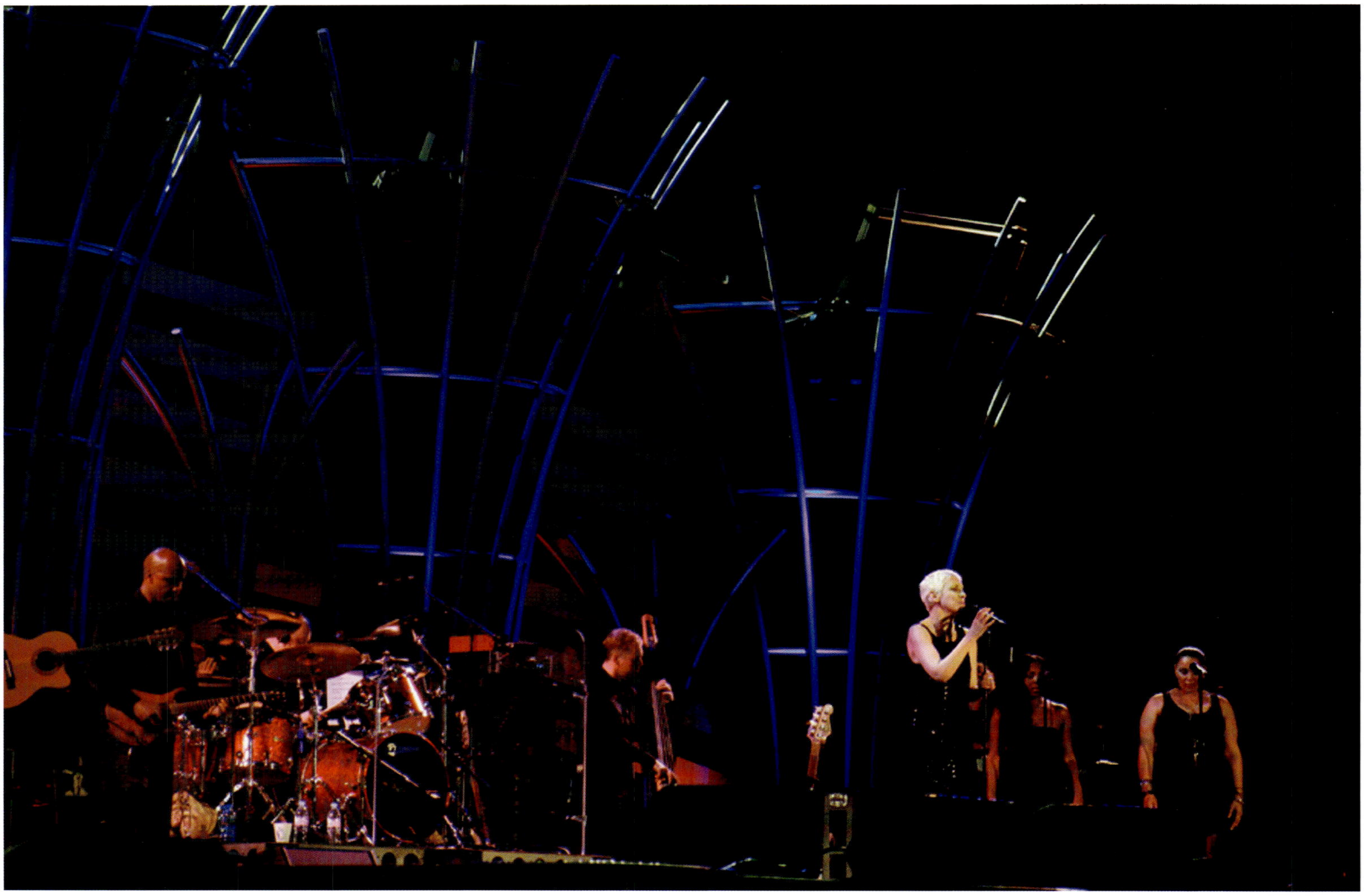

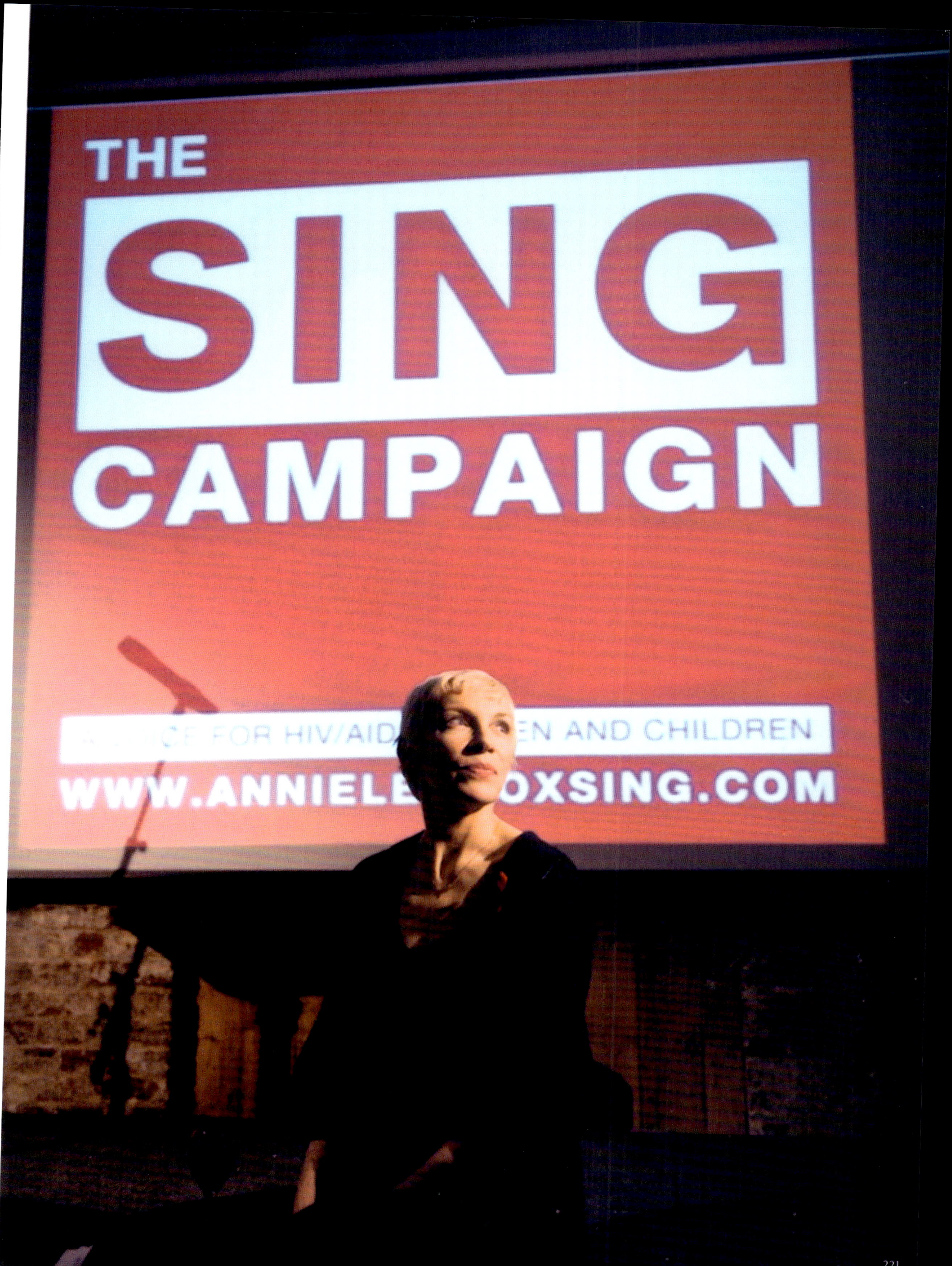
THE
SING
CAMPAIGN

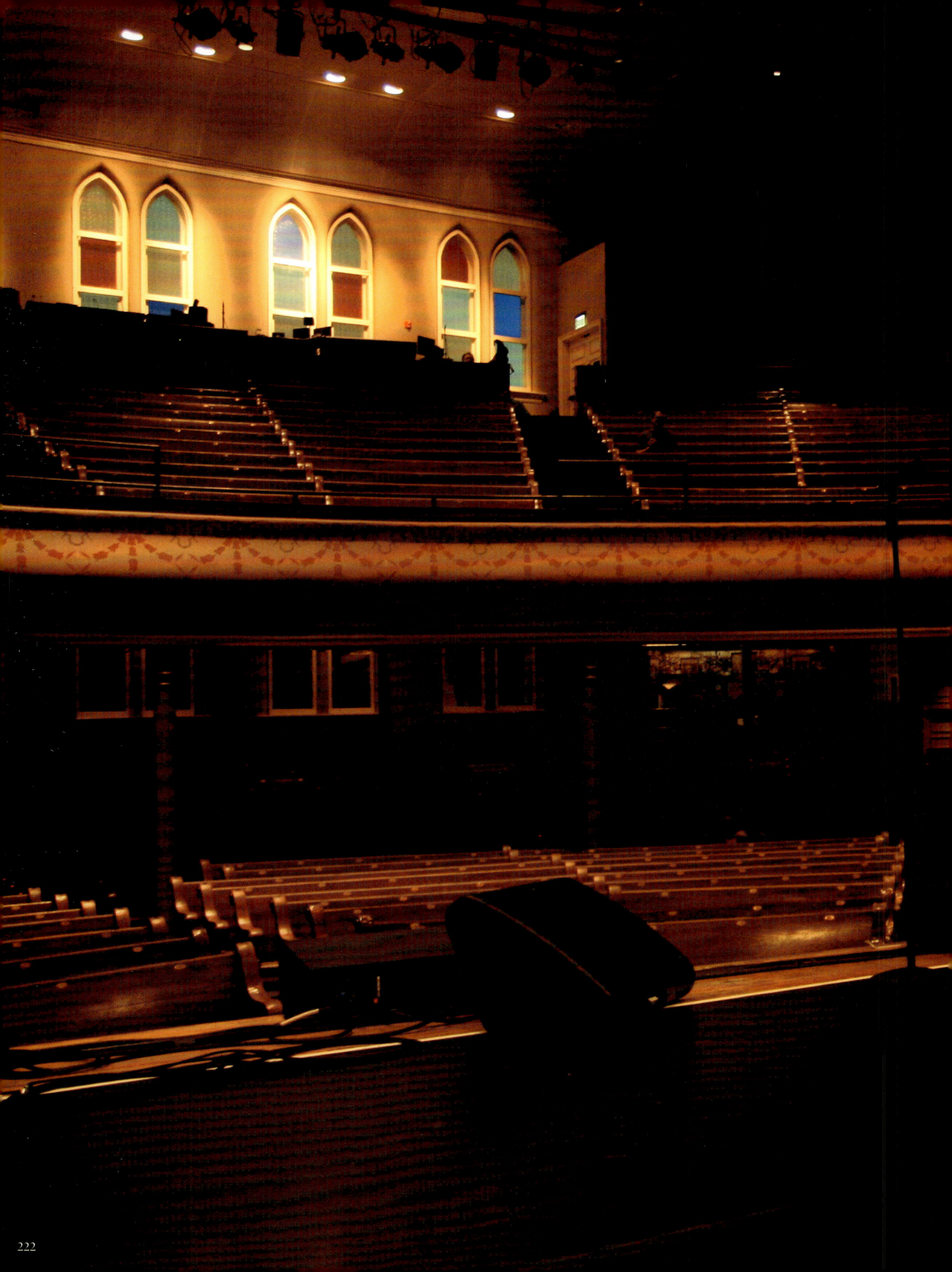

Sound-checking at the Ryman Auditorium in Nashville, Tennessee.
Such an iconic place to perform. It feels like you 'graduate' once you've played there – 'as ONE of the many artists and performers who've graced the boards along the way.

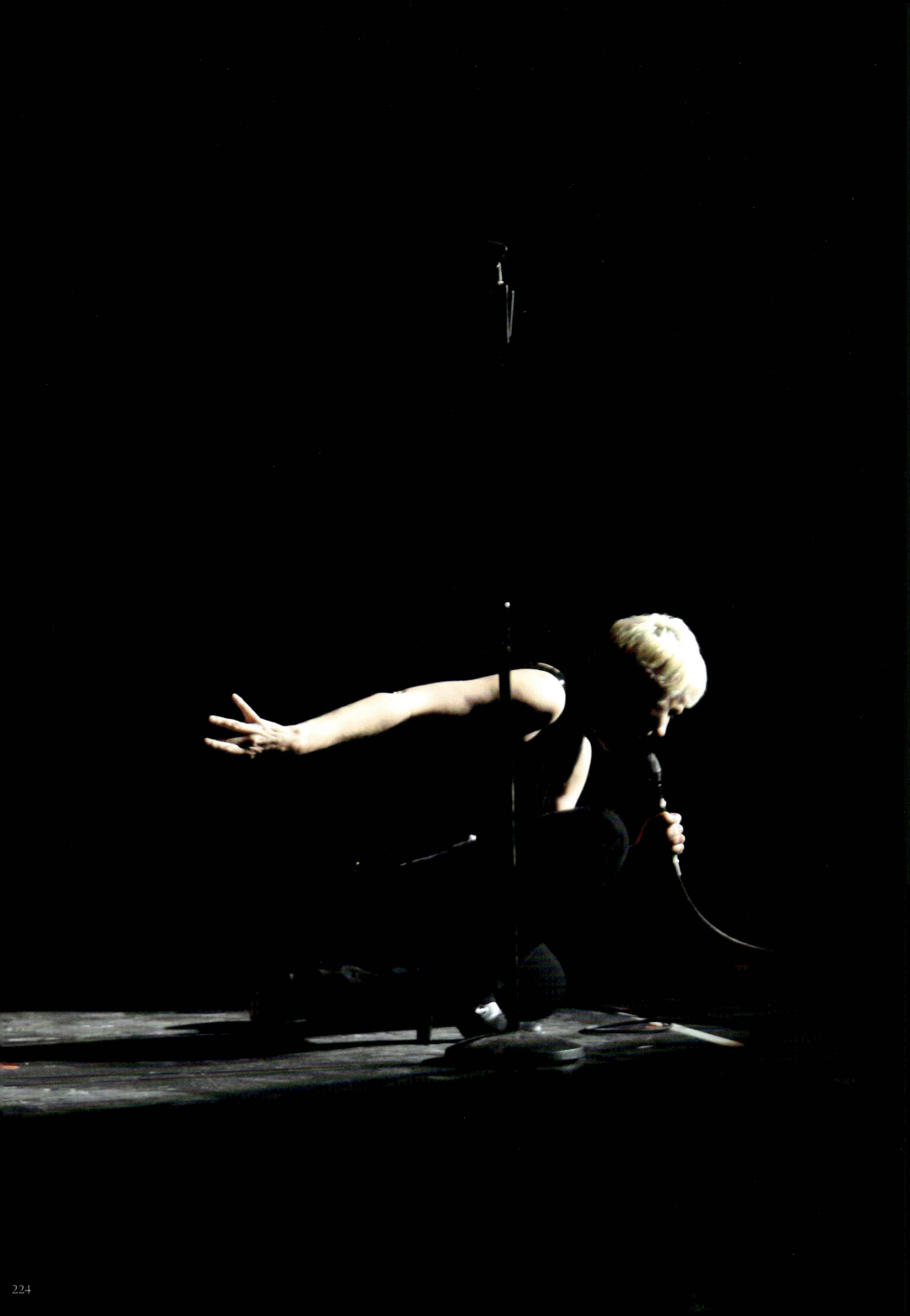

I chose this photograph because I feel it conveys the sense of vulnerability you can experience while performing on stage. After years of trying to overcome my own personal version of stage fright, I've found a better way to handle the situation. That doesn't mean to say that I'm completely over it, and that I don't get nervous anymore.

Every time you perform, you have to be totally in the 'now,' as you're compelled to come up to all the expectations you've placed upon your own performance,
As well as the audience's anticipation.
Most audiences don't suffer fools too gladly.
And being a lead singer can be incredibly intimidating if you let fear overtake you.
And there are so many things to be anxious about…
Including…
Equipment not working properly.
The microphone sounding muffled or too quiet on the vocal.
Feedback.
Instruments failing to come in, or coming in at the wrong place.
Failing to hear the band mix properly on stage.
Forgetting the lyrics.
Forgetting where you are in the song.
Not hearing yourself properly, therefore singing out of tune.
Tripping, sliding, or falling on stage…
Losing your voice.
Not being able to connect with an audience.
A hostile audience.
An indifferent audience.
A bored audience… You can tell!
Someone in the audience who keeps shouting for something incoherent and indecipherable.
Audience members who drunkenly insist on performing with you on stage.

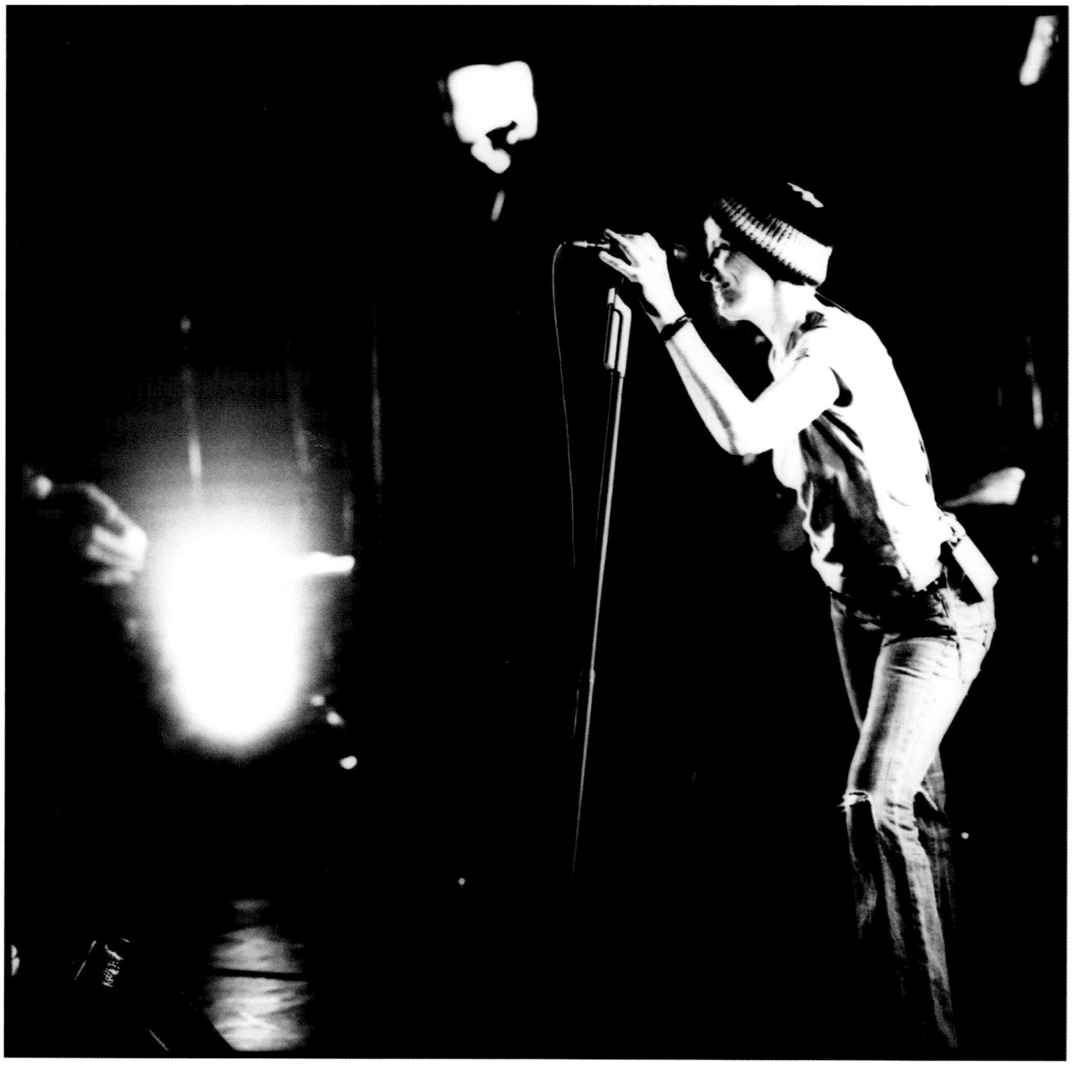

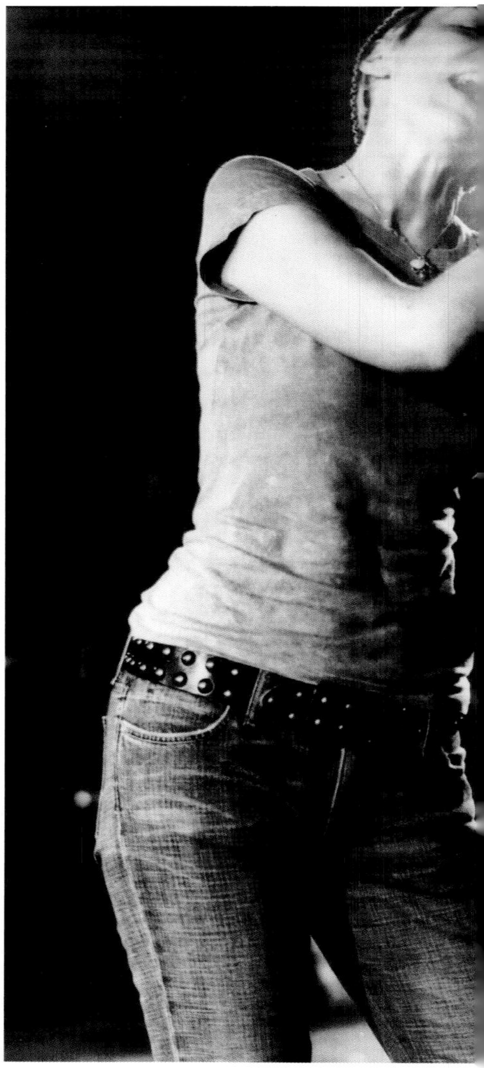

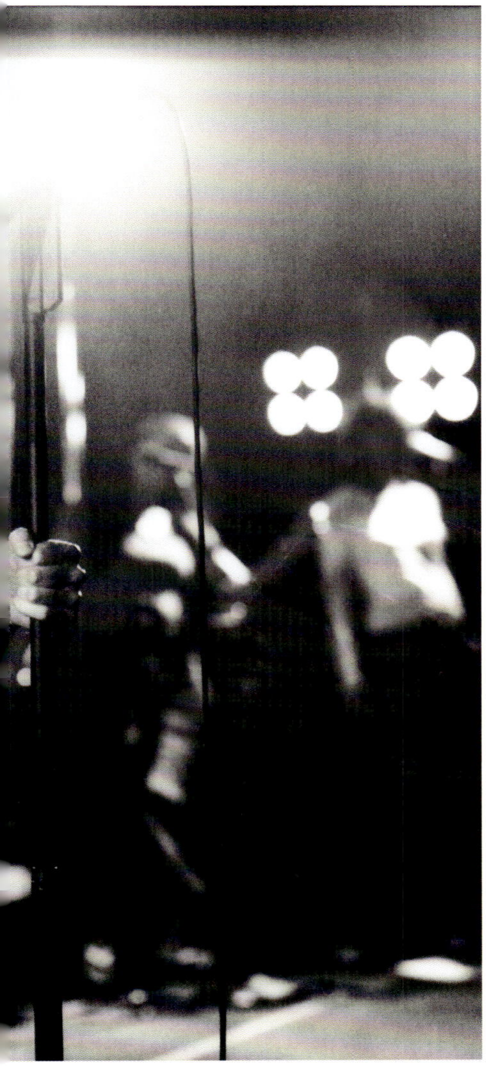

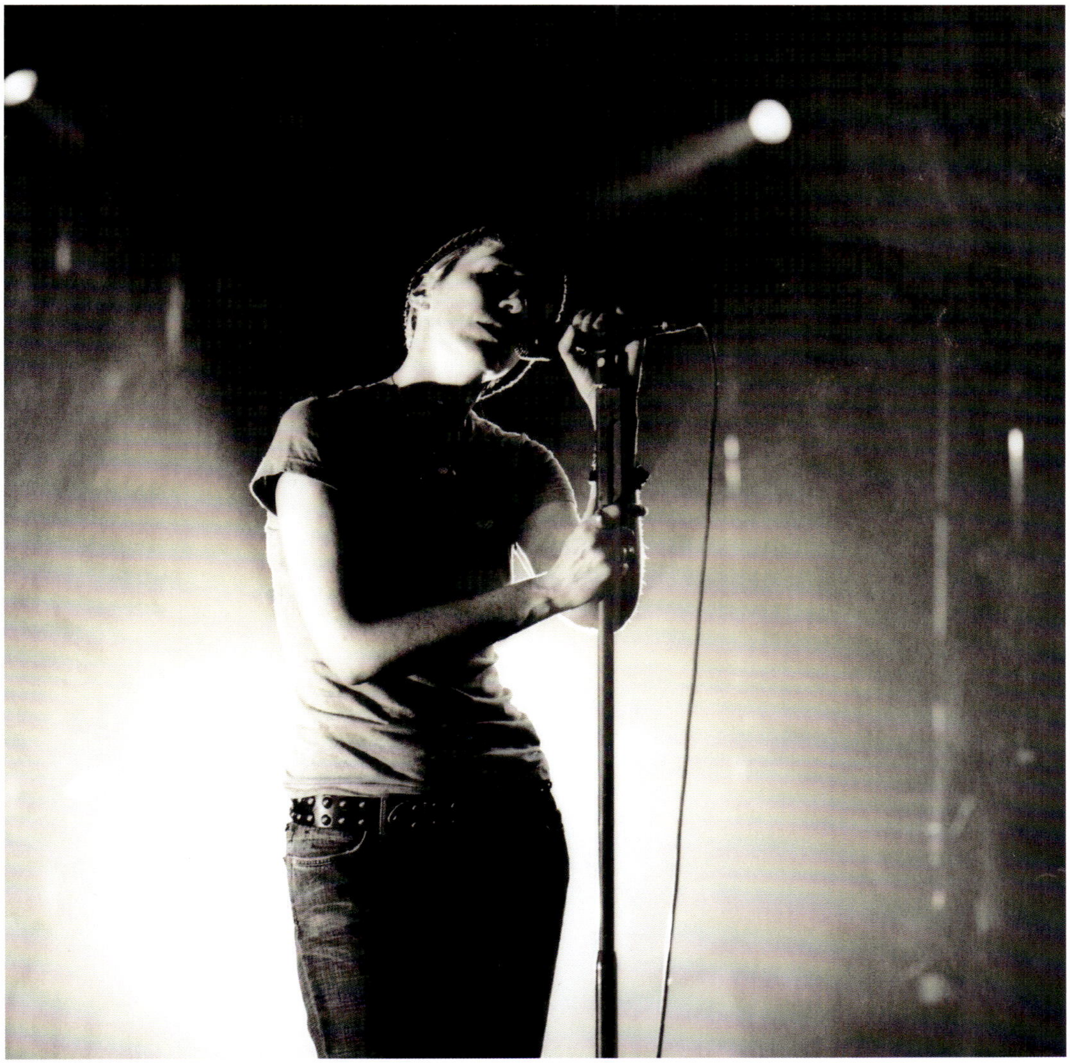

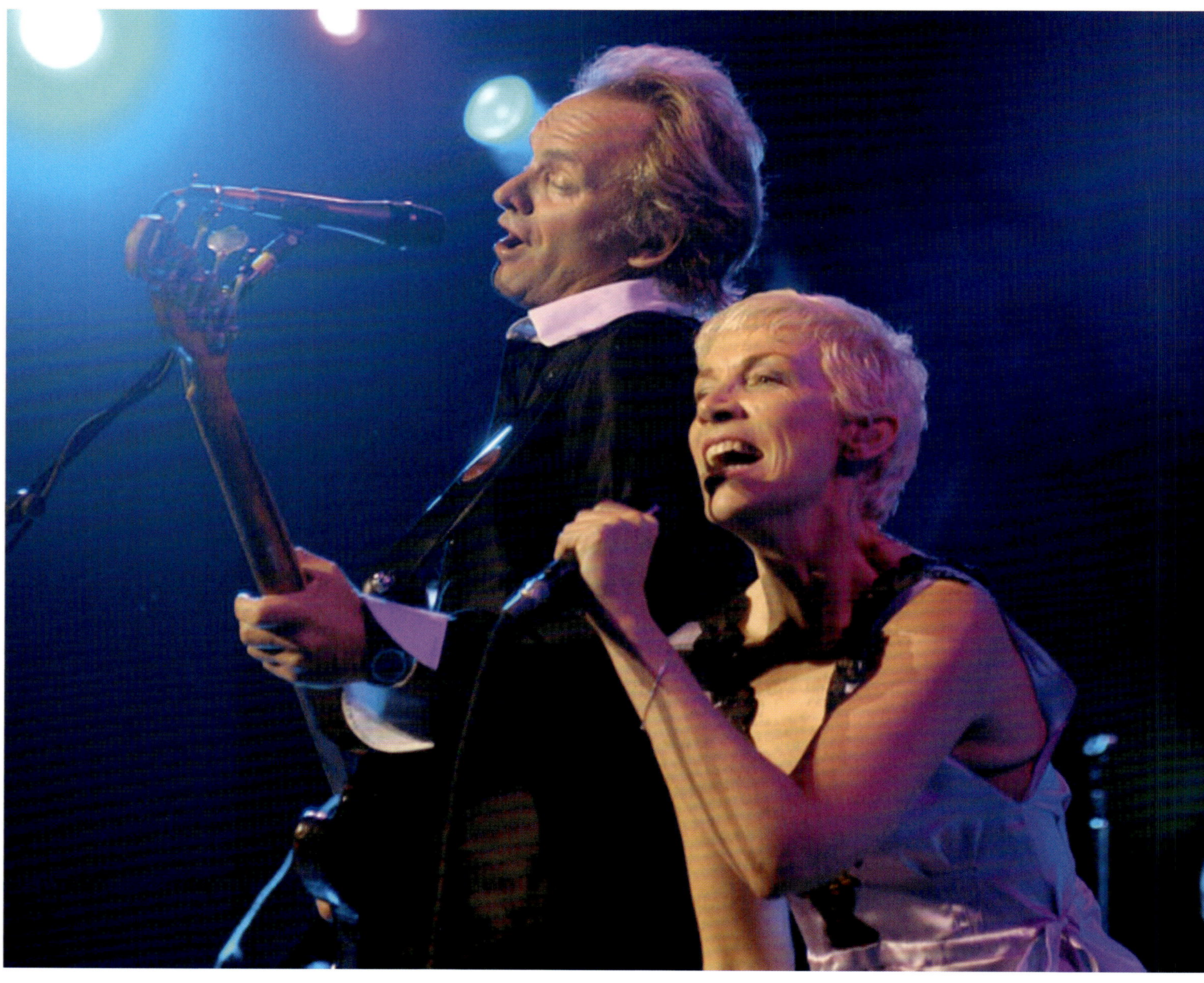

I joined Sting as a special guest on the American leg of the Sacred Love Tour in 2004… for 54 dates.

Looking back on this now I wonder how I did it, but somehow we all pulled it off. Sting and his band were exquisitely gracious and warm with us (my lovely band and I), and that made it far more achievable and fun.

It feels as if it happened only last year.

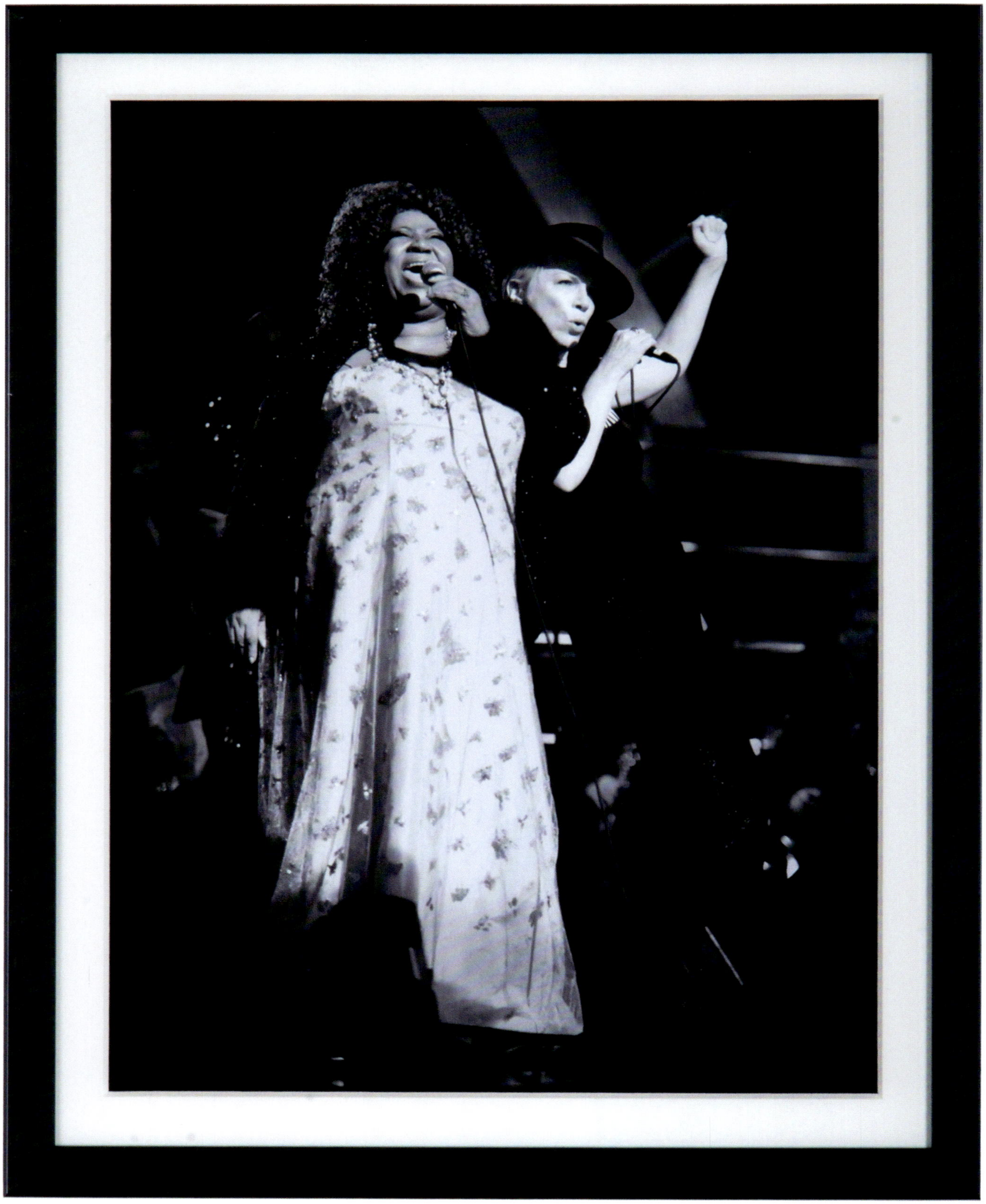

I had the true honor and privilege of duetting with the most legendary Soul Queen of all time… the GREATEST Aretha Franklin, at Madison Square Garden, October 30, 2009. We sang 'Chain of Fools' – an almost out-of-body experience. Afterwards I felt ten feet tall, the moment was so electrifying.

Rolling Stone

1290 AVENUE of the AMERICAS NEW YORK NY 10104

JANN S. WENNER
Editor & Publisher

December 1, 2009

Dear Annie:

Thank you from the bottom of my heart for being a part of the Hall of Fame concerts. It was an event that will stay with us the rest of our lives. These were some of the greatest performances I've ever seen and infused with the historical nature of the occasion and the fact that we were so joyously celebrating our life's work, an affirmation of a vision all of us have shared for years.

Thank you for coming a long way and for giving it your all.

All my best,

Jann

JSW/al

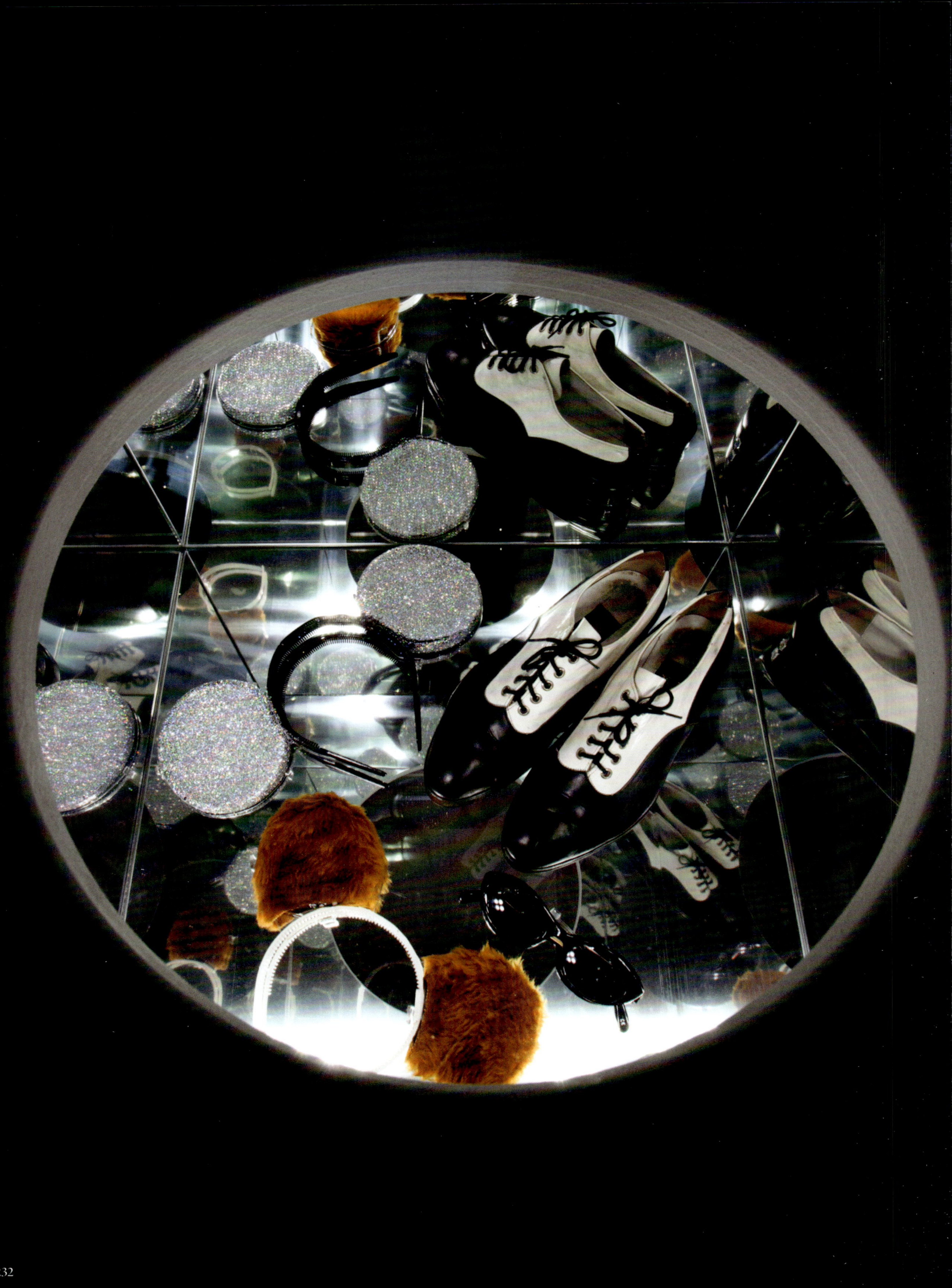

233

234

235

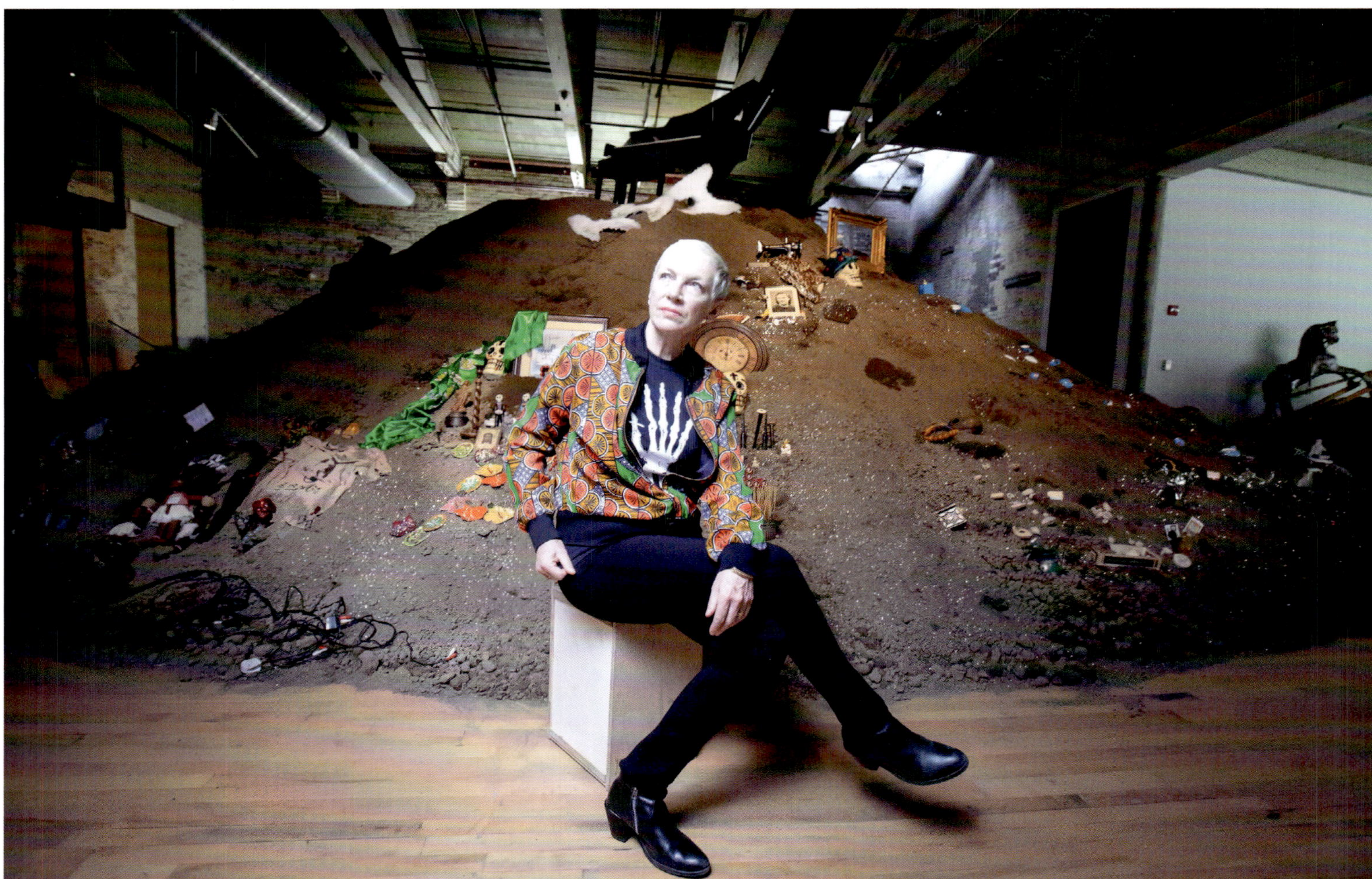

Sitting in front of the big mound of earth I'd envisioned for *Now I Let You Go*, an exhibition I curated at MASSMoCA in North Adams, Massachusetts, which was shown from May 2019 to February 2020.

The 'House of Me' exhibition traveled from the Victoria and Albert Museum in London (*pages 232–233*) to the Lowry Museum in Salford, Manchester (*pages 234–235*).

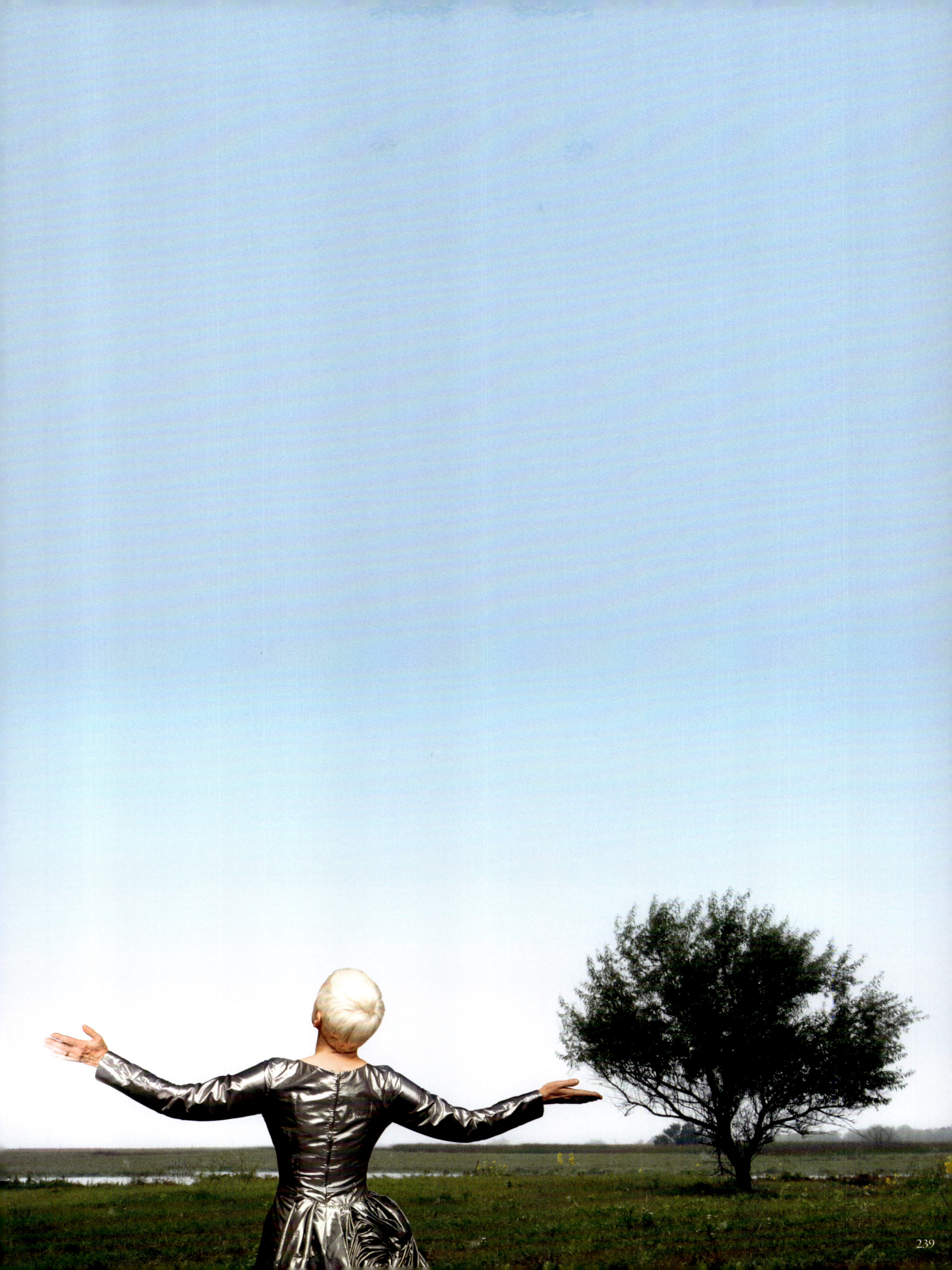

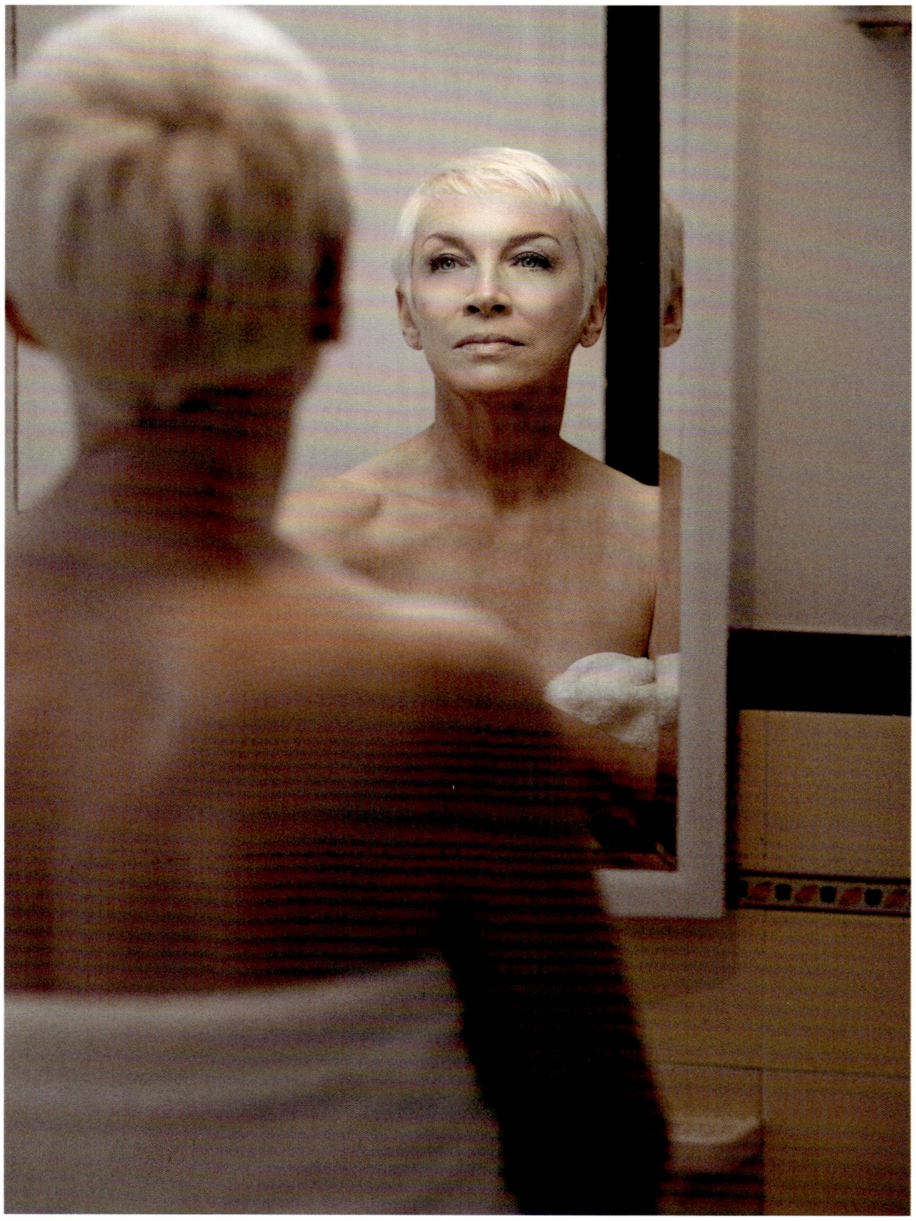

I've lived the life of a performer and worn many different hats, outfits, and hairstyles along the way.

I know the dialects of the three different aspects of life in North-East Scotland and my voice still carries their cadence with me wherever I go. There's also a touch of London in there too, as I did spend decades living in a wide assortment of places, all over the great urban sprawl.

I know how ecstatic it feels to have written and recorded songs, as well as the struggle to find words to arrive out of thin air when you don't even know what you want to say. At other times words arrive line after line, one after the other, and you don't really understand how it all came about…

I know about the long waits backstage…
Waiting for the time to start warming-up and getting prepared to go on stage.
This is the strangest time of all.
When you're completely suspended between 'before' the event and 'after' it's over.
There's nowhere else to be and nothing else to do, except wait and prepare.
Lay down on the floor and stretch out your body.
Gradually apply makeup while warming up the voice and praying that it's in good enough shape.
The time comes to start getting dressed.
Mentally checking everything through.
Then re-check again.
One more check.
Waiting to go on.
Counting time to go.
It's time to go!

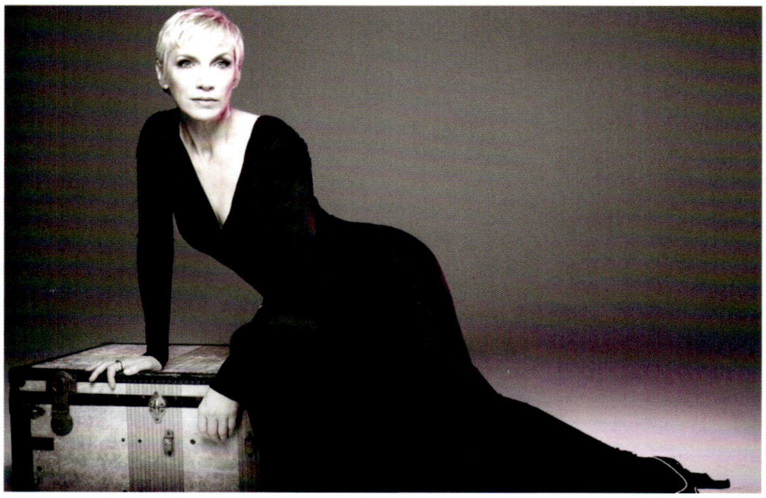

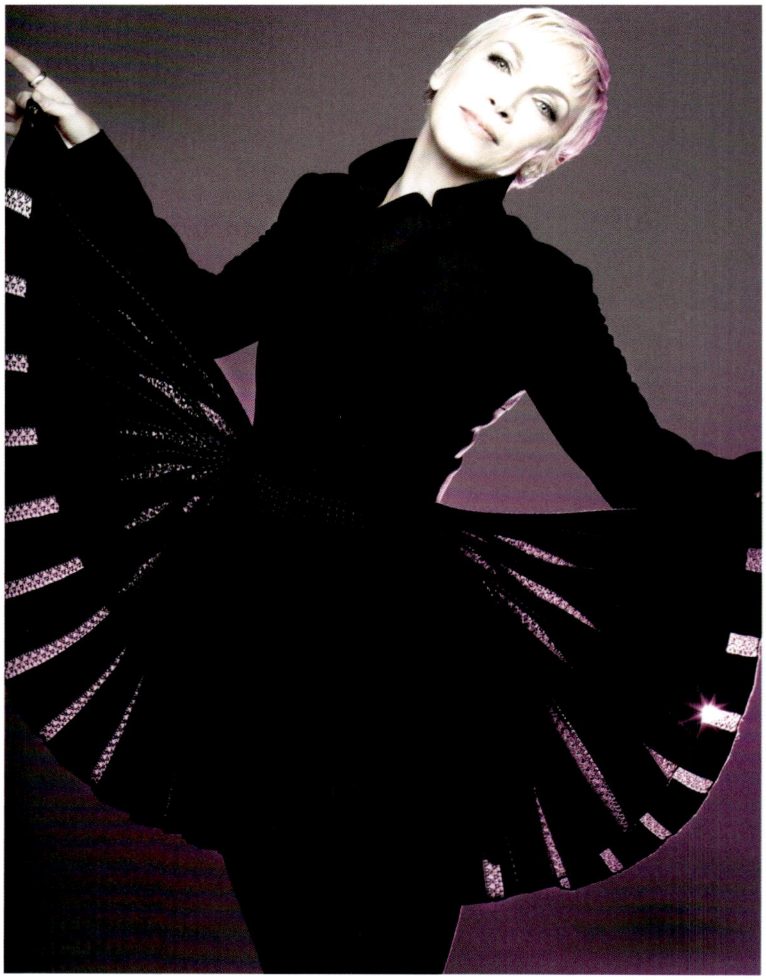

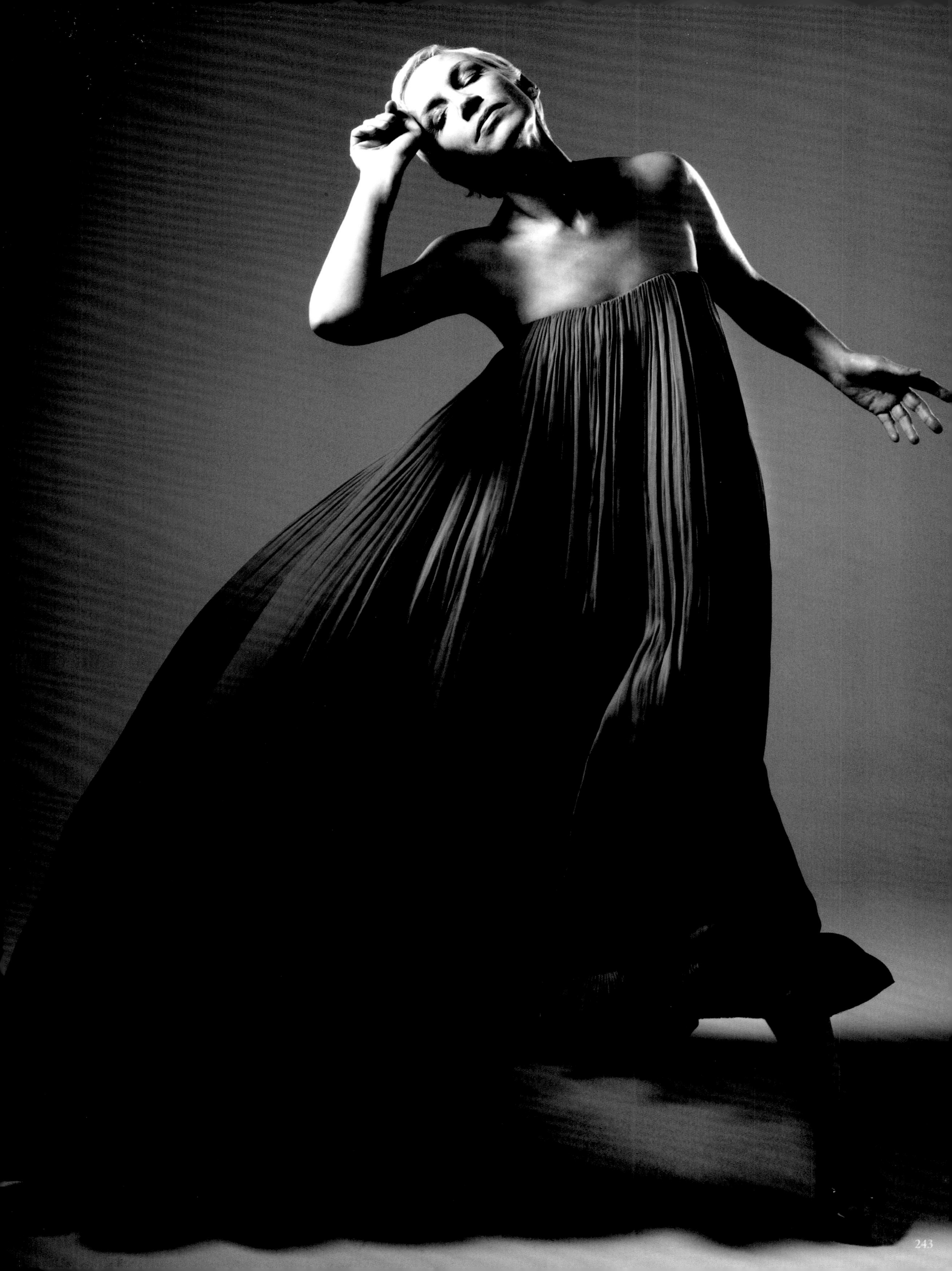

Every day I write the list
Of reasons why I still believe we do exist
A thousand beautiful things
And even though it's clear to see
The glass is full and not half empty
A thousand beautiful things
So light me up like the sun
To cool down with your rain
I never want to close my eyes again
Never close my eyes
Never close my eyes

The world was made
For you and me
To figure out our destiny
A thousand beautiful things
To live - to die
To breathe - to sleep
To try to make our lives complete
A thousand beautiful things
So light me up like the sun
To cool down with your rain
I never want to close my eyes again
Never close my eyes
Never close my eyes

245

Index

All images courtesy of Annie Lennox, with the exception of those
reproduced with the kind permission of photographers
and rightsholders noted below.

22, 23 © Pictorial Press Ltd. / Alamy
25 © Philip Grey
29, 46, 47, 101 © Gered Mankowitz
44, 45, 67, 68, 69, 70 © Peter Ashworth
48 © Geoffrey Angel-Attwood
52, 56, 58, 59 © Lewis Ziolek
54, 55 © Deborah Feingold
60–65, 71, 78, 80–85, 88, 89 © Steve Rapport / Getty Images
73, 74–75 © Brian Aris
86 © Mike Laye for *The Face* magazine, January 1985
98 © Derek Ridgers
104, 105, 106–107, 126, 127 © Henry Diltz
128, 129 © Claude Gassian
130–131, 180–181, 182, 183 © 2025 Artists Rights Society (ARS),
New York / ADAGP, Paris / Bettina Rheims
134, 135, 136–137, 138, 139 © Alastair Thain
142–143 © Edward Mapplethorpe
144, 145 © Adrian Boot / urbanimage
155, 156, 157, 158-159, 160 © Ellen von Unwerth / Trunk Archive
167 © Clare Muller
168-169, 170, 171, 173 © Satoshi Saikusa / Trunk Archive
174 © Michael Putland / Getty Images
175 © Dave Benett / Getty Images
186, 187, 188, 189 © Pamela Hanson / Trunk Archive
191 © Julian Broad
192, 193 © Kevin Mazur
196, 197 © Paolo Roversi / Art + Commerce
198, 199, 200, 201 © Javier Vallhonrat
202–203 © Andrew Macpherson
206, 207, 209 © The Richard Avedon Foundation
210, 212, 213, 215 © Annie Lennox and Allan Martin
236 © Eric Korenman
238–239, 240, 241 © Robert Sebree
242, 243 © Mark Liddell / Contour by Getty Images
245 © Tali Lennox

Front cover © Lewis Ziolek

FIRST PUBLISHED IN THE UNITED STATES OF AMERICA
IN 2025 BY

Rizzoli International Publications, Inc.
49 West 27th Street
New York, NY 10001
www.rizzoliusa.com

Written and curated by Annie Lennox
Copyright © 2025 Annie Lennox

Design by Brian Roettinger

Scanning and retouching by Sabrina Che

Publisher: Charles Miers
Editor: Jacob Lehman
Production Manager: Colin Hough-Trapp
Managing Editor: Lynn Scrabis

All rights reserved. No part of this publication may be reproduced, stored in a retrieval system, or transmitted in any form or by any means, electronic, mechanical, photocopying, recording, or otherwise, without prior consent of the publishers.

2025 2026 2027 2028 / 10 9 8 7 6 5 4 3 2 1
ISBN: 978-0-8478-7555-9
Library of Congress Control Number: 2025934674

Printed in Italy

The authorized representative in the EU
for product safety and compliance is
Mondadori Libri S.p.A., via Gian Battista Vico 42,
Milan, Italy, 20123, www.mondadori.it

Visit us online:
Instagram.com/RizzoliBooks
Facebook.com/RizzoliNewYork
Youtube.com/user/RizzoliNY